THE
WACCY
BACCY
BOAT
AND BEYOND...

Best Wishes

Phil Be___

Published in paperback in 2019 by Sixth Element Publishing
on behalf of Phil Berriman

Sixth Element Publishing
Arthur Robinson House
13-14 The Green
Billingham TS23 1EU
Tel: 01642 360253
www.6epublishing.net

ISBN 978-1-912218-56-1

British Library Cataloguing in Publication Data. A catalogue record for this book
is available from the British Library.

Phil Berriman asserts the moral right to be identified as the author of this work.

Printed in Great Britain.

This is a true story. Some names and identifying details have been changed to
protect the privacy of individuals. Some scenes and individuals have been partially
fictionalised. The threats, the voyage and the subsequent court cases are all fact
and a matter of public record.

THE WACCY BACCY BOAT

AND BEYOND...

PHIL BERRIMAN

CONTENTS

Introduction 1

Chapter One - Turning Points And A Slippery Slope To Trouble 3

Chapter Two - Denford Motors And The Aubriender 10

Chapter Three - I Was Just There To Inspect The Boats... 19

Chapter Four - The Melanie 26

Chapter Five - Mutiny On The Melanie 34

Chapter Six - The War On Dakar 45

Chapter Seven - The Dark Side Of Dakar 53

Chapter Eight - Pirate Rendezvous 65

Chapter Nine - Loaded To The Gunwales 72

Chapter Ten - The Doldrums: From One Extreme To The Other .. 85

Chapter Eleven - Smugglers' Creek 95

Chapter Twelve - Safe In Prison 104

Chapter Thirteen - The Devil's Convoy 108

Chapter Fourteen - The Dangerous Brothers 122

Chapter Fifteen - The Goldfish Bowl 134

Chapter Sixteen - Up From The Dungeons 149

Chapter Seventeen -
From Dedungeon To Defence, My Finest Hour 165

Chapter Eighteen - So Near Yet So Far 193

Chapter Nineteen - Fishy Business 205

Chapter Twenty - Conception..215

Chapter Twenty One -
The Cornish Maiden, Holyhead, A Strange Place 222

Chapter Twenty Two - The Schooner Rich Harvest 229

Chapter Twenty Three - Tyronio..236

Chapter Twenty Four - Two Boats And A Plan..................................242

Chapter Twenty Five - The Journey Begins...248

Chapter Twenty Six - Helgoland / Heligoland...................................258

Chapter Twenty Seven - Disaster 266

Chapter Twenty Eight - Round Two...275

Chapter Twenty Nine - Games, Set And Match 284

Chapter Thirty - Thailand - Land Of Smiles......................................300

Chapter Thirty One - A Murderous Voyage!.......................................308

Chapter Thirty Two - Eastbourne And Away 317

Chapter Thirty Three - Biscay, A Yachtsman's Nightmare...............322

Chapter Thirty Four - Robbery, Plain And Simple............................326

Chapter Thirty Five - Snortogrande..334

Chapter Thirty Six - Judge Fox And Victory!.....................................342

Chapter Thirty Seven - The Don Inda 350

Chapter Thirty Eight - The Final Blow..356

Chapter Thirty Nine -
From the Waccy Baccy Boat to CBD oil and changing lives 363

This is a true story.

*The threats, the voyage and the subsequent court cases
are all fact and a matter of public record.*

*Many of the characters are real but their identities are disguised.
Others are purely fictitious.*

INTRODUCTION

In September 1994, I was arrested in Smugglers' Creek near Falmouth with a record seizure of three and a half tons of hashish on board the schooner Melanie. A plot so dastardly and incredible led to my remand for fifteen months as a category AA prisoner, despite having no criminal record. Threatened with a lengthy prison sentence, my two co-accused took a deal. Against all odds, and risking the maximum fourteen years upon failure, I fought the case.

The jury heard tales of hard-core gangsters, guns, torture, blackmail, corruption and prison escapes, all the time surrounded by an armed security circus designed to intimidate them. But the pivotal point came when two regional crime squad officers were arrested for perjury on the judge's orders. He issued a gagging order on the press, I proved to the jury that I was in fear of my life and acting under duress, and I was acquitted by all twelve.

After weeks of scandalous events, in November 1995, I walked down the front steps of Exeter Crown Court a free man, much to the fury of my accusers, and the bewilderment of everyone else.

This book details the incredible true story of how one event after another, going right back to childhood, led to the schooner Melanie and my arrest at Smugglers' Cove... and what I did afterwards to take on the authorities, rebuild my life and end up where I am today, a happy man who wants nothing more than to help other people rebuild their lives.

CHAPTER ONE

TURNING POINTS AND A
SLIPPERY SLOPE TO TROUBLE

To understand how I ended up where I did, it's important to know what happened that led me onto that path.

I admit, I've been able to handle myself since the age of sixteen, if not earlier. I didn't have the easiest start in life. My dad Joe was the hardest man I've ever met and I inherited his right hook. And when I was younger, my older brother Jak also gave me plenty of motivation to learn how to defend myself but that's enough said on that. Needless to say, as I grew up in Teesside, I knew how to look after myself and I knew how to defend people who couldn't.

As I got older, it served me well and dispatched most unsuspecting fools who weighed me up and thought I'd be a pushover.

Jak, my other brother Alan, and I all worked at my father's aerial business from a young age. This provided good income for us as kids and we had more disposable pocket money than anyone else at school. I spent a lot of time chopping up old aerials to remove the steel from the aluminium and stripping the copper from the co-axial cable. It was really a man's job and very hard work, so hard that the others refused to do it, and my hands were always black and rough, but I split the cash with dad and made some serious money for my age. It also made me strong.

Anyone who knew me back then would say I was a good kid, hardworking, always prepared to stand up to bullies. I was even a cub and scout leader.

But one early evening in 1975, something happened that was to change the course of my life forever.

There were four of us in the car… an almost new BMW 2500 that belonged to my mate's father. Even though we were only eighteen, we'd persuaded him to lend it to us on pain of death if anything happened to it. We were out for the night with our girls and we thought we were the bee's knees.

We were in Wellington Street in my hometown of Stockton-on-Tees. My mate was driving like an old woman, petrified of his father and taking care of the car.

It all turned to shit as a battered Marina van smashed into us from behind. My mate stopped the car and looked around absolutely horrified. The state of the scrap heap behind us made matters worse… we just knew the driver wouldn't be insured.

We were just about to get out when the cheeky bastard drove off. Seeing red, my mate floored the auto BMW and we cut him off in seconds, chuffed until we saw the van drive straight at us, smashing into the nearside of the car and then reversing for another go.

I jumped from the car as the van hit the BMW a third time. I pulled open the driver's door to find a proper scallywag. The smell of whisky hit me. He was paralytic. The footwell of the van was awash as at least three bottles of the stuff had smashed. Cameras and other valuables were also strewn about. We found out later that he'd just been released from jail and had stolen everything, including the van.

I pulled out the keys. I never had time to think of any danger; the thought of this guy getting away and leaving us to explain the three separate impacts to my mate's father was just too much to contemplate.

But as he climbed out, he held a broken bottle by the neck. He swung it at me, and I simply sidestepped. He was an easy target and as he swung the bottle again, I smacked him bang on the jaw with my father's legacy, the good old right hook. He collapsed and was out cold. The police station was only two minutes away so my mate shot off on foot, keen to leave everything as it was to avoid any misunderstanding.

He returned a few minutes later with a young bobby who'd already been told the guts of what had happened. He was a big bloke, well-built with a hard, common face. I'd never seen uniform buttons so bright. He looked stressed and a bit menacing but hey, we were the good guys.

He cuffed the still unconscious scallywag, hands behind his back and sat on his chest while he radioed for transport. The prisoner began to wake up, mumbling about this fourteen stone copper on his chest. It was a big mistake; a sickening smash to the face from the copper's fist put him straight back to sleep.

The girls were horrified. They were really sweet and had never seen the likes of it. I looked at this copper with disgust. I'd never hit a man who didn't deserve it and certainly not one who couldn't defend himself. I shouted at him to stop, but he just glared at me and banged the driver's head on the pavement. Blood sprayed. I thought he was dead until I saw his feet twitching. I'd suffered too much at the hands of my bully brother to watch any more. I went over and pushed Shining Buttons off him and said, "Hey, mate… he's out cold; he's going nowhere, leave him alone."

He looked up, still snarling and spitting. "Piss off, son, or you'll spend a night in the cells with him!" He was clearly getting the same kick Jak had when he'd tortured us as kids. I took the copper at his word and pissed off. I'd never had trouble with the law and didn't want to start.

A few weeks later, I was driving my Lotus Cortina along Bishopton Road when a police panda with blue flashing lights came up behind. I stopped and who walks up to the car? Yep, Shining Buttons.

I wound down the window and said, "What's the problem, officer?"

He was half smiling; I wondered if it was the same copper.

"It's okay," he said, "you've done nothing wrong. But you know the other week? Well, the bloke has made a complaint against me because his cheekbones and eye socket are broken. I need you to make a statement saying that he attacked you more than once and that you did the damage. I'll back you up."

I couldn't believe my ears. I was furious. I'd never hit anybody on the floor, never mind in handcuffs. The next thing I said was to have a massive impact on the rest of my life; that's why I remember it, word for word.

"Listen, mate," I said, "what you did was disgraceful. You'd better leave me out of this or I'll tell them exactly what you did and what you said when I tried to stop you."

His face changed back to the one I recognised. He glared at me like I was shit.

"That's all I wanted to know," he said and off he went.

And so began a string of events, from having my car stolen, to being accused of stealing tax discs, to being beaten in a police cell even though I hadn't been charged with any crime. As time went on, I seemed to become more popular with the police who seemed to be very concerned for my safety. Whenever I ventured out in a car, they would take time to stop me to make sure it was roadworthy and would breathalyse me to make sure I was okay to drive. How very considerate of them.

The situation escalated to a point where I complained, and surprisingly my complaint was upheld. There was harsh action including demotion and suspension for all concerned. I'd won a victory against all odds. During all this time I'd been under a lot of stress with the case coming up. I'd often asked for help from God and my spirit guide. My prayers had been answered. It felt like a victory... as if I could get on with my life.

What I didn't realise was that this was a catalyst for years of harassment and victimisation that was to change me from an honest, hard working lad with excellent prospects, into someone who despised the police.

I ended up moving away to work, and when I finally returned to Teesside, I hoped that the crusade against me would have stopped. I decided a 'proper' job would put me on the right track. I'd always wanted to be a fireman. Everybody, including the police, likes firemen. They're heroes in every sense of the word and after all the trouble I'd had, I decided I wanted to join the fire service.

I was accepted and went to train at Aldridge near Birmingham. I got right into it. I'd been handling ladders and heights, helping my dad with his business, since the age of eleven. The fire brigade training is notoriously hard and many recruits don't make it. You're pushed to the limit as soon as you arrive.

The Silver Axe is awarded to the recruit with the most points at the end of the course. I was seventeen points clear when we were sent to Birmingham for the final week to face the dreaded Breathing Apparatus section. Beneath the old headquarters was a maze of tunnels fitted with cages like big rabbit hutches. We were pushed to the limit in simulated situations. Trapped in the cages with barely enough room to move, let alone drag ourselves through, in full kit and BA gear.

Many who'd endured months of hell failed the BA course and were discarded immediately with no second chance. It's a physical and psychological nightmare designed to put you in a worse situation than you're ever likely to encounter in a real fire. But the secret is to be aware that it's only a simulation. The instructors were (or were supposed to be) on hand outside the cages with their advanced breathing sets to pull out anyone who flipped out with claustrophobia or panic attacks as their air began to run out in the black smoke-filled tunnels.

I was partnered with Barry Sneddon, a guy who was as keen as me and second in place for the Silver Axe. As we completed our last test, we emerged from the tunnel with our warning whistles blowing. This lets the wearer know there is less than five minutes of air left in the tank. One rule that had been drummed into us was: if your whistle is sounding, never… ever… go back into a situation for any reason.

There were no instructors at BA control, only recruits whose job was to log men in and out. The instructors should've been at all the nasty points, but they were all chatting halfway down the tunnel complex; we'd passed them perhaps seventy-five metres back.

We were about to take off our gear when we heard a blood-curdling scream and shouts for help. At first we thought it was part of the test to see if some mugs would enter the tunnel while their warning whistles were activated.

Mugs Berriman and Sneddon decided that something was really

wrong and it didn't matter about the whistles in a simulation. We went back into the tunnel to find a recruit impaled on a steel rod which had detached at one end and was now like a meat hook, stuck under his armpit and through his shoulder.

His mate was powerless, as he couldn't exit the cage without climbing onto him. By now the poor bastard had been screaming for a couple of minutes. Blood had filled up his fire boot dangling six inches from the floor and was now pouring out of it.

We unhooked him and walked him screaming like a pig for thirty metres into the light of the BA control. When the instructors finally arrived from their cosy chat, I was furious and blasted them for neglect of duty. We travelled home that night chuffed to bits. We were heroes even before we'd passed out!

We were summoned to the headquarters at Middlesbrough to see Bill Cooney, the deputy chief. We thought we'd get an award or at least a pat on the back but were sacked on the spot because we went back into the tunnel with our whistles blowing.

Apparently the training school didn't want us back. They'd messed up and wanted to avoid a claim against them from the injured man.

I protested and demanded the opportunity to prove our case. The union rep was present and backed us up. Cooney gave us one week but despite being handed the evidence of signed reports on the incident from fellow recruits, he just glared at me without reading them. He told us to get out. I was gutted and wanted to bash him.

Three days later, I was stopped in my car by who else but Shining Buttons who took great pleasure in telling me that a word had been put in on my behalf. My career as a fireman was over before it started.

I went back to the motor trade and always made enough money to maintain a decent standard of living. I became good friends with nightclub managers, started to live the high life, and my reputation of being able to look after myself was paying off. I was doing well for myself, importing left-hand drive American and German cars from Holland. I bought my first Porsche 911 and drove it back through Dover. It was this car that started my dealings with her Majesty's Customs and Excise. I'd driven through the night, only to get the car ripped to bits by a full team who'd been tipped off I was carrying drugs. They found nothing. They were furious, but I'd done nothing wrong. It was the start of a long and bitter relationship.

During this time, I started to get roped into escapades that, looking back, I should have kept well away from. I'm sorry to admit it, but it was just a natural reaction. I felt victimised by the police and I found myself mixed up with villains because we had a common enemy.

Then I met a girl, and the age old story, she got pregnant and suddenly I was a father. After my baby girl's birth, I took stock and realised I'd become too fearless. I began to worry about it. I couldn't believe some of the things I'd done and now I had something that scared me. My baby! I was very protective and realised I'd been lucky not to have been jailed on a few occasions.

But, underworld tongues were wagging, and I'd gained a notoriety that I didn't deserve... or did I?

CHAPTER TWO

DENFORD MOTORS
AND THE AUBRIENDER

One day around this time, I was approached by a proper switched-on traveller who offered me a proposition: I would buy the scrappers, he would pick them up with his Hiab wagon and bust them with his two sons, sell the bits and account to me. All of this for half of the scrap value of the remaining shell.

Scrap was on fire at the time. The deal later increased to all the scrap value when prices settled down. It always puzzled me why he wanted to work 'with me' as he insisted. One day, I finally got into his head. He wasn't registered with the authorities, he was ill and scared to go to the doctor. Frankly, he'd accepted he was going to die and wanted his family in a normal house and his kids to learn the trade. They were two good hard-working lads who never gave me any grief.

I finally persuaded him to register and seek help. He did and discovered he had some glandular disorder that was treatable. He eventually went on to get better and use all I'd taught him and his sons to set up his own yard. I was perfectly happy with him doing this; he and his sons helped me, as much as I helped them.

I concentrated on the motor salvage business and bought as many cars as we could to break. All my parts were tested, dismantled, cleaned, labelled and priced according to availability. I was no charity. I made sure I had the stuff that was in demand. I bought it all, whatever the price, even from other yards. I maintained the demand and prices. More than anything, I made damn sure our customers were respected!

Everybody in the motor trade came to know that if you had something to sell, you went to Denford Motors. I'd walk round other yards buying the 'jewellery'... carburettors, starters, radiators, alternators, bumpers, headlights, and get my men to take them off properly. The owners would be laughing at me in the pub but I'd be laughing at them in the restaurant at 4am with champagne, fillet steak and a beautiful girl by my side. I made a fortune and nearly all cash.

In the eighties, joy riding became the regular sport of the North East trainee villains. Lads would go out for the night in small groups armed with a screwdriver to do the door lock and a short piece of scaffold to 'pipe' the steering lock. They just nicked the fastest car they could, rifle the glove box and then thrash it around the housing estates before setting it alight or dumping it in a beck.

That progressed to removing the wheels and tyres, then the seats, bumpers/spoilers and other parts to upgrade, for example, a standard 1300 escort to look like an XR3i. So their prime targets would be any hot hatchbacks or Cosworth.

The insurance companies made matters worse. If they recovered such a car, they'd write it off simply because the parts that were missing would cost more new than the car was worth.

But then it was sold to a salvage dealer who knew whoever bought the car would steal another to get whatever was missing – wheels, tyres, front and back spoilers – to repair it. 'Stolen recovered cars' were sold by the insurance companies' own salvage agents to anyone who had the cash.

Each time one was sold, another similar car went missing to donate all the bits to repair it. This went on and on until it became an epidemic.

Then there were the burn outs. The insurance companies' agents would sell half a ton of twisted metal, along with the all important chassis tags and documents, sometimes for thousands of pounds. The shiny replacement that would inevitably get nicked and have its numbers changed to become a 'ringer', would cost the next insurance company dearly.

Most of the time, the dealer would scrap the junk and sell just the document, tags and receipt, or just the receipt. The car crime epidemic was created by the greed of the insurance companies who tried to minimise their losses while knowing full well they were perpetuating the problem.

The biggest screw up was the Q plate. The authorities decided to Q any car made up of parts that couldn't be identified or age related. Instead of solving the problem, it opened the floodgates. No longer did you need to buy a write off, you could build a car from stolen parts, provide a few receipts and a week later you had a car complete with a new identity, on a Q registration.

Worse still, the car was stamped by the local plod or tax office with a set of standard stamps which could be bought by anyone for £30. Every 'twocker' (taking without the owner's consent) had an Escort Cabriolet or an RS Turbo. Amazingly Q cars, Jeeps and Transits became much sought after. Anything on a Q was worth good money.

The answer was on the V5 document, which was usually very vague. Make: Ford. Model: Escort. Year of manufacture: not known, registered April 1st 1992. Engine number: None. Chassis number: None. A Q-registration chassis number would be stamped somewhere obvious, usually on a strut top and that would be all the plod had to check out a car.

An old Mark 2 or 3 Escort could be bought on a Q for say a few hundred pounds. They would almost invariably end up as the latest model RS Turbo or convertible. There was hell on. Insurance companies wouldn't touch the original cars; they became group 15 or more. Even a Ford Transit diesel became an insurance problem because they were so easy to steal and Q. All a thief needed to do was weld in a new step and the number was gone!

Dodgy firms would apply for V5 documents in false names and multiple occupancy addresses. Once the document arrived, a twin would be found then a triplet until there could be five or six identical cars with the same Q plate. If the job had been done properly and all the numbers removed, the end customer usually had the car re-registered on an age related number or another Q by plod, who spent half their time tracking down Q plated cars and checking them out. These cars were eventually known as 'Dupes', from the word duplicate.

As a result of this total farce created by the insurance companies, I made stacks of money. I realised there was tons of expensive late model parts being smashed up, dumped or scrapped because they were left over from a ringing operation. I advertised to buy just parts.

Of course, I accept that some of the parts must have come from stolen motors, but that's an occupational hazard of the salvage business. When a car was 'rung', the operation left a legitimate, damaged car that needed to disappear. Because we completely dismantled every vehicle before crushing and scrapping the shell, we were the preferred buyers for every car ringing gang in the north. But we were legal.

After a few twenty four hour lock ups in police cells relating to engine numbers on stock I'd bought to be straight, I decided to investigate the problem. My business was to buy and sell parts for cars. I recorded the calls when I rang the police stations in all areas of the north with the same question:

"I'm a salvage dealer," I'd say, "and I have a man with a pick up full of engines at my gate, some damaged, some not. A couple are late model and although I want the engines at the price he's asking. I'm a little suspicious and worried that some might be stolen. Can I give you the engine numbers so you can check them on your computer?"

The police would reply, "No sir, we cannot supply you with that information under any circumstances."

I rang the DVLA headquarters, only to get the same answer. I was amazed. The numbers related to the car and not the part. From that day, I removed every unique number from every car, engine, gearbox and other parts. I insisted on this, before it was stacked in the yard. We went through more power file belts, than any other sundry in the workshop.

If you bought a replacement engine, gearbox or full body shell from Ford, it came without a number. I've even bought ex-police

Granada 4x4s from an auction without a single identifying number other than the registration plate. I stamped my own identifying numbers on the parts I sold.

Many forces tried to prosecute me for this practice, none succeeded. We never stole anything. We bought and sold parts and took enough reasonable precautions (within the limitations of the information available to us) to ensure they weren't stolen. The police hated me, watched me and investigated me. But they never got me for anything. I really enjoyed making serious money in that grey area of the law.

I was getting one over on them. If an insurance company lost money then I was happy. They'd screwed me over twice by then, once with a fire and once with injuries from a car accident. It always put a grin on my face when I sold an engine that could have indirectly been paid for by them.

As always, I was looking for new and interesting ways to make a few quid and in 1988, I travelled to Spain by car, bought all the local papers for the classified ads and was busy comparing prices of cars, trucks, machinery and boats, when I noticed an advert for the Aubriender.

She was laid alongside the old Customs Quay which had been sold to a company which was building high-rise waterfront apartments. She was a 117ft former Royal Navy minesweeper of the Fairmile B Class, built of mahogany in the double diagonal style. She'd been converted at various times in her life for use as a booze cruiser, rum smuggler and more recently a houseboat. My head filled with all sorts of ideas and plans for this vessel.

The ship had been used as security with a bank based in Gib. The owner had defaulted, leaving it in the hands of ex-pat, alcoholic squatters who lived on board and sold various bits of her to anyone who wanted them.

The hull and machinery were all there but there was no steering or controls... just an empty wheelhouse. I expected it to fetch about £30,000. A handful turned up in time for the start, including the bank manager and auctioneer.

I was well nervous; I'd been to many auctions but never one for a ship. The auctioneer asked £3,000 and up went my hand. It turned out to be the first and last bid. Everyone else had come out of interest only. A very embarrassed bank manager and auctioneer hastily conferred, then offered the ship to me for £4,000. I couldn't believe my luck.

I immediately shook hands on it and gave him £1,000 cash deposit in exchange for the already prepared contract and receipt. The whole transaction from bid to receipt took less than ten minutes.

As I was trying to contain my joy, a car full of businessmen turned up in a serious panic. They'd come to bid for the ship but had been delayed at the infamous Spanish frontier. The bank manager tried to get the auctioneer to restart the auction. But the sale stood and I owned a ship. I was offered £24,000 for it there and then. I refused and told them it was not for sale.

My plan had worked very well. I'd earwigged a bunch of British guys in a big Mercedes looking around the boat on viewing day. They were from Malaga and had every intention of paying up to £35,000 for her. I noted their car registration and posted a note to the local Customs' office.

"Dear Sirs. It would be seriously in your interests to be very vigilant at the border crossing on Tuesday between 9am and 11am. It is my information there is likely be a consignment of hashish carried by a car (not known) entering Gibraltar and also that a Mercedes 500 Reg XXXXXX will be carrying a large amount of cash. I want nothing for my help. Regards P."

The main problem with Gibraltar is the tension with Spain. The Spanish border guards often make life a misery by checking lots of cars, some smuggling cheap tobacco. Such was the price difference, there was huge smuggling going on by sea and land. Delays entering and leaving Gib are commonplace even now. They will not let you jump the queue without a flashing blue light.

I suspect the Brits were late for the auction after being delayed at the border. Was that wrong? Slippery maybe, but I was only telling the truth. Of course there'd be cannabis passing into Gibraltar; it was a daily affair and common knowledge. People were caught every day. A 'consignment' could be worth only £10 but the tip off would cause a huge tailback of cars waiting to be searched. Furthermore, I heard them saying, they'd be carrying a large amount of cash. All true, officers!

I liked owning a ship, which I now describe as a 120 foot motor yacht. My plan was to sail her back to England and refit her closer to home, before returning to Spain as a floating hotel and water sports centre. I thought if I could get her to pay her own way, I could have a real nice situation there without it costing me an arm and a leg. I could split my time between home and my yacht, on the Med.

A guy turned up, looked around and told me that he would supply a crew through an agency "all above board" and fuel and give me £20,000 when my boat was delivered to the UK.

I was very confused. "What the hell are you on about, mate?" I asked.

He replied in his thick Geordie accent, "The job man. Yee knaa. The job."

It finally dawned on me that someone had told this bloke that I'd be up to let him use my boat to smuggle tons of hashish. I told him, "No!" I had to choose my words very carefully. I'd met some of these guys, one named Henry had steered him my way. They were pretty high up the scale of first division villains, and I didn't know where this guy ranked.

What I did know was, from that moment, we were watched day and night by one agency or another! Frankly, I didn't care as I had no intentions of doing anything illegal. I was making more than I could spend at home without actually breaking the law.

It was my dad, Joe, who helped me get the Aubriender out of Spain. I'd learned to sail the hard way. In 1971, my father bought a boat first built in 1900 at Cowes. The Kestrel was a gaff rigged yawl, 36ft long including the bowsprit. It hadn't one piece of labour-saving gear or modern equipment anywhere. We joined the Hartlepool Yacht Club much to the horror of the members. We didn't fit in at the club house as my old man was working men's social club material and it showed. We'd turn up in a dirty old Bedford van with ladders strapped to the roof. On board would usually be hell. We didn't have the likes of Henry Lloyd insulated sailing suits and boots. Instead we three brothers fought over a couple of pairs of yellow waterproofs stolen from ICI. We were drilled and bawled at until we learned that we couldn't sit and enjoy the experience; we had to work all the time. We got into difficulties on at least six occasions when I was on board and called out the inshore lifeboat to help.

Back to the Aubriender... and as we sailed into the Straits of Gibraltar, I felt a fantastic sense of pride. This boat was humongous compared to anything I'd ever owned or sailed for someone else. Several storms and dramas later, we berthed at Cadiz Yacht Club. I decided to refit Aubriender there and sail her back to the Med. And that's where I met Robin when a Spanish frigate came into the harbour with a small wooden yacht, a little like the old Kestrel lashed alongside. She was the Matilda of Wight, now black with soot and almost sinking. Robin told us his story in his best public school voice while hand-pumping the waist-deep black sludge and at the same time trying to boil a kettle to make tea. I sent for our petrol-powered bilge pump while we listened transfixed. He'd had just gone through a nasty divorce. So he said, "Bollocks," bought a boat and set off from the UK to cruise the Med. He explained he'd been ripped off, got caught in a storm and his newly acquired boat started to fall apart when it got wet.

I watched him searching through black flotsam until he found and unscrewed a bottle containing milk; he sniffed it then asked if he could make us a cup of tea. We stood on the wall looking down on this impossible bloke with his totally impossible story and started to laugh. He looked a bit confused, so I had to explain. "Listen mate, you've been through hell and back. You look like a seagull washed up in an oil slick! Your boat's sinking and all you can think about is a good old cup of British tea. That'll sort the job out, what? Get out of there, you daft twat, and let us get the pump aboard!"

He looked at me like I'd gone too far... but, that's just how I am... I say it like it is. Four showers, plenty of grub and cups of tea later, his boat was out of danger and we had a drink. We should have guessed; the guy was an ex-SAS captain. Two out of ten people you meet in marinas are ex-SAS, bank robbers, tax exiles or spies; they're nearly all bullshitters who're running from the law, creditors or the CSA, but this guy was for real.

One day, he asked me what I was really up to. I had no idea what he was on about.

"You're being watched and I mean watched closely," he said.

He'd been watching our spies for three days. I suppose it was in his training. I'd like to think I knew when I was being followed at home, but I'd no reason to think the car squad or my archenemy Shiny Buttons would have any interest in me in Cadiz.

He was right on the money. But why watch us? We'd had nothing but chew every time we went through borders, or perhaps it was because we were acting like a bunch of twats, lording it around Cadiz with sports cars, power boats and jet skis. They were probably wondering what else we were doing on the quiet. So here we were, 1,700 miles from home, and still getting constant attention.

Soon, the Aubriender looked the part with her new lines. Another deck had been added, creating a wheel house and separate luxury quarters for me and my guests. At deck level we had a bar, lounge and dance area. Below was the galley, heads, engines and cabin accommodation for twenty six people. I decided I wanted the Costa del Sol for Christmas and she sailed beautifully through the Straits of Gibraltar right back to the place we first found her. Within days of arriving, we were under surveillance again. It was fairly obvious that the police and Customs were still convinced I was smuggling cannabis. Meanwhile, I was having a lovely time within the law. Just!

Not long after all that, and a son later, I ended up single again. I bought a yard in Bowesfield Lane in Stockton to expand into and put the Aubriender up for sale as a going concern. Denford Motors was doing great. My business model was paying dividends. I was enjoying life again.

So how did I end up with the Melanie at Smugglers' Cove?

CHAPTER THREE

I WAS JUST THERE TO INSPECT THE BOATS...

I got a reputation for finding bargain boats and fixing them up, something I loved doing. One such call led me to the Michelle Louise and a disaster of a trip where we ending up limping into La Caruna. Spanish Customs immediately stormed the boat looking for the huge amounts of cannabis resin they'd been 'told about'. Of course they found nothing, because we had nothing. But, typical of Customs in any country, they trashed the parts of the boat that were not already destroyed. We ended up taking her back to the UK where Customs had another go. It was also extremely clear that the authorities were still absolutely convinced we were in the cannabis smuggling business. We were on a list.

It was around this time, I got in real trouble. John Hannibal, an ex-boxer, then security operator I knew from Leeds, so nicknamed because of time served for biting bits off people, attacked me with one other for no apparent reason in a Stockton nightclub. It would be over twenty years before I learnt they'd been paid by two drinking pals, Charlie Chopper, a nightclub operator, and agent of my arch enemy Shining Buttons, and a rival salvage operator whose business my own success was affecting. Although the top of my ear was bitten off, I was still standing when they ran losing blood and reputations at a rate of knots.

He traded on fear. With his reputation crumbling, he tried everything to regain it, including sending a wannabe to shoot at my Porsche on the drive. I refused to be intimidated by them, and finally after a year, people around me were starting to worry.

I contacted a guy I knew who ran with a gang big enough to resolve the problem, without hurting anyone. Hannibal was woken in the night, and left in no doubt he would be punished severely if anything else occurred. Job done, all I had to do was pay the bill. Unfortunately, when you lie down with dogs, you get fleas. I was summoned to a meeting with a gun-toting gang of villains from Newcastle, headed by a guy called Cordite, where it transpired that they too had always believed my wealth came from cannabis smuggling. They wanted me to find them a boat suitable for transporting gear from Morocco. I was pretty horrified, but could see why they wanted me. They knew nothing about boats and needed someone who could keep their mouth shut. I had no intentions of doing anything other than finding a boat, so had nothing to worry about.

I made the mistake of recommending a yacht owned by a friend of mine. With the deal agreed, their skipper Frank Waleing sailed it from the island of Mallorca to Estepona on mainland Spain, but, it later transpired that on route they collected the hashish, landed it, then said the vessel was faulty, demanding their money back, all the time telling me they'd lost over a hundred thousand pounds. I'd been mugged into providing them a boat for a run, which was successful, but now they didn't want to pay, and wanted more! They insisted I was responsible for huge losses, but all the time, they were playing me.

I identified perfect boats, went after them and each time… problem after problem, beset by constant surveillance. I was mixing with some dangerous people, and even though I kept on insisting that I was just there to inspect the boats, it was never that straight forward. At one point I found myself in Turkey, there to inspect a boat, looking at 880 kilos of cannabis, just lying there in a pile. That's the same weight as a VW Beetle!

Cordite was pushing me to be involved in his operation, and was making sure I was in deep enough that it was hard to walk away. If I wasn't jumping through hoops for him, he'd have one of his extended gang of mercenary enforcers, such as Terry Dactyl from Hartlepool, to cause some grief out of nothing so I'd need Cordite to resolve the problem, but I'd had enough. I couldn't fight them, I had to escape. My business didn't need me personally by then. I had the Michelle Louise in Hartlepool marina, loaded up with food, fuel and water and fully intended to be gone. I pulled a big bag of cash together and was about to tell my kids and their mother the plan, when something happened that changed everything.

Someone arrived at my door to tell me Cordite's reign of terror was over. He'd been arrested for kidnapping and torturing a rival gang member in broad daylight.

I was ecstatic. It couldn't have come at a better time; I didn't have to run anywhere.

But my joy was very short-lived. Amazingly, Cordite was released after the victim had exonerated him by statement. I was petrified. I knew they were daft. But this was a horror story, proof positive that I was knee-deep in shit with unhinged lunatics who were capable of anything!

Within just a few days, and maybe in answer to my prayers, the tables turned once again. The rival gang member (after being shot at in the street) came clean, and implicated Cordite as his kidnapper. The police entered him into the witness protection program and moved him into a safe house in the South. Cordite was rearrested. My own situation was fast becoming critical. I knew the surveillance had been stepped up to twenty four hours a day and I was due to be arrested for what they believed was my involvement. Someone had gone to a massive amount of trouble to get me to Turkey to set me up.

I racked my brain for a solution, until I had a plan! I found a telephone box and called the Customs' hotline. I said I wanted to give information about heroin smugglers, but wanted to speak to officers based in the south as I believed there was corruption in the North East police and Customs. I explained I was a marine engineer, a buyer and seller of boats, which was basically true. I told them I'd been sent to Turkey by some North East gangsters to look at a yacht which I'd 'suspected' was going to be used for the movement of cannabis, a drug which I personally thought should be legal.

I was prepared to name the two Turkish men involved because they'd mugged me into being present with 880 kilos and 'Mafia' when they knew fine well, I was only there to survey a boat on behalf of a firm. I explained how scared I was and that I'd decided to risk trouble and inform Customs. The agents listened intently and took notes. I basically told the truth apart from who I was, and the fact that I knew the Turks were Customs' operatives targeting me. I stressed that I was a boat expert being paid to do a job and not a smuggler. It worked. I've never heard nor seen any of the Turkish men since then. I went back to my life, knowing Cordite would be in no position to mess my life up for quite some time.

Since Cordite was safely locked up with no prospect of bail, the surveillance on me was vastly reduced. I still intended to take the Michelle Louise to Mallorca, but there was no longer pressure to scarper quickly.

Then my world was upside down... again! Cordite, aided by an armed gang, had escaped from a prison van en route to Newcastle Crown Court from Holme House Prison in Stockton. Many people, including me, believe this escape to be suspicious in the least. On the day of the escape, the two most dangerous men in the North were transferred to court in a taxi mini-bus with a civilian driver, instead of a high risk armoured truck previously deployed.

I put my escape plan into overdrive; I wanted my boat out of Hartlepool and fast. My dad took her down to Torquay and with my pride and joy safely out of reach, I breathed a long sigh of relief.

I was planning to get away myself when my doorbell went at one in the morning. My security camera displayed my worst nightmare... the unmistakable figure of a man I didn't think I'd ever see again. It was the most wanted man in Britain, the now infamous Peter Cordite.

He'd had grown his hair and beard to look like a mad Highlander. He looked at me through his glasses and blurted, "Surprise surprise!"

There was no point in showing fear; it would only spur them on. They trade in fear rather than a fair price or negotiation. I'd already contemplated this situation, and calmly took them through to the lounge and shut the blinds. Cordite said he wanted a "ride out of the country" on my boat. Saying no wasn't an option.

I explained that I was sorry and I would help if I could, but it was too late; my boat was almost in Mallorca. I was feeling quite relieved and chuffed that I'd had the foresight to scupper this very scenario, before it could happen. My self-satisfaction lasted only a few seconds as Cordite exploded, "You're a lying bastard. The boat's sitting in Torquay and you better get your bags packed, you're taking me, tonight!"

My head was whirling. I was speechless. How the hell did he know? Of course any pretence of camaraderie was now out of the window after he knew I'd tried to deceive him. Let me be very clear about my choices at that very moment. I knew Peter Cordite was a desperate, escaped kidnapper and torturer, looking at twenty years in jail; he had access to guns and gangsters who'd do his bidding at the drop of a hat. He mysteriously knew the secret location of my boat some three hundred miles away and was sitting in my house.

They knew that I lied about my boat on which he was pinning his hopes of an escape! Deep, deep shit came to mind.

Preferring not to have my two children burned alive in their beds, I took him to Torquay. The weather forecast from the harbour master was good. We cleared formalities and set off. The next stop was Spain.

Everyone on the boat disliked Cordite. He was lazy, arrogant and quite useless. He refused to pull his weight. In fact, he treated my beautiful yacht like a building site bait cabin, leaving fag ends and rubbish wherever he'd been. I lied again to my crew saying he'd paid good money for the trip, so he wasn't expected to work. But Cordite would talk to me like we were alright and I responded likewise. This was self- preservation really. I wanted him to understand why the Michelle Louise wasn't suitable for smuggling.

As we got within 60 miles of the Spanish coast, the weather started to blow again... right on our nose. The waves whipped up and banged us head on. We made slow but sure progress through the night. Cordite was caning the cannabis he'd brought and started to get very paranoid and afraid. He came up from below scared shitless, wearing two of the five lifejackets on board. If the shit hit the fan, one of us would go without. Next morning, Cordite came up on deck and pushed past me as the boat rolled violently. He almost fell overboard. I grabbed his life jacket and for a split second thought very hard about the consequences of an accident at sea!

I often contemplate where I would be today if he'd fallen into the Bay of Biscay. The truth is, I don't think there'd have been a queue to save him. And I still wonder, what made me grab his jacket.

The weather began to ease off and the sun came out to play. Cordite had clearly had enough; he'd been petrified and hadn't slept for two days. We were off the north coast of Spain and he demanded to be let off.

Nobody wanted him on board anyway so it was decided to head towards La Coruna; I'd been in there a number of times and knew there was a visitors' pontoon at the yacht club which was pretty lax on security. We could probably land Cordite without a problem.

He announced he needed me with him as he had no clue how to get anywhere. He had a point. Few people spoke English in the north of Spain. It wasn't like the holiday destinations of The Costas.

Cordite's thick Geordie accent and limited vocabulary made him difficult to understand in the UK, never mind in the Basque region of Spain where the dialect is quite different from the rest.

I did say it was impossible to go with him as I was needed on board. But the alternative was much worse; he'd have to stay on board until we arrived in the south, at least five days sailing plus a fuel stop. I'd put my crew through enough shit so I jumped ashore with him and went straight to the airport by taxi. It was still early morning.

A short uneventful flight to Malaga and we were in a taxi to a pre-arranged apartment in the city. After a cheap restaurant meal, I was to stay the night and head off in the morning. He continued drinking and smoking copiously… much more than ever before. As far as he was concerned, he was now safely on the Costa del Crime; a big hitter, on the run, with a pocket full of readies.

That evening, I discovered a much darker Peter Cordite. He

assumed the role he'd been dreaming about since his childhood. A true mobster, ruthless and feared by everybody! As far as he was concerned, this was the beginning of his meteoric rise to the top of the criminal elite. The Costa del Crime was now his for the taking.

If I wasn't convinced he'd call his merry henchmen back in the UK and have my family hurt or worse, I'd have been gone. It was like a gangster movie. He was naively thinking every villain on the coast was going to lie down for him and do his bidding.

Yes, I was scared of him because I wasn't prepared to murder someone. But he'd lost the plot big time, thinking he could take over down there. In Newcastle, he was just a bully with a big stick; far more successful organisations and gangs on Tyneside weren't scared of him and his arch enemies just laughed at him.

The next day he picked up a new phone and had a couple of meetings with some crooks before telling me that there was a load of hashish to be collected off Lareche on the Atlantic coast of Morocco to go to the UK, and that his crew were taking my boat. Or else!

The fuel capacity and distance to travel made the plan impossible. "Well, you'd better get another boat then, and sharpish!" he said.

I made my way to Gibraltar to meet the Michelle Louise. I sent the crew home but a lad called Graham stayed and I kept him busy with little jobs. For the record, he had absolutely no idea who he'd helped transport, or what type of shit I was in. He was labour only. His family were straight military or ex-military men.

It wasn't long before I was approached through Cordite by a guy called Bill Stunbury who operated an unofficial labour agency called the Marina Helpline. He seemed to know everything that went on in the port. He introduced me to a man called Tonio Lara who had a 42ft aluminium schooner called Melanie.

CHAPTER FOUR

THE MELANIE

The Melanie was available for bare charter and came without a skipper and crew. Lara was a smuggler and had bought the boat for a future venture. She was moored in the adjoining Shepards Marina and was more or less ready to go. He insisted on a contract of terms. We would charter the Melanie and he would have a charge on the Michelle Louise as a deposit to the value of the charter. If anything went wrong, the contract would keep them out of jail.

It was expressly agreed that this contract was solely for that purpose and that Lara and Stunbury were to be paid very handsomely as part of Cordite's operation.

I saw this as an end to it; I had to get my father to come out to sign the documents as the current bill of sale for the Michelle Louise had his name on it. I said it was to register the boat in Gibraltar to avoid paying VAT in Europe. Bill Stunbury took charge and organised a skipper and mate with 'experience' for the job in hand.

The skipper, Dave, had his own little yacht and Bob, his mate, seemed like a good hand. Dave and Bob also agreed to say they'd stolen the Melanie if they were caught on the proposed jaunt. For this, they'd be 'looked after' while in jail. Yeah, right!

Unfortunately, the replacement parts arrived with one of my mates, Jimmy the Dip who was now fully aware of what was going on. I had to put him in the picture when we took Cordite to Torquay.

I bought three tickets home but Jim insisted he wanted to stay. His partner Trish was away and he clearly fancied posing as the skipper of my yacht while I was back in the UK. I discovered years later that he'd even borrowed a couple of grand from Charlie Chopper saying it was for me. Cheeky bastard!

I told him to keep out of the business with the Melanie and only observe the movements. I also insisted he did not tell Graham anything about her or anything to do with Cordite and Co. I paid him for his time and expenses, which would see him okay for the holiday he'd mugged me for.

I left Graham with a wad of cash to cover expenses and sundries along with a list of jobs to do on board while I was gone. I insisted he should not give any of the cash to Jimmy without my express permission. I flew back to the UK with my fingers crossed that all would go well. Cordite would finally leave me alone and hopefully smoke himself to death, with all the money he made.

I'd been very careful to keep everything to do with the Melanie completely secret and took great pains to get 'lost' and create diversions. I knew the agencies were watching my yacht and they would believe that we were re-registering her to avoid VAT.

As long as Jimmy stayed away, the only connection to me was a piece of paper to be used by way of an alibi should the worst happen. I'd left code words and virgin phones to communicate safely. I knew that every phone box in Gibraltar is recorded 24/7.

It's such a small place with so much dodge going on, it'd be stupid not to. If anything was going to go wrong, it wasn't going to be down to me. I was turned over by Customs coming in, but had nothing to hide. It was time to relax, for a while.

The Melanie began to navigate through the notorious Straits of Gibraltar and then south down the coast of Atlantic Morocco. Infamous as the busiest hashish collection point in the world was a port called Lareche, or rather, the area of ocean just offshore.

Sailors en route to and from the Canary Islands or the Caribbean would report fishing boat crews offering to supply cannabis resin in quantities ranging from 250 grams or nine ounces (a nine bar) up to a bale weighing around 35 kilos (a packet).

Much larger quantities took a few hours or up to a couple of days to organise depending on the quality required, but only after the cash had been flashed. Collections already paid for or prearranged were conducted after radio transfer of fictitious boat names, call signs and passwords.

There were some very rich fishermen in those days; everybody was paid right down the line. Stories of royalty, beachside palaces, secret caves and fast launches were common. Even patrol boats were said to be involved.

A levy of around $30 per kilo was allegedly paid by the suppliers to ensure safe passage from the mountain growing regions to international waters.

If the Moroccan navy or Customs hadn't been bribed, it was customary to pay various decoy boats to act suspiciously to confuse the assets of the authorities. Of course, this may have all been bullshit. A lot of disinformation is used to drive up the prices or give confidence to buyers.

"Don't worry, my friend, everybody will be paid. You'll have no problem, I swear it," is pretty much a standard saying in the business. The Moroccans in the hashish trade are slippery individuals. They have to be. Their jails are pretty grim and the business had attracted the likes of Peter Cordite who, let's be clear here, didn't have a shilling in the project.

He was the transport. He'd negotiated a fee to collect and deliver the goods to the UK. He would also profit as his gang distributed the product back home when it was 'on the floor'. Everyone else was risking their liberty, investment, boats or hashish.

With most of the firm only participating through fear or the promise of money from a fugitive in hiding, the chances of a happy ending and getting paid were pretty slim!

The Melanie returned to Gibraltar after four days at sea. The message was relayed to me that no contact had been made with the Moroccans despite hundreds of radio transmissions. Both sides insisted they'd been on station at the correct times and co-ordinates and had broadcast the correct codes.

Because the communications were coming and going through Cordite, anything the least bit technical was lost in translation!

Despite his brief experience at sea with me, he couldn't comprehend the geography involved. He'd been told the pickup point was "around the corner from Gibraltar". He thought the crew was lying when they reported vicious tides and rapidly changing gale force winds in the notorious Straits. He was only eighty miles away and the weather was great!

Adding to the confusion were the various levels of anti-surveillance telephone etiquette adopted by others in the conspiracy. Because Cordite did none of this, most people refused to plainly spell things out to him for fear of being recorded.

Cordite smoked copious amounts of cannabis from the minute he woke up until he passed out at night. Even in Newcastle he was paranoid, but on the run in Spain, the hashish was a much higher grade. He'd have a passing thought and turn it into suspicion before his tunnel vision set in and consumed him with rage.

When things didn't go to plan, the last person he could imagine at fault was himself. I was always well aware that my cognitive ability was compromised when I was stoned or pissed. I was careful not to make important decisions or judgements, until I was totally straight.

Three attempts were made to rendezvous with Cordite's purported partners over the weeks. Jimmy gave me very sparse details and despite my warning to keep clear, had somehow managed to become Dave's crew on the second and third failed attempt. I was furious.

Then Bill Stunbury from the Marina Helpline rang. There was a problem.

Dave, the skipper, had left Gibraltar in a hurry with his own boat. Bill said Jimmy had bashed his mate to get on the second trip... then he'd bashed Dave in a drunken row after the third trip.

He also said he now needed to take the Melanie across the Straits to Ceuta, a small Spanish enclave on the Mediterranean coast of Morocco. Cordite had arranged for new crew members Geoff Burge and Gary Parkin to take over. They'd both been missing for a few weeks.

A midnight call from Cordite was to have devastating consequences. He was on a bender, screaming down the phone that he was going to have my kids killed and me tortured if I didn't meet him in Spain within twenty four hours to explain myself.

In a blue cannabis-induced haze of semi-conscious psychotic paranoia, he believed he'd been double crossed by The Fixer from Blackburn and accused me of collecting the elusive ton of cannabis and taking it to Sweden in the Michelle Louise.

He was clearly more dangerous than when I'd last seen him. His criminal empire was crumbling in Newcastle, he was losing control and his gang members were looking after themselves, rather than being at his disposal. Cordite simply wasn't bringing home the bacon.

I bought a three day return ticket and flew out to Gibraltar. I first confronted Jimmy to get his side of the story. He admitted he'd ignored my instructions, crewed on the Melanie, then recruited Graham Cavanagh to crew under him. He'd also relieved Graham of the cash I'd left him to finish my boat, telling him I'd said it was okay and that it was for fuel.

He'd been pretending he owned the yacht, partying and snorting coke with some scutty tarts and spending my money. His face was covered in scabs and his knob and gums were infected. I could have bashed him, but they'd already drawn enough attention to warrant a full Customs' search, after returning from a failed rendezvous.

I should've known better. After all… it was Jimmy the Dip! I couldn't really blame Graham. He wasn't the sharpest tool in the box and I'd left him with a first division, sneaky bastard, con man. What would his family say if they found out he was now an international drug smuggler?

I did manage to establish that they had definitely been at the right place for the exchange so it was pretty certain the other side was lying. Dale Gordon told me Geoff Burge was en route from the UK, and I was to wait for him.

Strangely, Burge called to say he was en route to the airport but didn't arrive until the next day. More significantly, he was a different man to the game bloke I'd met before.

He was withdrawn, nervous and didn't want to talk. I pressed him and he told me his wife had just had a child and was giving him a hard time about the trip. It made a bit more sense then.

I told him the Melanie was across the Straits and left him in Gibraltar while I rode across the frontier to Spain on the Virago motorbike I'd brought down on the boat.

Cordite brought a skinny, pale young woman who looked like an addict to our meeting. She waited in the car while we sat in a bar. I have no idea if he was shagging her or if he'd brought her to help him find his way. He was bouncing mad. He'd clearly been getting the run around off The Fixer and his Moroccan contacts.

I soon convinced him that we had nothing to do with it. As he'd sailed across the bay with me, he had a reasonable idea of the time scale involved. I'd brought a chart and explained the mileage and time it would take, also the fact that both boats were still in the vicinity of Gibraltar meant his reasoning was impossible.

I thought it strange how he was so easy to convince after the threats he'd made to get me to travel, but I was accustomed to dealing with his mood swings and put it down to his drug use. Apart from anything else, I'd have been long gone, had I conned him and taken the cannabis to Sweden.

He gave me some written instructions and code words for a new job. A 'contact' would be collected from Casablanca on route to the Canary Islands, where a load would be transferred at sea.

The idea of the contact travelling on board was to negate any trust issues after the three failed attempts to collect the previous shipment. All I had to do was pass the information to Geoff Burge and be on my way back home.

I rode back into Gibraltar a much happier man until I reached the boat. Bill Stunbury said Geoff had left for a flight back to the UK. I raced to the tiny airport but couldn't find any trace of him. The inward flight hadn't even landed yet. Perhaps he'd gone to Malaga Airport by bus? I was devastated. I'd only left Cordite two hours earlier... now I had to tell him his skipper's arse had gone.

I called him to break the news. Naturally he went ballistic and blamed me. He said he wanted me to take the Melanie to Tenerife, where he'd have the crew waiting. I refused point blank and hung up.

I called Mel, the mother of my two children, but couldn't get hold of her. I called her step dad Malcolm who worked for me in the yard. He told me she was at a caravan park with the kids for a few days. I left instructions for her to call ASAP.

My intention was to get them somewhere safe to give me a bit of breathing space to work out what to do. I thought I could find Burge or Parkin and talk them round. Anything, except get on that yacht.

Cordite was a very accomplished liar who would manipulate people into doing his bidding by pure deception. He was certainly no academic, but he'd managed to control an organised gang of thugs, robbers and drug dealers in a tough city. He had to have some skills and acumen as well as a lot of bottle.

Of course, if anyone realised they were being lied to, they could hardly confront him and risk a beating or worse. He ran his empire on lies and fear. It would be much later when the mysteries regarding the disappearance of Frank Waleing, Geoff Burge and Gary Parkin would be solved.

My next move was determined by a devastating phone call. It was so terrifying I still remember it word for word because it was a direct threat to my family. Someone knew I'd been trying to contact them and even more menacing was that Mel, my kids and my parents were being watched.

"Now then Mr Berriman… just to let you know… your kids are having a nice time in Flamingo Park in a blue caravan and your mum and dad walked across to the Malleable Club last night at about nine o'clock. Now stop messing about and get on with it!"

There was no clue to who it was, but it certainly wasn't a northern accent. I called around for more than an hour before it was confirmed they were indeed at Flamingo Park caravan site in North Yorkshire and in a blue caravan.

I couldn't believe Cordite had the resources to tap my phone or even to follow my family. It was odd because my partner Dawn was by far the easiest person to locate as she was living at my house and Cordite had even met her. Strangely, her name was never mentioned. I spoke to Cordite on the phone.

He denied all knowledge and repeated, "The contact in Casablanca is waiting."

His tone was menacing and cocky. He knew the score. He refused to provide expenses for fuel or stores, saying I'd brought more than £2,000 with me and should use that for now. I was in shock, how did he know so much? There were a number of options regarding the money; the lads in the yard and Dawn knew how much I'd taken from the till. Also, I'd been searched by Customs at the airport. Alarm bells were ringing very loudly. Who or what organisation was providing him with information?

I had no choice but to take the threat of violence to my family absolutely seriously. Cordite knew I was scared of nothing. He'd seen that with John Hannibal, Terry Dactyl and also in the Bay of Biscay. But he knew I feared for those close to me and was fully aware of the ruthless and violent bastards he ran with.

There were some in his gang that 'got off' by terrorising vulnerable people. Most worryingly was that they seemed to be able to get away with it. It was almost like they had a licence from the police who were either completely useless or were running paid informants or undercover operatives among the gang.

In any case, it was best we set off from Spain by ferry to Ceuta.

CHAPTER FIVE

MUTINY ON THE MELANIE

I'd already sent Graham ahead to keep an eye on the Melanie. As usual, we found him horizontal with a fag in his mouth. We'd arrived in time to catch the supermarket for supplies and topped up our tanks with fuel and water.

A middle aged geezer was hanging about asking questions. In those days, it was a badly kept secret that there was always 'work' available for game crew in that area. This particular guy had already spoken to Graham a number of times and was waiting to proposition me.

My bullshit meter went straight into the red. He was dressed in a bright purple shell suit, new Nike Air trainers and a full range of gold bling, more typical of Jimmy Savile than a drug smuggler. He was overweight and clearly struggling in the heat. He purported to be based in Ceuta, recruiting and co-ordinating 'transport', the term used for the movement of drugs across the Straits.

I didn't need to be Sherlock Holmes to see he'd just arrived. He was dripping with sweat and had red sunburn... he even had a white circle under his medallion! His tracksuit and shoes looked like they'd been bought at Malaga airport the day before. Although Ceuta was Spanish, it was just as mucky as Morocco only a mile away. In this transit point in and out of Africa, our new friend stood out like a pig at a Muslim barbecue.

At a nearby bar, he tried to order lager instead of beer or cerveza and wondered why the barman looked confused. He also struggled with the exchange rate. He told me the border was over the mountains an hour's drive away. I knew it was five minutes on a bus. He was without doubt the most useless undercover operative I'd ever met.

He looked and acted like a typical Brit on his first trip abroad. He even wore a fake designer baseball cap. There was no point in fobbing him off; Graham had already told him the Melanie was working.

Within just a week of Jimmy transforming him into a criminal, the dozy bastard believed he'd developed the skills to determine who was or wasn't a fellow smuggler. "He's alright Phil, I didn't tell him anything," he said. "Just that he'd have to ask you himself."

What a prat!

I told the Walking Shell Suit we'd be there at least three days waiting for instructions and for the fog to clear. If we'd not received instructions by then, we'd consider a proposal from him. We ordered some tapas and continued drinking beer and brandy until after midnight, by which time he was absolutely hammered and staggered off looking for a taxi.

Back on board, I told my crew to make ready for departure while I familiarised myself with the radar equipment. Despite drunken protests, we slipped our lines and headed out without lights and through the two harbour piers in almost zero visibility. Using radar alone and totally blind, we motored north for two miles, turned west and transited the notorious Straits of Gibraltar.

There was method in my apparent madness; the three days of forecasted fog meant almost zero wind compared to the normal gale force winds in that area for three hundred days a year. This would make for a smooth trip under motor. Tarifa, close by, is a Mecca for wind and kite surfing. Our drunken spy would still be in bed by the time we cleared the Straits into the Atlantic Ocean where the wind and visibility was perfect for a cracking sail to Casablanca.

Instead of taking the shortest route close to land where the tides and currents need to be considered, I sailed out a further twenty five miles before turning south. Inshore in those waters, local fishermen and their tuna nets were a nightmare, often spanning a couple of miles and mostly unlit.

For that reason I'm never one to put into port for the night.

Better to stay away from land and other boats. As Jock Smith said, "Rocks sink boats, not waves." A true pearl of wisdom!

Deep water is much safer and not nearly as rough. We didn't need to worry about anyone looking for us… there was no co-operation whatsoever between the Moroccans and the Europeans.

In twenty four hours we'd done more than two hundred miles. I didn't fancy Casablanca; it was too commercial for my liking. A British registered yacht would attract too much attention. I had a North African pilot book on board which showed a small marina ten miles north of the city. Mohameddia was where European and American sport fishermen kept boats all year round, just to chase the elusive Black Marlin in October and November.

After checking the tide to make sure we had enough water to cross the bar, (a sand bank) at the harbour entrance. We entered and tied up. We cleared Customs and immigration smoothly by saying we were on route to the Canary Islands and needed urgent engine spares. If you have no good reason to be calling into Morocco, you'll set alarm bells off.

I even asked the marina manager to identify an official Perkins Engine dealer in Casablanca and to arrange a taxi for us next day. I tipped him with a carton of Red Marlboro, the brand expected by every official in Africa. We had a large stock of whisky and cigarettes for just that purpose. As usual, we had visits and inspections from various uniforms and dealt with them all in the same way.

The next day Jimmy and I taxied into Casablanca. At the Perkins' dealers, we hopped on another cab and asked for Bogart's Bar as instructed by Cordite. The driver was clueless and must have asked a dozen other drivers at the rank before dropping us at an international phone booth to check the instructions.

The predominant second language is French and back then, very few spoke English. We were working with a phrase book, a pad and a pen. Progress was frustratingly slow and Cordite was as much use as a chocolate fireguard.

We waited around all day, calling him every hour to see if he'd any more information. But to no avail. We managed to pay a hotel receptionist who spoke good English to ring around to find the bar. We gave up late at night and returned to the boat.

This farce went on into the third day by which time I was getting really pissed off with Cordite. He clearly couldn't organise a piss up in a brewery. Finally, we found a guy in a cafe who said there was a themed lounge inside a hotel called Cafe American, which had pictures of Humphrey Bogart and the movie Casablanca on the walls. It was the only clue we had. I called the Geordie idiot and told him what we'd found.

"Whey eye man…" he said. "I told yee; it was Bogart's Bar!"

Needless to say, our contact was not there. We returned four days in a row between 8pm and 10pm, before a middle-aged Spanish bloke called Miguel turned up.

The next problem we had was that he didn't speak a word of English and his Spanish was from a region called Galicia in the north which is nothing like the Spanish I could get away with. Galicia was also home to some pretty busy smugglers and more worryingly, the Basque terrorists ETA.

I'd heard many stories about fishermen collecting cocaine from ships en route from South America as well as hashish from Africa, and then landing them with all of the agencies 'boxed off'. Some of the profits went as bribes and some went to fund the Basque resistance. Of course, that could be bullshit.

The reality was that vast profits were made by criminals under the guise of noble causes, as in any country with a civil dispute. In any case, we were a bit worried about our passenger!

We still made him welcome. He clearly had no idea of the details of Cordite's screw ups; the arrangement was for Cordite's crew to pick him up to co-ordinate a meeting at sea off Tenerife. The three failed meetings off Lareche had infuriated everybody.

I tried but couldn't make him understand that we were only delivering the boat. Next day, we slipped out at first light. Miguel was keen to avoid the proper departure protocol and it wasn't long before a patrol boat was in pursuit. With no chance of outrunning it, we slowed and pretended to be ignorant as they came alongside.

It soon became obvious Miguel could speak French as he tried to explain away our sins. It looked like we would have to follow them back in until I came up with $100, two bottles of J&B Whisky and four hundred Marlboro Reds (African for "forget about it"). We were soon on our way.

I set the autopilot a course for the Canary Islands and sorted out the crew's rotas and maintenance schedules before rolling a big joint to enjoy with my very large brandy. I knew I'd be doing the graveyard shift in the dark, so it was my time to relax while everything was going well.

The weather conditions were spot on for a fast passage. The ocean was teaming with wildlife and the lads were sick to death of me shouting "whale" every half an hour.

I prepared a steak dinner and checked our position. We'd made good progress. Miguel was pleasantly surprised at my cooking, especially as we had a good stock of Spanish red wine, bought very cheaply at Ceuta. I found his Spanish difficult but could still communicate in a fashion. Jimmy and Graham were limited to fewer than a dozen words: vino, cerveza, capitan, si, gracias…

Nightfall came, the lads went to their bunks and I stayed on watch in the cockpit while Miguel mooched about below. After a couple of hours, I called him to take over while I took a dump and made coffee. When I returned, he'd disengaged the autopilot and was heading south instead of south west, causing the sails to flap a little.

I just thought he was getting a feel for the wheel and left him for a few minutes before re-engaging the pilot to bring her back on course. It was then I realised he had no intentions of going to Tenerife. He was absolutely adamant that we had to go to Dakar, the capital of Senegal. I'd only heard of Dakar because of the Paris-Dakar rally on which Mark Thatcher, the son of the ex-Prime Minister Margaret, made a tit of himself.

We argued as best we could, given the language barrier, until I had no option to agree to change course, despite having no charts for that area and not enough fuel or fresh stores. I asked him what bearing we should steer. He didn't know but, indicted south until we saw land again, and then we should follow the coast.

I was extremely suspicious. I suspected Miguel understood more English than he was letting on because he listened intently to weather forecasts and other radio transmissions.

The yacht was worth some £70,000 and could easily be re-registered in a place as corrupt as Senegal. All the pirates would need to do is shoot the three of us at sea. Nobody would dream of looking that far south. We'd declared our intention to go to the Canaries and if we didn't turn up, they'd assume we'd been lost en route.

A huge consignment of drugs runs into millions of pounds and a lot of jail time. Acquiring a boat is a very difficult task without leaving a paper trail of contracts, bills of sale, Customs clearance, immigration and passport numbers at every port. We were heading into waters and countries where life was very cheap and anything can be achieved with a fistful of dollars.

We had no idea who we were dealing with at the other end or what they intended to do with us. We were three potential witnesses who could link them all to a multi-million pound conspiracy, resulting in a serious spell in jail. We were in real danger; it was a good job I had the graveyard shift, as I wouldn't have slept anyway.

I spent a long night shift contemplating our position. I knew Cordite wouldn't give a damn about us. He'd go along with anything to get into the big league, and the big league would do anything to keep him out!

He was already a bloody liability who would become much more dangerous if he had a big score under his belt. He was already on the run, making it risky that he wouldn't pay up once he had control of a shit load of product.

He'd already been a target of various gangsters in the UK; a truck load of money would make him an even greater target. I decided to head for the Canaries by hook or by crook.

Any ship's compass has a number of magnets positioned around it which are moved to swing the reading. A new boat builder needs a professional to come and swing the compass to produce a certified graph called a Deviation Card which shows how far it deviates on whichever heading. This is because any magnetic influences created by steel or other magnets – in say loudspeakers – in the vicinity will give a false reading called deviation.

Another factor is the variation. A marine chart always has a compass rose printed on it displaying the amount of variation for that area. Also, True North and Magnetic North differ. A navigator must take both factors into consideration to determine the correct compass heading to steer. Miguel was no navigator!

At 5am while everybody was asleep, I pointed the boat southwest and swung the compass to read south. We were out of sight of land anyway. Only I knew where we were heading. We had more than a thousand miles to go before we would sight land again.

I calculated about a week's sailing before we would see one of the Canary Islands. I didn't know which one, because I removed the internal fuse from the GPS system so there was no way for anyone to determine where we actually were.

It was old-fashioned navigating, or 'dead reckoning' as it's known. For almost a week, the other three thought we were about to sight land on Mauritania. In fact, we were hundreds of miles off the coast.

One day, our guest heard a conversation in Spanish on our VHF radio while he was on watch. He waited until the conversation finished and called them, despite me objecting to him breaking radio silence. After a short conversation during which he made notes, it transpired he'd been talking to a ferry from Cadiz in Spain, en route to Tenerife.

We could see her on the horizon. In any case, she had to be in range of the VHF which is only about twenty five miles ship to ship, depending on the height of the antennae. I pretended to be flummoxed when he said we were approximately one hundred and ten miles north east of Tenerife. He was pretty pissed off, as were Jimmy and Graham. They all thought I'd lost the plot… pardon the pun.

I pretended to spend hours fixing the GPS before putting the fuse back on the printed circuit board and firing it up. We plotted a position and ran for two hours holding south on the compass before taking another fix. The resulting line showed we had travelled south west. I did it all in front of Miguel and let him come to the conclusion himself that the compass was seriously inaccurate.

He was feeling pretty chuffed with himself while I acted like an amateur in awe of his brilliance. I still had to find a way of stopping off at one of the islands before we went to the dark country. A little bit of fiddling in the engine bay caused the motor to surge up and down as though it was conking out. I insisted we head for land on safety grounds. If the engine failed, the batteries would go flat and we'd have no GPS.

He'd obviously lost confidence in me, but had to agree with my logic. Thank God for that. I set a course for Morro Jable at the most southern tip of the island of Fuerteventura which, roughly translates to 'strong winds'.

A couple of days later, Jimmy came into my cabin frantic to wake me up. I'd only been asleep four hours after being awake the previous twenty eight in rough weather. When it calmed right down, we'd gone back to full sail and I'd gone to bed, leaving strict instructions to inform me of any changes. However, they'd taken it on themselves to make an executive decision to let me sleep as the wind picked up.

Their thinking was that I'd make them help out with the night shift if I'd not had enough sleep. I knew there was something badly wrong by the look on Jimmy's face and the fact that we were heeled right over. The wind was already at gale force and the lazy stupid bastards hadn't reefed the sails. We were crashing along flat out and the sea was building up as we approached land in shallower water.

From the cockpit, I could see the lighthouse for Morro Jable. We were doing nearly 14 knots with wind on our starboard side picking up more rapidly and gusting to over 50mph. The sea was almost following us, making it dangerous to change course with so much sail up. I pushed open the hatch and called the lads to get harnessed to a jack line and get on deck to reef some sail. I reckoned it was going to get rougher before we reached port. The sails and rigging were at the limit. I was surprised and well impressed with them.

The motor conked out of fuel. We were heeled so far over the fuel pick-up pipe was sucking air. I pushed open the hatch and bawled at three wide-eyed faces as a wave came over and almost knocked me out of the cockpit. The hatch closed.

I lashed myself to the wheel and kicked on the washboards which come up from the cockpit floor to stop water flooding in. The hatch didn't open. I kicked again. I slackened off my safety line to reach the hatch but it was jammed. I swung on the boom and booted it until it cracked and slid back along the runners. Then I realised it'd been bolted from the inside by my shitty-arsed, mutinous crew, who flatly refused to come up on deck!

In all my years of racing offshore, I have never seen anyone refuse to soldier in a shitstorm! The mentality of hiding below is crazy. If nobody helps, there's a much bigger risk of losing the rigging. Below decks is the last place you want to be when it happens.

All three of them were white and frozen with fear! Shouting at them made no difference at all. I caught another wave in the face and coughed it all up until my gob was full of phlegm. I leaned forward and spat it into their faces before pulling the hatch shut. It was the most angry I'd ever been at sea. What a bunch of cowardly wankers.

With no other option, I held my course; I knew the consequences of broaching would be catastrophic with full sail. One of the masts would go soon after the rigging popped. I wouldn't have enough time to let slack out myself, thanks to the three shithouses below. But I had more urgent things to worry about as some of the gusts were almost knocking us down flat.

The boat was designed as an ocean racer and had very little superstructure above deck so she quickly came back up. It seems much worse than it is because when the boat heels that far over, there is hardly any sail area in the wind until it bounces up. The danger lies when 'the knockdown' happens on the crest of a wave and the momentum causes capsize! A schooner has a sail in the middle known as a 'fisherman' and while all the others are triangular, the fisherman has four edges. Quite a bit of the area is high up the mast compared to the other sails, which taper significantly by comparison.

I decided to sacrifice this sail to reduce the risk of disaster. I knew I couldn't get it in because I couldn't leave the cockpit as the auto pilot had no chance of holding the course in that sea. I always have a sharp knife in a sheath lashed in the cockpit for just such an emergency. I took it and slashed the fisherman 'sheet' (rope/line to control the angle of the sail) away from the winch head. The sheet whizzed through the blocks (pulleys) and whipped out into the darkening electric sky as the sail shredded into a hundred pieces during a heart-stopping minute of deafening, screaming thrash. I cowered for cover while the debris wrapped itself around the stays and rigging.

I'd now lost a quarter of my sail and had a little more confidence of making it to port, even though the wind gusts picked up another ten miles an hour. Thirty minutes of adrenaline-fuelled fighting at the helm and I got inside the cover of land. The wind subsided to a steady gale, backing off as it changed direction a little after shearing off the hills on the island.

I steered upwind and engaged the auto pilot while I went on deck to drop the sails. I left the foresail part up (reefed) to keep a bit of way on should the engine not start. I also made ready the anchor for the same reason. There are no brakes on a boat with no engine. I was determined to bring her onto the dock myself to show the three little shitty-arsed piggies hiding below, what this big bad wolf was really capable of.

The engine was air locked as expected so I tacked (zigzagged with the wind at alternate sides) in between the piers and landed her beam on to the marina's reporting berth without using the anchor. I'd already made up the mooring lines and dropped the stern line over a bollard as we passed it. When the line went tight and the boat swung in, I was up on deck and jumped onto land with the bow line.

As I walked away, I dropped the bow line on to its bollard. It was 10pm, with no one on duty. I continued walking for more than a mile until I found a bar. There I stayed until they threw me out at

4am, pissed as a twat! Luckily for them, no lights were on when I returned. I found my bunk and slept.

CHAPTER SIX

THE WAR ON DAKAR

When I woke with a screaming hangover, the boat was spotless and shipshape. My pitiful crew had worked their bollocks off to make up for the day before. There was little point rubbing their noses in it as their heads were already down as far as they would go. They'd already made crew declarations at the marina office as Miguel spoke the lingo.

I hadn't seen any paperwork so I still didn't know his real name. I was cheered that he'd lost his bottle the previous day and that made me top dog! I decided to front it out with him and voice my concerns. I was going to call Cordite and I wanted him to tell me his name to verify his position and authority to change the destination.

Miguel refused at first but I stood my ground. He'd taken all our passports to the office. I threatened to go and get a copy of the declaration and clearance form before he agreed. I still went to get a copy and checked everything was above board. He was on record as being on the boat which allayed my fears that someone intended to do away with us and use the vessel.

Miguel was much more compliant after I'd spat in his face. He could hardly look me in the eye. He'd fronted himself as a fearless operative but when the shit hit the fan, he'd run for cover like a pussy! I was back in charge and told him straight; we were staying another day to get supplies and that he was paying for them and the fuel.

We still had more than a thousand miles to go to Dakar and the tanks were empty. He agreed and parted with a slack handful of cash saying "completo". That means "full" and suggested to me he meant that was all he had with him. It was enough for everything, including something nice to smoke.

I called Cordite but he made no sense. He just said that a crew would be waiting wherever Miguel took us. He thought Senegal was a place in Tenerife and started ranting and raving because we hadn't arrived at our destination. He slammed down the phone. Clearly, he was having an unhinged, paranoid moment; everyone was lying to him. I'm sure Geography wasn't in his curriculum while he was robbing the other school kids of their dinner money.

I called him back and told him it would be another week before we could reach Dakar. For almost a minute, he screamed like a demented clown. I could hear him smashing things. This time I hung up to call Dale Gordon and Bocksy (the fixer) to make sure they knew things were beyond my control, and to get assurance that my children would be safe.

The weather forecast was too good, meaning we'd largely be motoring in searing heat without the strong trade winds. I'd already noticed the gearbox was a bit too noisy for my liking; I checked the fluids and resigned myself to that fact that some systems are noisier than others.

After the third day, we could see mainland Africa on the horizon. All I had was a North Atlantic routing chart to work with, which hasn't nearly enough detail for proper navigation. But if sailors hundreds of years ago managed to get where they were going, I was sure we could manage.

To find Dakar, all we had to do was follow the coast south. The city would be easy to spot as there wasn't much else of significance en route.

After another twenty-four hours of blistering heat, the gearbox shit itself, banging and clattering like some twat locked in a coalhouse. We stopped the motor and began to drift slowly south in the trade currents. I knew the problem was terminal!

Unless the wind picked up, we'd be at sea at least another week. I went into the engine compartment to disconnect the propeller shaft from the broken gearbox so the prop would turn freely rather than act as a brake. Graham, holding a torch, said he'd seen "something like that in the forward cabin, under the bunk".

Behold! While they'd been mooching about, they'd spotted a brand new gearbox wrapped in plastic. Clearly, Tonio Lara had known the gearbox was on its way out and bought a spare in advance of it falling apart. The typical Giblet arsehole was too tight to fit it. "Fix it when it's broke" is a stupid policy at sea.

The engine compartment was a confined working space, especially in 38 degrees. But I had everything unbolted in just over four hours and ready to pull the box clear of the engine. After an hour's break for food, we lashed a line to take the weight and tried to lever it free. It wouldn't budge more than a few millimetres.

I double checked everything was unbolted and tried again. Still it wouldn't budge. We banged wedges in the gaps, crow bars… you name it. Something was badly wrong. This part of the operation usually took less than an hour. We were puffing, panting, bleeding and sweating like pit ponies for six hours before we gave up.

Using a makeshift flexible drill shaft, a twelve volt light and a mini board camera from a web cam, I checked inside the bell housing where the starter motor had been removed.

I could see the flywheel and gearbox shaft had seawater ingress, probably from a previous flooding or leak from the oil cooling heat exchanger which uses raw water to cool the gearbox fluid. It was in a terrible state. The main input shaft was seized solid due to electrolysis, which happens when two different metals react in seawater and bond together.

I sprayed a lot of solvents and even diesel fuel into the spaces in the hope of loosening whatever was seized before retiring for the night. We had every sail up to catch what little breeze there was, but still we managed only three knots. Walking pace!

We tried again from first light to nightfall – sixteen hours of hard toil. I was absolutely screwed. We gave up. I reckoned I'd lost a stone in four days of trying. We managed to move it about an inch. For two full days, it didn't move anymore and there was nothing else we could try. We only had limited tools and equipment. Finally

I had to admit defeat; this particular job would require serious heat, probably from an oxy-acetylene burning torch.

We resigned ourselves to a long, slow passage. At least our sunshine cruise had a good supply of everything we needed. Except women of course! My only concern was Cordite's paranoia. I hoped to be able to get a mobile signal as we got closer in to land to explain the delay.

It was futile. I had to accept that the further we got down the coast, the less it was going to be like Europe. In truth, we had no idea what to expect. I had zero knowledge of Senegal or Dakar. I quizzed Miguel, but he knew little more than me; only that there was an International airport and a busy fishing port.

After almost another week of blistering, relentless heat, the frustration was getting to all of us and the atmosphere deteriorated to tetchy arguments. As each Friday came round, Jimmy would descend into a dark mood, he knew that as always, his partner Trish would be out partying.

Although he had the morals of a scrap yard dog, he didn't trust Trish one bit since she'd discovered coke. She'd caught Jimmy out cheating many times and she'd paid him back a few without him knowing. Every Friday, he was like a woman with the worst PMT (post monstrous tension). Nobody could cheer him up.

This Friday was no exception. It was 40 degrees; the sails had been flapping and banging all day in a dancing breeze. He'd been on the wheel for six hours and made only seven miles when he exploded into a rage, smashing empty San Miguel beer bottles all over the deck.

I grabbed him by the neck and quickly overpowered him before he did any serious damage; he'd had too much sun and alcohol and completely lost the plot. I kept hold of him while a horrified Graham and Miguel looked on. I made him take salt tablets with sweet tea and rolled a nice big joint to share while I gave him a bit of 'counselling'. Just as he was pulling himself together, the wind started to gust and finally settled to a steady breeze.

As the sun went down, the boat was sailing smoothly at six knots, hardly fast, but after twelve days of virtually drifting, it seemed like we were flying. It lifted our spirits. Then, as if it couldn't get any better, we saw artificial light on the horizon. Could it be Dakar? Only a GPS fix or a light house sequence would confirm it for sure.

The GPS only supplied co-ordinates which would normally be transferred onto a detailed chart. In our case, 3mm represented 60 miles (one degree) on our old routing chart which clearly stated that it was "not to be used for navigation".

We concluded that as near as damn it, our journey was almost over. There was only the light house to spot which, according to our information, could be seen for 60 miles in good visibility at night. We couldn't see it but assumed we were too far inshore. We headed out to 40 miles offshore to keep clear of any rocks, sunken obstructions or fishing nets. Without a chart, we'd need to wait and follow another boat in or risk a disaster.

Any sailor, even a tanker captain, relies on 'pilot information' which these days is displayed on a chart plotter or a laptop. But back in the early nineties, small vessels mainly relied on a pilot book for a specific area.

An up to date pilot book gave the skipper information about depths, obstructions, hazards, radio channels, facilities, safe channel lights and buoys. Everything needed for safe entry into an unfamiliar port.

We had zero information and really didn't want to be getting into any shit. Following a local, reasonably sized vessel is always a good idea in such circumstances. Furthermore, it was dark; despite my crew's eagerness, I didn't want to be arriving until the morning anyway.

As we got closer, we could see fires burning all across the city. It didn't look good. Miguel was clearly worried and had no explanation. We were probably twenty miles out when we started to hear explosions and gunfire. A couple of helicopters were buzzing around randomly.

We were absolutely gob smacked. It was obviously some sort of coup or civil war. We'd sailed thousands of miles to a war zone. Cordite and Co had really messed things up! I made my intentions very clear; no way, as long as I had a hole in my arse, was I taking us into that port!

The risk of upsetting Cordite, his thugs, and our friendly pretend Basque terrorist, paled into insignificance at the thought of burning tyres around our necks and hundreds of drug crazed rebels firing AK47s into the air. Not my idea of a cruise destination, that's for sure!

I decided not to get any closer. I didn't want to go anywhere near their twelve miles of jurisdiction and stayed out in international waters. We would wait until the morning and see if there were any vessels coming or going.

Miguel could speak French and he assured me that was the second language in Senegal. The plan was to find out what was occurring by VHF radio. If that failed, we would edge closer and hope for a mobile phone signal.

The fighting became more intense as midnight approached and then seemed to die down to almost nothing. This was very puzzling. We imagined all sorts of scenarios. Had there been a coup? Was it successful? Was it a random attack by rebels? What should we do next?

We knew we'd be an easy target for looters on the rampage. Without a gearbox in the port, they'd be able to catch us by swimming, never mind a 'war canoe'. There'd been horror stories of civil unrest and gruesome accounts of atrocities in various parts of Africa at that time.

We racked our brains to remember which countries were affected. But Jimmy and Graham were hardly into current affairs. They rarely got past the tits on page three and the football at the back of any newspaper.

As the sun came up over the now silent city, once fierce fires were spewing smouldering columns of lazy smoke against the pale watery skyline, marking the areas where the devastation was worst.

It had been a long, hard and worrying night.

An hour later, the first fishing kayaks ventured from the port. We could see with binoculars they didn't have lights, never mind a VHF radio. With no motor, we had no way of getting within earshot of them. The wind was extremely light and Dakar is on an outcrop of land, on an otherwise straight coastline with north to south currents.

It was hard to keep a steady course. We didn't want to call the port radio in case it'd been over-run by rebels; how could we trust whoever answered? It was 11.30am before a motor fishing vessel came headed towards us.

A ship's VHF has a low power setting which can be used ship to ship without everyone else listening in. We waited with baited breath until they were close enough before Miguel manned the radio. He called for twenty minutes in French and Spanish. Finally, I tried in English and got a reply.

His English was only just understandable, and I'm sure he thought the same about mine. But after about five minutes, we arrived at a startling but welcome revelation; there was no civil war, no bombing and no rebels. It had been the President's birthday with street parties, bonfires and fireworks. The helicopters were the president and his entourage, visiting various gatherings.

We did feel daft! We'd been shitting ourselves for twenty five hours for nothing. What a relief! We were battered and desperate for sleep. We'd smoked joint after joint, in fear of our lives.

I set the sails up for a steady run in and went to bed for a couple of hours, leaving instructions to wake me as we approached. It was four hours before I was back at the wheel. The entrance to the port was sheltered from the prevailing wind, so we were whispering along at less than three knots, but at least we were making way.

I ignored the crew who wanted to hail a tow. I didn't want any claims of salvage or ridiculous excuses to levy crazy charges on us. I knew of dozens of such horror stories, including mine with the Michelle Louise. It wasn't going to happen to me again.

It was one of the best accomplishments of my sailing history and I give the credit to my dear old dad. Back in the days of our old gaff rigged yawl Kestrel, we had no engine most of the time and he would say, "How do you think they did it before engines?" He'd make us tack into Hartlepool, refusing to use the engine, even when it was working.

I tacked our way through the busy port, upsetting numerous craft. Skippers yelled and horns blared but I ignored them completely. My concentration was intense. Finally, I told the crew to drop all sails and landed perfectly against the dock side. We'd made it. What a relief!

CHAPTER SEVEN

THE DARK SIDE OF DAKAR

I'd picked a large wharf to come alongside. The port stank of rotten fish and dirty oil. It was absolutely filthy. It wasn't long before we were inundated with locals offering all sorts of services and wares, many trying to get on board. It was a nightmare and we seriously weren't in the mood for visitors. I'd only slept for a few hours and the others were desperate to be stood down.

We slackened the lines and I left Graham with a boathook to keep us a couple of meters from the dockside and stop the marauders jumping onboard. He only spoke limited English to start with and was easily the best at pulling a 'dunno mate' face. We had a nice cup of tea and relaxed before the officials arrived. How English!

We said we were en route to the Caribbean when the gearbox failed; it didn't take much believing as the engine compartment was obviously like a bomb site. Red Marlboro and whisky were in big demand and after the fourth different uniform had left, I was starting to get pissed off.

The next to arrive was a doctor saying he was from the department of health. He wanted to see our vaccination cards; apparently he was worried we might catch some diseases. It was the last straw; I asked what diseases we needed vaccines for and he named a few like Dengue Fever, Yellow Fever and Malaria.

I showed him all our anti-mosquito medicine and documents which proved where we'd been. But he still wasn't happy. Then I asked him how much to vaccinate us as he was carrying his black doctor's bag? He opened his bag revealing it was empty. He smiled as I dropped in two hundred Marlboro and he was gone. Africa!

They wanted us to move from the wharf as they were expecting a ship. Of course we had to bung them to tow us further round the docks, close to a tuna canning factory. The stench was gagging, absolutely sickening. All the rubbish, fish carcasses and floating shit had been blown into our corner. I was heaving in no time.

I knew the port captain spoke better French than English, so Miguel was dispatched with a carrier bag full of goodies and some American dollars to bribe him for a better berth. Within an hour, we were moved to the next section. It still stank, but not nearly as bad. From the minute you arrive in these places, they work tirelessly to relieve you of as much money as possible.

Miguel arrived back with two big local guys who'd been assigned by the firm to look after our boat and keep the marauders at bay. They spoke English in a fashion and I made it quite clear that they were not to go below decks under any circumstances. They agreed, so we fed them the same food as ourselves which they seemed to appreciate greatly.

I was told our contacts would meet us the next day. I didn't want to get off the boat, but I had to make some calls to let people know we were okay. Miguel stayed elsewhere that night. Jimmy and I ventured out; I didn't really trust our boat sitters. We had to present our passports to get in or out of the port area. We found the nearest hotel with a bar and ordered cold beers before calling home.

Dawn simply didn't believe what I told her. She thought I'd been partying. I'd only bought a three day return ticket to Gibraltar and I'd been away more than three weeks. She was furious, but I couldn't explain fully what was going on for security reasons. That only made matters worse. Let's face it; we could hardly believe what had happened ourselves!

Jimmy had much the same problem, so we resigned ourselves to the fact that we would be home in a day or two and could tell the whole story then. A couple of cold beers later, we walked back to the port. Inside, half a dozen little huts offered drink, music and a full range of prostitutes.

Graham was awe-struck at the women chasing him and shouting

compliments. Bless him. I led him to believe they just loved white guys because their own men had nothing and mistreated them.

He could have his pick of any of them, because they'd come from their tribe in the jungle to find a 'Bwana' white man! He'd never been abroad before and suddenly he was in deepest darkest Africa where every local girl thought he was a millionaire playboy on a beautiful white yacht.

He took it all in and went to sleep with all sorts of notions going on in his head. Next morning, he asked how much money he was owed in wages.

"Enough to buy one of them, mate," I said.

We packed our bags ready for the off and waited around for Miguel to turn up. I'd made a list of all the jobs that needed doing and compiled a book of instructions for the machinery, equipment and fittings on board. Without these, it would be a nightmare for the new crew. We'd only recently discovered some things, such as a fuel transfer pump and still had a full tank in the stern.

There were instructions for everything, based on our experiences on board. Miguel finally turned up with three 'engineers' with burning gear to remove the old gearbox. I asked about our tickets home.

Miguel just looked at me puzzled and said, "No comprende," and indicated a meeting was arranged later with English speaking bosses. Oh what joy!

The gearbox bell housing had to be burned away so they could get to the shaft. Even after it was heated to a cherry red, the shaft still wouldn't come out. I told them to chop it off to get the box out, and then weld something to it so that a slide hammer or hydraulic jack could be used to part it.

It finally came out after eight hours. The boat reeked. The 'engineers' hadn't showered for a while, that much was obvious. I insisted they washed on board and gave them some old clean clothes before we fed them with a decent meal and a few beers. They loved us for that. Within an hour, I had the new box fitted. The Melanie had propulsion again. We showered and waited for Miguel, who'd promised us a steak restaurant.

He finally arrived at 8pm in a big old Mercedes driven by a local.

We locked up the boat and left our two watchmen on deck before clearing immigration out of the port and on to a hotel restaurant. We'd already eaten some decent steaks and sunk a few beers by the time four men turned up to join us.

We were introduced and moved to a bigger table in a private function room. They were all classic middle-aged Arabs, dressed in fine suits, sporting moustaches, big jewellery and sunglasses. Their entourage of six local women and one teenage boy arrived a couple of minutes later, herded in by another Arab. He was clearly a go-for in a cheaper suit and wearing a plastic watch. It was obvious the women were rented for the amusement of all. But not the boy; he sat next to one of the men who fondled him occasionally, much to my discomfort.

Two of the Arabs spoke decent English. They said they were Egyptian but I had my doubts. They were evasive when pressed. They certainly weren't good Muslims, that's for sure. Even though they pretended to be flash, I saw through them. The food was expensive and they'd timed it just right after the kitchen had closed, so they didn't have to feed anybody else.

Rather than buy drinks at hotel prices, they soon ushered us out to a nearby club "where everyone can relax". The club was mostly outdoors but we were ushered into a small lounge inside. They gave the girls a few dollars to eat at the snack bar while we talked.

One of them, Momet, who seemed to be the boss, produced a bag of cocaine and began to chop it on the table. He didn't seem bothered when the waiter came in with a tray full of bottled Heineken. I got the impression that this was their regular whore hole; they could do as they liked as long as they flashed a few dollars.

He gestured to us to use the drugs. I politely refused. So did Graham who was a coke virgin. I wanted to keep my head together and although I gestured to Jimmy to refuse too, and even kicked him under the table, he quickly and defiantly snorted all three lines on offer.

Jimmy had briefly ventured into the world of drug dealing and should have recognised the purity after the first line. But, ever the greedy arsehole, the Dip was doing an impression of Al Pacino in

Scarface. Much to the amazement of our hosts, he asked for more and snorted that too!

In ten minutes, any hope of intelligent conversation was lost… he was out of it! Wide-eyed and belligerent, he screamed, "Where's my bitch? Where's my black bitch?" as he fell backwards off his chair pulling the tablecloth and everybody's drinks with him.

The evening descended into chaos. The only thing we learned was that they expected us to supervise all of the servicing and repairs and there would be more 'engineers' arriving the next day.

We managed to load Jim into the car as he shouted at the women to join him. Three piled into the back and lay across us; their little luminous dresses hiked up revealing bare arses and shaved pussies. The smell was quite awful as they wriggled around trying to grab our cocks and shove their tits at us.

They weren't much classier than the tarts in the port and must have cost all of ten dollars each. I spotted another club with flashing lights and ordered the driver to stop. I managed to persuade the girls we were going in. When they climbed out, I threw some dollars into the road and told the driver to leave them… much to the fury of Al Pacino; he'd announced he wanted to bugger all three! Ha! The cockroach!

Graham and I hit the bunks and left him on deck talking shit to our watchmen. By morning, they'd done three litres of whisky and nearly two hundred cigarettes; Jimmy was still in a coma when some guys arrived to repair a damaged sail.

The GPS set had played up time and time again. There was a much better commercial set fitted, but there was no antenna for it. Although I'd provided Momet and his merry men with the commercial set's model, serial number and the address and contact details of the agents in Dakar, I was a little disappointed that they sent a guy with an electrical meter and a soldering iron to look at the old one instead. But hey, it wasn't my problem.

But he could speak good English and I quizzed him about the Egyptians, managing to get the address of their hotel. I jumped in a taxi, and saw them leaving on foot. I followed them to a cafe a few hundred metres away. I casually walked in and joined them.

They were surprised and asked how I found them.

I said, "I just asked the taxi driver to take me to the Egyptian men's hotel, and he did."

This put them off guard. I'm sure they wanted to remain anonymous.

First off, they refused to buy the antenna for the GPS as it was $300. Typical! The whole operation depended on exact meeting points at sea, both to collect and then to transfer the drugs near the UK. And they wanted to rely on a dodgy old GPS rather than spend their coke money on an aerial.

The real bosses and financiers of these deals have no idea how much of the 'expenses' fund is creamed off for high living, drugs and prostitutes. This type of dimwit is responsible for many failed jobs because they rob money from everywhere, Silly bastards!

Historically, the hashish business was run by well-to-do, intelligent university hippy types, who understood the importance of planning and proper funding. By the time the bank robbers and gangsters got involved, it all turned to shit, with petty criminals they met in jail becoming lieutenants in charge of funds in faraway places.

Consequently, you end up with cash-rich amateur crooks pretending to be the main men. They live the high life which costs more than their personal expenses or wages. So they lie and steal, putting the job in jeopardy. Of course, they're not telling Mr Big about the coke, champagne and rented bum holes. Oh no! They're supposed to be working!

Finally I got round to us. "Where are our flight tickets home, when do we leave?" I asked.

The two English speaking guys glared at each other, then translated what I'd said to the others. They had a short conversation in Arabic. What I'd said, judging by their body language had come as a shock.

My heart sank because I knew what was coming. I could feel the banging in my chest and a sharp pain at the base of my spine as the tension built up.

"Well?" I asked firmly, glaring at Momet.

He raised his hands like he was carrying a big bowl and

smiled. "Mr Philip, there are no tickets for you, I know nothing about this."

I tried hard to stay composed as I explained what was supposed to happen. They insisted they'd been told we were meeting the supply ship, and there was no other crew. I was shaking with rage. I slammed down on the table and left before I did something I'd regret.

My two eager crewmen were waiting at the boat for news. They expected to be paid well and be given tickets to London as promised. I went below and made a big joint before I devastated their worlds.

I was surprised how well they took it. Then it dawned on me that neither had ever had a pot to piss in and a big pay day was something they'd been chasing, since bullying their way onto the boat.

I, on the other hand, couldn't spend what I was earning and had all the trappings I could want. They knew they were close to the dope and weren't going to get a lot for delivering an empty boat. They wanted the big score!

I called Cordite. There was no other crew coming. He blamed the problems with the gearbox and the time it'd taken us to get there. It was all bullshit. I refused point blank to sail it and hung up. Next, I called Dawn and asked her to go to a secure line. Calling from a different phone, I told her to collect some money from my business, buy us some flight tickets and bring them out on the next available plane.

She refused… I was shell shocked! I explained we were in really serious shit, but she wouldn't talk about it; she didn't believe me. She point-blank refused and put the phone down. I thought she must have been threatened by someone in the gang or even the police. It would be a lot later when I found out the truth.

In any other circumstances, she'd have done what I asked without question. It wasn't like I was asking her to commit a crime. All I wanted was a route out. She'd already been involved and knew fine well what was happening. I was completely devastated and more than a bit worried.

To add custard to my shit crumble, I returned to the port about an hour later to find a car waiting outside with Momet and two nasty looking natives standing by it. There was no point in making a scene; life is pretty cheap in these places and witnesses are easy to buy off. I got in the car and was taken back to the night club. It was daytime, so it was shut. The security guard let us in and we were ushered to the outside area under some palm trees.

Momet didn't look happy... neither did his two gorillas that were in combat stance, expecting me to kick off or run. I couldn't hide the fact that I was weighing up all the options. Running was pointless; the cleaner had locked the gate behind him. If I'd fought my way out, where was I going to go? I knew I had little choice, but to front it out.

I knew they needed me or they would've taken me elsewhere to do me in. I decided to act cool despite my heart banging like a bass drum at a miners' march. The next few minutes of awkward silence reminded me of a scene in a bad gangster movie where I was expected to beg for my life. Instead I was in a boxing stance. I didn't exactly fancy my chances, but there were no weapons on show and I wasn't going to be even bitch slapped without putting up a hell of a fight.

It was like a Mexican standoff. Momet was puffed up, trying to look angry and nodding his head at them to commence the beating. After three attempts, he was starting to look stupid as his henchmen demonstrated that they were just for show, or hadn't been paid enough to get rough.

The security guard came onto the scene and something was said in French, probably, "We need help."

One of the heavies finally made a lunge at me. Instead of backing off, I stepped forward and caught him clean on the chin with a knockout right hook.

Except it didn't knock him out! He rolled over and got straight back up, albeit a bit wobbly. It was as good a punch as I had in the locker and I'd had the element of total surprise. I knew I was in trouble! I put my hands up in the air to surrender as the guard hit me on the back of the legs with a baton. I crumbled to floor and got a taste of the dirt as he hit me again across the back.

It didn't seem like they wanted to hurt me, it was more to show who was in charge. It might have gone on for a bit longer, but someone was banging on the gate. In came the other four Arabs with an older, tall guy.

They immediately remonstrated with my captors and a short row broke out. I didn't fall for it. They were doing a stage managed 'good guy, bad guy' routine. The old guy gave me his hand, pulled me up, dusted me off and sat me down before ordering drinks all round.

The big guy I'd hit was looking pretty sheepish, rinsing blood from his mouth where I'd knocked a tooth out and split his tongue. It emerged he was a professional boxer in the city. At nearly seven feet tall and four stone heavier than me, he looked a scary bastard. The others were laughing at him, so I took the initiative and offered to shake his hand.

He'd made a move and underestimated an opponent he didn't know by stepping forward; I'd got the drop on him. In the ring, he'd have got a standing count; out in the street, one to one, I'd have booted him before he got up. He took my hand, nodded his head and gave me his tooth for a memento. The drinks arrived and we sat down as though nothing had happened.

The old guy was known only as El Capitan. He was Cuban and had a face a dog wouldn't lick, even if it was covered in marmite. He looked like he'd been fed with a catapult as a baby and had teeth like two rows of bombed out houses. In short, he was a big ugly twat. He was sixty plus but you wouldn't want to mess with him.

He spoke English with a deep gravelly voice as he explained what I already knew. The group was sorry but were only passing information from very bad people. It was out of their control. My family was in danger and there was a lot of money at stake. He said I had no choice, they were desperate. "The ship has been waiting months," he said, "and they will pay you one million Great British Pounds."

There was no point arguing. We were between a rock and a hard place. I'd already contemplated our position and knew I'd have to play along or they'd murder us and use the boat anyway. There were clearly a lot of people in the conspiracy and a boat load of money at stake. Three lads from the North East going missing was a small risk by comparison, considering where we were. I could hardly imagine the idiots in Cordite's gang giving a damn about us.

Jimmy and Graham were already up for it. And so it was to be. For the sake of my family, I would kill or die… whatever!

I got back to the boat and drew up lists of jobs and items we needed. We were leaving in two days with El Capitan to meet a ship and collect five tons of hashish from Afghanistan. Where the hell they were going to put five tons on a forty two foot yacht was another matter.

I was told we were collecting diesel fuel from the supply ship, so cleaned all the water storage tanks out for extra capacity. This, along with quite a few 25 litre drums, would give us the range we needed to motor most of the way north against the prevailing Trade Winds and currents.

We bought a shit load of bottled water along with our supplies which would easily last us four weeks. At an average seven knots speed over ground, we would sail one hundred and sixty eight miles per twenty-four hour day. With not much over three thousand miles direct, it would take three weeks on auto pilot… five hundred hours. The Perkins engine used a little over a gallon an hour at cruising speed. My extended capacity of six hundred gallons would do the trick.

The extra fuel weight would be an issue at first, but reduce by the time we got into any shitty seas, further north. We'd be seriously overloaded, but if the load was spread out properly, it would help with stability. I doubted that we'd have enough room below for five tons, and we'd definitely be low in the water, especially at first.

We went out on the razzle on our last night with more than a little trepidation. On returning to the port, we passed a chubby native girl who'd been chasing Graham persistently for five days. He pulled on my shirt and said, "Please can I have permission to go ashore, Captain?"

I pulled out $50 and gave it to him.

"What's this for?" he asked.

"In case you need a hotel. Be back in the morning, before noon."
He was gone.

By the time I'd rolled a joint and got a drink, Jimmy too decided he wanted to go back out. I also offered him money, but he said he wouldn't need it as his girl had her own place.

I replied, "You're as green as him, you daft twat. You don't think she fancies you, do you? She'll want paying!"

The silly bastard looked at me like I'd hurt his feelings. Although he had more scars on his face than teeth, Jimmy could pull a woman with his patter. The stark realisation that he was about to pay for sex hit him hard. But the fact he was going to be at sea for some time, and had been without sex since the sluts in Gibraltar who gave him the pox, made him get over it quickly; he took the money, forty fags, a bottle of J&B and jumped off the boat.

"What about you?" he asked.

"Don't worry about me, I've got three coming here in ten minutes now you two have gone," I joked. I'd never been able to get my head around the prostitute thing. I preferred to believe the gold-diggers that threw themselves at me really fancied me! Ha ha. The thought of those poor girls being abused by some of the animals in the port turned my stomach; I pitied them.

The likes of Jimmy and Graham would certainly be a welcome change, and I was sure they wouldn't come back with any money! I needed to be alone (apart from the watchmen on deck) to contemplate our position.

I knew this bunch of idiots had no intentions of paying us anything, even if they made top price for the cannabis. The gear had obviously been sitting about out at sea for a long time. I was told the ship's engine was broken and they were drifting offshore, waiting for spares.

I realised this was the same ship that the Fixer from Blackpool had asked me to meet off Ireland in March. Then, when we'd set off from Cueta, she was supposed to be off Tenerife, more than a thousand miles north. If she was drifting, she would be heading back south, so it made sense.

The Trade Winds are so called because the old Square Riggers and other highly inefficient sailing rigs relied on seasonal weather patterns to cross the oceans. For most of the year, the largely northerly winds and southerly currents would carry a vessel south from Europe to the Cape Verde Islands and across the Atlantic to the Caribbean and the Americas.

Coming back the same way would take three times as long. So a vessel would sail north up the coast of America before crossing The Atlantic. When today's adventurers row across in little boats, they take advantage of these systems.

As the supply ship had supposedly set off with twenty five tons on board, there was no way they could enter any port for repairs until they'd unloaded at sea. No bloody wonder they were desperate.

Of course I had no idea how much they'd already got rid of. I didn't have a plan, only to comply with them. Anything could happen en route, but at least my family would be safe if I was seen to try my best.

If all went to plan and Cordite got possession, the likelihood of anyone else getting paid was slim, never mind us. I'm sure that's why the professional smugglers had been screwing him about for so long.

This load was obviously a desperate mission... much more difficult than a thousand miles from Morocco to the UK. The organisers would have become more and more desperate as the ship drifted further south, away from profit and into trouble. That's why they allowed Cordite and his gang into the big league; they probably had nothing to lose. I went to sleep lonely, drunk and stoned.

CHAPTER EIGHT

PIRATE RENDEZVOUS

Much to my annoyance, Jimmy couldn't get his arse out of his bunk until after ten and then he was about as much use as a chocolate fireguard. Graham turned up at noon on the dot. I quizzed him about his night, if only to brighten the day up. He'd gone to her home and met the family before spending the night on a dirty mattress on the floor. At least she had her own room.

It all sounded pretty sordid but the lad had a spring in his step, no money left and a cock like a blind cobbler's thumb… for which I dispensed some antibiotic cream. He had to shave his pubes later or learn to walk sideways like his new guests. I put the pair of them on antibiotics for three days as a precaution. These daft twats were in their late thirties. I think their idea of safe sex was: always put your money in your sock, and never tell them your real name!

I sent Graham for some last minute supplies including batteries, 'skins' (Rizla papers) and some fishing hooks. The big ugly Cuban arrived with nothing but the clothes he was in, fags and a loaded Colt revolver in a holster. I showed him to his bunk and left him with a bottle of rum while we made ready and motored out into the busy port under a lot more control than on the way in.

The port officials had clearly been bribed not to worry about departure clearance as they closed their window shutters when they saw us approach. I'd already been told to go straight past and was happy to oblige. We were short on decent fags, but I'd bought a carrier bag full of local weed from our watchmen. It smelt much stronger once we'd left the vicinity of the tuna factory.

Soon, we were into the open away from the stench. The fresh, clean air made us realise just how bad it'd been. El Capitan emerged half-pissed. He obviously didn't want to be seen on board in the port. He gave me GPS co-ordinates to set a course. I was shocked to find out we were going south again for at least a day.

Everything was working fine; the new gearbox was quiet and smooth and we seemed to have more power. The old one must have been sapping the power due to worn parts. We headed on a south west course for approximately 160 miles until we were level with the Gambia and 120 miles offshore. We were cracking along at 9 knots making good time.

Every half an hour, we would call out a code word on the VHF channel 8 (low power) and check the radar. At 9am I spotted a target twenty miles away, just as I received a faint garbled reply. I woke the Cuban with a coffee; he poured half out, filled it up with rum and drank it in one.

Within half an hour, we could hear the other station clearly and after confirming code words, I was confused to hear him say, "I can see you on my radar. We will come to you." That's the last thing I expected from a drifting ship with a broken engine!

I was suspicious, but it was hardly relevant at the time. We both sailed towards each other; I calculated from the radar they must have been doing at least 7 knots. Within an hour, we were close enough to read the name on the bow without binoculars.

The Kelaha IV was a coaster approximately two hundred feet long and in a terrible state. No wonder they couldn't come into port. I supposed it'd been hacking about the coast of Pakistan where it was registered. Clearly there was little regulation; I remember thinking the tug in Campbeltown was a rusty bag of shit. But I couldn't imagine this steaming far from land, never mind around Cape Horn!

The crew looked like a bunch of desperate marooned pirates; filthy, unshaven barbarians, they wouldn't have got a job on Captain Barbossa's ship the "Black Pearl". As we closed, they began to make preparations for us to come alongside. They were still moving slowly forward to maintain heading and reduce the rolling.

There was a fair bit of swell as I neared their starboard side. I could clearly see she was rolling too much to be safe. I span the wheel to get clear but the Cuban pushed me over, grabbed it and turned back into the ship as a line was thrown down. I screamed at him to pull away but backed off as I looked up at the bridge and saw an AK47 assault rifle pointed right at me.

He shouted at Jimmy to take the line and tie it on. Jimmy complied as best he could; the lads were both terrified at the sight of the gun and frankly so was I. We were going to sustain damage, but I had more to worry about than the boat.

My brain was exploding. Scenarios flashed through my head. Were we to be murdered at sea as I'd feared weeks earlier? I contemplated the Cuban's revolver as the line tightened and pulled us into contact with the rusty battered hull and her squared, protruding rubbing strake. The strake immediately destroyed our fenders and started to tear into our aluminium skin above the water line. Jesus! These men were crazy!

As the ship rolled, the crosstrees, the part of our rigging apparatus that pushes the wire rope stays away from the mast, caught on the ship's handrails and twisted them. We were now locked together as the ship rolled again causing more severe dents in our hull. I shouted to Jimmy to untie us, but he'd lashed the line in a hurry and had no chance while it was tight.

I screamed at the Cuban, holding on in the cockpit, "You stupid idiot, you're going to sink us, do something clever!" He was pissed, panicking and useless. I jumped into the cockpit to grab the big knife. For a second he thought I was going to gut him. I knocked the gear lever into forward to give Jimmy some slack and jumped on deck ready to cut the line if he still couldn't untie it.

As the ship rolled again, the crosstrees unlocked from the handrails and nearly took one of the crew's head off with a wire stay. He was knocked to the floor with blood gushing from where his ear had been. Another of their crewmen took a fire axe and brought it crashing onto the bollard, parting the strained line with a loud twang.

Our boat lurched forward still under power. Because the line had been cut high on the deck, it fell into the sea and quickly wrapped around our propeller. The useless Cuban bastard should have knocked her into neutral as soon as he saw the line fall into the water.

In only a couple of seconds, nasty noises came from below. The propeller stopped dead but the engine was still in drive. The flexible coupling was destroyed, freeing the shaft to whip around in the engine compartment. I pushed the daft twat out of the way and hit the emergency stop button.

We drifted clear but after less than one minute, we'd sustained serious hull, rigging and mechanical damage. Mayhem! The adrenaline was surging through my veins as I forgot all fear and launched into a tirade of abuse, shouting and clapping at the Cuban who was still sitting on the floor in shock. Dickhead!

I sarcastically congratulated the captain of the ship via VHF on his crew's professionalism and to report we had no drive. To my relief, he apologised profusely for his crew's stupidity. If they intended us harm, he would hardly be eating humble pie.

Next it was the Cuban's turn. "And what the hell were you the captain of… your local, bloody football team? You useless bastard! Look at the damage!" He hung his head in shame… as did the coaster's crew as their captain bawled at them in Arabic from the bridge.

We launched our little RHIB from the deck and I went on board. The crewman with half his ear missing was concussed. They had no medic and only a very sparse first aid kit. I'd brought mine along from the Michelle Louise. It had nearly everything a trauma team would need.

I ordered some clean boiling water. We had two choices: just tidy the ear up or attempt to stitch it and risk infection. It was going to be a mess anyway so we sedated him, cut the raggy bits off and dressed it. I gave them a high dose of antibiotics for him to take for three days and left a fresh dressing.

I told the captain I would try and fix our boat. The rigging was an easy repair although it wouldn't look good; the hull was quite dented but thankfully, still watertight. The prop coupling would need something fabricating. He said we would have to use the sails if we couldn't fix it. Then he asked for food. His crew were starving.

They'd been on very short rations for six weeks as a re-supply boat hadn't turned up. They'd been promised fuel and stores two months earlier. Hence they were drifting about… they only had enough engine fuel for a couple of days steaming. I sympathised with them. They looked terrible and given what I already knew about the people we'd dealt with, I got the distinct impression they'd also been misled.

The horrible idiots in Dakar who posed around the city with whores, rent boys and cocaine, hadn't even given the Cuban a bag of groceries for them. I sorted them out a selection of food, drink and fags. They were ecstatic.

I set about the coupling, spending eight hours sitting in the bilges. I fabricated a replacement with two pieces of hardwood ply, eight pieces of high pressure hose all fixed together with eight bolts. It was a brilliant job, considering we were more than a hundred miles offshore. It worked fine.

By the time darkness was falling, the coaster had used our RHIB to ferry nearly 100 sacks of cannabis resin, each 'packet' weighing about 35 kilos. I told the captain to stop; there was no room for what we had, never mind any more. The last load still came, making a round number of 100 sacks. They were in such a rush, a couple of sacks went to the bottom, and they didn't bat an eyelid.

I radioed the captain about our fuel.

Another bombshell.

"We have no fuel," he replied. "We have no instructions to give you fuel."

I jumped into the RHIB, shot across and boarded the ship. I was shouting and cursing at the Cuban who was already extremely unpopular with the crew.

They'd not even had a coffee for a month and were all ganging up on him. I could see why he brought his revolver; there were some desperate looking bastards, I can tell you.

Finally, they agreed to give me what diesel they had in the bottom of a tank for the auxiliary generator but only in exchange for some more supplies to see them through a few days. It took another two hours to fill our plastic drums with 180 gallons, less than a third of what we needed. And it was filthy.

The Cuban came across with two crewmen in a little rowing boat because the front of the RHIB floor had been ripped from the inflatable tubes as the two lost sacks were thrown in; it was now useless for carrying anything heavy. They began to ferry the fuel and lifted the drums onto our deck.

I sorted out another five plastic carrier bags of supplies for them, including 400 cigarettes, coffee, tea, juices, tins, a range of dried food and ten cases of bottled water. It meant we would have to be careful but what choice did we have?

We worked ourselves to a frazzle, stashing everything as low as possible in every conceivable place. When they'd brought the last of the fuel over, they fired up the engine and headed back to where we'd first spotted them. I wondered what the hell they were doing, but it was none of my business. After an hour, their stern light disappeared on the horizon.

I heard a faint crackle on the VHF. It was a southern English accent hailing the same call sign we'd been given. They obviously had another rendezvous scheduled at the same co-ordinates which accounted for their hasty behaviour. I'd already had a feeling there was someone else coming as I picked up a bit of the Egyptian's conversations.

Quite often, such an organisation would be tasked to bring a cargo within range of other smaller vessels. They would expect to get paid, whatever happened to the gear afterwards. Their job is over once they unload to the corresponding passwords. The Europeans clearly hadn't been able to organise things properly.

There'd be plenty of transport up near Spain or Northern Morocco which could blend into the traffic. The gear they had was worth at least the same as the Moroccan commercial blend, but lack of fuel, organisation and commitment had seen them hanging about for months.

Very large RHIBs stay up to one hundred miles out in the Med off Morocco, because they'd be impounded if caught inshore; even if empty. They meet other boats for stores and crew changes while waiting for a job.

They come onto the beach for loads then rendezvous with the customers far away from the patrol boats. When it's all unloaded, they still have to stay out. At the end of the season, they'll use the RHIB to land gear on a beach or up a river in Spain or Portugal, usually until they get caught.

It's a suicide mission, but the jail time given in Spanish courts is nothing compared to the UK and the rewards for the brave Moroccans are extremely high.

CHAPTER NINE

LOADED TO THE GUNWALES

We fired up our motor and headed north. The sacks were jammed everywhere. We were walking on them two deep. I tried to listen for further transmissions, but heard nothing that made any sense.

The lads went below to sleep, absolutely shattered. I broke open one of the sacks. What the hell? I might as well try it! I immediately noticed the hessian sacks were mouldy inside, clearly this stuff had been hidden for some time in a damp, dark place deep inside the rusty old tub. However, each slab was wrapped individually and well protected.

It was foil-packed, disguised as commercial Cajun sauce mix in approximately nine ounce portions, four portions to a kilo. On the street, it would be described as 'Paki Black' or 'Soft Black'. It wasn't the usual stuff on the street in the North East... it was better. I rolled and smoked a number of joints, relying on the autopilot, while I dizzily pondered our position.

It was an excellent smoke and certainly did the trick, especially as we were free and clear of the 'Pirates of Karachi'. Any more disasters would be down to us. We just needed a plan. The wind was light but steady; the sea state was so calm, I even had a few drinks. It was a very pleasant shift; I let the lads sleep for over 12 hours and I never heard a peep from them.

They woke up starving, just as I was starting to flag. Both were bright and cheerful. It was a lovely day and Jimmy went below to the galley to rustle up some food. I'd spent all night munching pistachios and was looking forward to something cooked. Within a minute, we heard him cursing and banging about. He came up in a right state… I thought for a moment we must be taking water, but he blurted out, "We've been robbed; the dirty idiots have robbed us. Come and have a look."

We followed him below to the stern saloon and galley; all the cupboard doors were open, the seat cushions were strewn about and the lockers beneath them were also open. At first, I thought Jimmy had found it like that, but it was him who'd opened everything to check inside.

We had indeed been robbed; most of our supplies had gone. The Melanie had split accommodation, forward and aft of the cockpit. Nobody had been in the galley or stern saloon since the last of the fuel had been transferred. The greedy, horrible, thieving bastards! They must have rifled a locker each time they'd come on board.

We spent an hour in shock trying to remember what was in each space. In addition to the food and drinks, they'd swiped the Marlboro and only left some of the French cigarettes we'd bought in Dakar to top up supplies. We couldn't for the life of us understand how we hadn't noticed them bring stuff up the hatch and onto the deck.

Finally, we found how they'd managed to pull it off. There was a watertight hatch into the galley where they tied their row boat to our port side. We'd always had it shut with the four fasteners screwed up tight. Only one remained. One of the coaster crew must have been hiding down there for a couple of hours and passing stuff out each time they set off back to their ship.

We were seething. I couldn't believe our bad luck. If I'd sorted out their supplies after the fuel arrived and not before we'd have noticed immediately. We were gutted! They'd systematically picked the best stuff, leaving us with nothing but shit and not enough for the three weeks we'd be at sea. Even that calculation was now null and void as it depended on us getting enough fuel to motor all the way.

I declared a state of emergency and ordered an inventory from Jimmy of every morsel of food and drinkable liquid. I insisted that Graham searched the boat afterwards. I knew Jimmy only too well. Sure enough, we found a couple of plastic bags filled with tinned goodies that he'd salted away, probably weeks earlier.

He hung his head in shame until I told him we wouldn't still have them if he hadn't hidden them. He'd been caught red-handed again, but still made out he should be in charge of the stores. You'd think he'd bought them with his own money. He was priceless that bloke.

We divided everything by thirty, which was my revised estimate of the number of days we'd be at sea. It amounted to very meagre rations indeed. We weren't going to starve, but the quality was going to be shit and fluids would be in very short supply.

Each person would be given their share once a day in front of each other. There would be no exceptions! We stored all the provisions in boxes in one cabin and I held the key. There was no way Jimmy would be 'dipping' into anyone else's share.

I decided to make more room and move weight lower down by decanting the drums of fuel into the tanks. Before the first twenty five litres was transferred, we realised we had another serious problem. Some of the fuel was okay and some of it was shit. We'd been screwed again. They'd given us the dregs from the bottom of a tank. It would have blocked our fuel lines, the filters and the water separators.

I had to devise a system so that only clean fuel would be put into the small 'day tank' in the engine room which held enough for at least twenty four hours. Under normal circumstances, an electric pump would top this tank up from the main tanks through particle and water separators. But the system simply wouldn't cope with the shite they'd given us.

I made a siphoning apparatus which would only reach half way down a drum. Only the top half of the fuel would be siphoned out into another, completely clean receptacle, until it was full. This would be left to settle, before only the top half of that was siphoned into the day tank.

Water and impurities always sink to the bottom of diesel fuel. This was the only way of guaranteeing that only clean fuel would reach the engine fuel filters and ultimately the engine. I rehearsed the method three times with the lads and reiterated the importance of the process. Even Graham could recite it perfectly.

It was made law that we had enough completely clean drums of fuel in reserve so that the process would never have to be carried out in rough seas. This would hamper the settling stage. When I was absolutely satisfied that they both knew the importance and the method, we stood down and I cooked a decent meal. I had a beer, a whisky and a nice smoke before going to sleep ready for another graveyard shift.

Six hours later, all was well except that Jimmy was also asleep after having broken the first rule of no drink or drugs during a watch. I was always able to operate with a mild joint and knew my limitations. But Jimmy was just born greedy. He was surrounded by tons of the stuff. He just couldn't stop himself. What a bastard, I bollocked him and gave him some jobs to do. I stood Graham down and gave him permission to have a cup of tea and a joint as he'd done more than his fair share.

Twenty minutes later, I left Jimmy on watch and went below to find Graham building a huge joint on the saloon table.

"What the hell are you doing, son?" I said.

He looked up with a dumb, wry smile. "It's a five-skinner, Captain. I thought we could share it."

"Bugger me," I said. "I hope you bought enough skins?"

"Yeah, I bought two packets," he replied, not realising that the magnitude of his stupidity was about to be laid bare!

An average pack of Rizlas contains twenty five cigarette papers; an average joint uses three papers. By my reckoning, he'd bought enough papers for sixteen joints between three men. If he continued to make 'five skinners' he'd only bought enough for ten smokes. And no, he wasn't joking!

There are no corner shops or service stations at sea. If you don't get it before you sail, you won't get it until you come back in. I'd tried to drum this into them every time something ran low or ran out! "Work out what you'll need and make a list." I was speechless. All I could do was shake my head at him in disbelief.

I waited until we'd smoked the mega-joint then put the remaining skins in my pocket before alerting him to his new predicament; he would be spending a considerable amount of his spare time carefully emptying cigarette carcasses and painstakingly refilling them with a mixture of tobacco and cannabis. Later, I nicked some copper pipe and brass fittings from the engine compartment and fabricated a 'hubble bubble pipe'.

We were making pretty good progress. After four days, we could run the engine at just 1,000 revs and still manage 6 to 7 knots with the sails well trimmed. This reduced the diesel consumption considerably and extending our motoring range. I knew there'd be more wind further north, but that'd be a couple of weeks away.

My plan was to meet the Mable E Holland at sea to cooper the load on board; we'd then clear Customs empty and spend a day or two in port. We'd meet up again at another pre-determined spot and collect half of the gear, which we'd hide before moving up the coast to land it. The other half would be split again and both boats would then land a quarter of the load.

I changed the appearance of the boat from the air and sea. I'd brought along a twenty five litre drum of light blue paint to change the deck from white.

Next we removed the name and stencilled "Diamond White" on the bow, the stern, the RHIB and the emergency life rings. We sheeted the RHIB as it was red and easy to spot, then painted the white fenders black and tied them to the push-pit. We then painted the life-raft orange and tied every line we had to the safety rails.

We even went as far as to tape the wire stays with white electrical tape, move and fit dummy antennas and stencil trade names "Furuno" on the "Raytheon" radar dome. By the time we were finished, Diamond White looked completely different from the vessel that left Dakar.

We were feeling pretty chuffed with our efforts when the engine misfired and stopped dead. The vast majority of times a diesel engine stops, it's fuel starvation or contamination. But this doesn't result in a misfire. Rather it loses power and peters out. I was worried. The wind and sea were light so I waited until the engine compartment was cool enough before draining water and shit from the filtration system. Jimmy and Graham hung their heads in shame.

"What the hell did I tell you?" I ranted and shouted until they finally confessed their sins.

"We did what you said with the siphon and didn't find anything left in the bottom so we didn't bother anymore because it was a nightmare," they said, still thinking it could easily be rectified.

I bled clean fuel through to the injector pump and tried to start it without success. The problem was much worse than we first thought. I had to remove and dismantle the injector pump which is major surgery even in a workshop. It's a job for a specialist and took more than eight hours. When it was finally stripped, my heart sank; the main drive shaft in the pump had seized and sheared in half.

It was lubricated by the diesel fuel, not by lubricating oil. Water in the diesel had turned the filters to mush and caused them to collapse; when the pump finally overheated, a 'steam pocket' had formed, pressurising any lubricating fuel away from the bearing and causing the total failure.

It was completely screwed. I did try to join it with molecular chemical metal and thin threaded bar. It took two days and lasted ten seconds and did even more damage. Only a replacement would fix it. No more bodges were even remotely possible. To all intents and purposes, the engine was scrap metal until a replacement injection pump could be bought at the Bosch agents, probably costing a couple of grand.

The cost was irrelevant. The logistics were impossible to say the least! I could have lit a joint with my rage alone! There are no words to truly describe the dark hours following this catastrophic diagnosis.

Any hopes of getting back safely fell apart with the pump shaft.

I thought I was going to burst a blood vessel and ordered my crew to get out of my sight and stay there for their own safety. I'm ashamed to admit I would've attacked and beaten them at the drop of a hat! I cleaned up and lit a big joint. After the third joint and a couple of stiff whiskys, I was ready to explain our predicament.

Because of their gross negligence, dereliction of duty and total disregard for specific and vitally important instructions, we had the following problems, not in any specific order:

Propulsion power: We were now at the mercy of the wind – or lack of it – and the current which was always going south. We would likely die if we didn't risk incarceration by stopping somewhere to re-supply.

Electrical power: The engine charged the batteries which would soon be flat; that meant we would no longer have an autopilot meaning a minimum two people on watch with one at the wheel 24/7. We had no lights, radar, navigation, VHF, music, hot or cold running water. The remaining charge in the batteries was all we had. We were hundreds of miles offshore, knee deep in shit!

Morale was rock bottom. I struggled for two days to pull myself together. The lads had to live with the fact that it was their fault entirely. But I have to give credit where it's due; they got on with it without complaining. We were snatching sleep whenever we could; there was no point in any shift pattern. We couldn't sleep unless we were ready to pass out.

I began to search the storage spaces that weren't filled with our cargo. I found a bust small suitcase generator; it seemed someone had tried to fix it and given up. Parts were scattered between some paint tins.

I cobbled and bodged it back together, nicking odds and sods from the little outboard motor on the RHIB. After two days it was finally running. It knocked out only a small amount of AC 220 volt current, but it was a start. I repaired a broken cordless drill charger and wired it to a single 12 volt battery taken from the battery bank.

After half an hour, the battery was sufficiently charged to fire up the radar for a few minutes. It wasn't going to power the autopilot, but with nearly five gallons of petrol we had left for the RHIB, we could briefly check our position on the GPS and use the radar, VHF radio and lights in an emergency. It wasn't much, but it lifted our spirits enormously.

Unfortunately, what little wind there was came from the north, the very direction in which we wanted to travel. So, we sailed at least thirty degrees off our target heading to make any 'way' or speed at all. There's usually more wind near the coast, but we obviously needed to stay clear of land and the recognised shipping lanes.

Rather than regularly zigzag, I decided to head further out on a course for Canada. If anyone was looking for us by air, they'd be checking on similar boats heading north. When we'd sailed far enough northwest, we'd head northeast and appear to be coming across from the United States, rather than from Africa.

The days were long and boring, especially as we were short of decent food and drink. We did come across some spectacular wildlife, which I'm sure was because we were off the usual routes and were sailing instead of motoring. Dolphins and whales were a regular occurrence and a welcome break from the monotony, although Jimmy and Graham often refused to come up on deck to watch them.

One misty morning, we witnessed a spectacle which has never been surpassed. It started with a dozen or so dolphins in the distance as the first sunlight broke through. As usual, I shouted to the lads. Even if it annoyed them, it was still a break from the misery that had engulfed us.

I started to think I was hallucinating and mistaking wave tops for these fine animals. The wind had picked up a little, but not enough to blow the surf off the top of waves. I shouted again to the crew, this time with extra urgency. Something was very different; either I was losing the plot or we were heading into the middle of a phenomenon I'd never heard of, let alone seen.

Reluctantly they mustered enough energy to surface above deck muttering about their dolphin-daft captain.

"Look, look, what do you see?" I said.

"Bloody dolphins. So what, we've seen 'em before, for Pete's sake!"

"No man," I said. "Keep looking, all around you!"

And so it went on until they began to realise that there seemed to be hundreds coming towards us from all directions.

We broke out the binoculars and passed them about in disbelief; there weren't hundreds, there were thousands. At least three thousand, probably more but this story is already unbelievable by any sailor's standards.

There were dolphins all around us for as far as we could see. It was almost as though they were coming from the oceans to meet up for a party and we were on the dance floor. We were sailing through a massive jamboree of performing animals... many jumping, twisting and somersaulting together in what looked like choreographed displays. As long as I have a hole in my arse, I know I'll never witness anything like it again in my life!

I didn't even know that different species mixed. They were so close we could identify at least ten different types. There seemed to be very large pods of particular types arriving from every direction, before they split up and went crazy. I'm sure the 'know it alls' will be saying they were hunting a shoal of sardines but I've seen that many times and on this occasion, there was no evidence of any feeding going on.

I can best describe it as a festival, a marine Glastonbury or Olympic Games. I'm not saying there wasn't a sardine shoal about, but I'm sure there was more to this than a feeding frenzy.

They were showing off, performing and competing. The whole thing went on for an hour and had me buzzing for days. I still love to watch dolphins near our boat, but mainly because it reminds me of that day. And I know what you're thinking. Yes, I was stoned. But it did happen. I swear!

Nearly all sailors believe that the dolphins play by riding the bow wave of vessels. They seem to take it in turns, sometimes two or three competing for prime position. But one night, I discovered the truth.

There is a phenomenon created by a substance known as Phytoplankton Algal Bloom, luminous algae right at the bottom of the marine food chain. It can range from green to pink, depending on different factors. The water seems normal until it's disturbed, then it flushes with luminous colour. A vessel breaking the surface leaves a ghostly trail. It's like a special effect in a movie. When it's very plentiful, even a fish leaves a track.

One night, the sea was thick with it and dolphins were playing in our bow wave. This time, they were leaving very significant tracks. My interpretation of what we witnessed that night is that the dolphins hide in the bow wave, so that the fish ahead can't detect them, with their 'sonar'.

When they're close enough, the dolphin powers out, snatching two or three fish, before circling into the queue for the bow wave again; I watched fascinated for hours. There was so much of the luminous algae, I could even see the tracks of the sardines.

An otherwise very dull week was brightened up one Friday night by flying fish. These creatures are quite fascinating and very common in the warmer climes of the Atlantic. They're usually about a foot long and 'fly' to avoid predators such as tuna, dolphins and marlin.

They flick their tails up to seventy times a second to launch before their big glider- like fins come out. The average glide is about fifty metres, one metre above the surface. They can use the wind or updraft from waves and have been recorded to fly for forty seconds, at seventy kilometres an hour.

Most mornings, there'd be up to a dozen on deck; I thought they were inedible but have since learned they're the national dish of Barbados.

This boring Friday evening, Jimmy was going through a particularly bad depression. He was reluctant to do his shift on the wheel. Clearly, he was thinking of his missus getting dolled up for her night on the town. He'd been spoiling for a row for a couple of hours. He wouldn't pick on me though; he'd rather give Graham a hard time.

Finally, I had to step in and tell him off. He spat back at me until the tempo was raised to a shouting match. I told him we realised it was Friday and why he was being a pain in the arse. But it didn't mean he could dodge his shift so I said, "Forget about your lass, do your shift and get your arse on the wheel, while we have a cuppa!"

He cursed and muttered, but finally took the wheel with a face like a bulldog licking piss off a thistle. We went to the stern saloon to smoke and take the piss out of him.

We could see Jimmy's arse and legs from where we were sitting.

Every time we laughed, he'd accuse us of laughing at him. We heard a slap then a bang as Jimmy fell backwards. Instead of his legs, we could see his head in the cockpit with a flying fish flapping out of his mouth.

Well, we were both dumbstruck at the sight of it wriggling and flapping on his twisted face. Poor bastard… he was mortified. He spat it out before screaming and jumping about like a lunatic.

We rushed up to see him stamping on and splattering the fish into bits on the cockpit floor. He was wide-eyed, bleeding from the mouth and properly losing control. He launched at Graham… I had to overpower him and hold him down. He accused us of throwing it at him until he realised we were in the stern section with no access forward. We couldn't have been the culprits.

When he finally pulled himself together, he vowed he was going to "eat every one of the slippery bastards from now on. I don't care if they poison me!"

Stitching and dressing his mouth should have taken no more than half an hour, but we kept descending into fits of uncontrollable laughter; it was two hours before we settled down. Next morning 'cock breath' as he was now known, found four of his new friends on the deck, which he cleaned, grilled and had on two slices of dry toast.

I didn't want to try the fish. Although it smelt pretty good, they were all fins with only a thin body and were full of fine bones with little meat. We weren't starving yet. Jim insisted they were okay although I half expected him to be ill. Rather than wait for more to jump on deck, I thought a bit of fishing might break the monotony.

Graham rooted through the cupboards to find the hooks he bought in Dakar. "We'll catch some big buggers with this, Captain," he said as he offered up a huge tuna or shark hook.

"No mate, we want something to eat, not break a record, fetch me a much smaller one," I said.

"They're all the same," he said. "Are they too big?"

I should have known better than to send him shopping and expect common sense. The hooks were nearly four inches long and absolutely useless! That was the end of that plan.

The next day, in very light winds, we were only doing a couple of knots when we spotted a giant turtle casually plodding along ahead. It didn't seem bothered as we changed course to have a closer look. It was almost alongside when Jim jumped on deck with a big knife; he looked scared, but was clearly going to have a go at killing the animal.

The boat was almost stopped when he ordered Graham to get the boathook. He put the knife between his teeth like a pirate and made ready to jump in. "Stop, stop, stop," I shouted. "We can eat it," he shouted back.

The last thing I wanted to see was Jimmy mindlessly stabbing this beautiful creature half to death before it dived down and suffered a horrible, lingering fate at the jaws of the local sharks. This beast must have weighed 450 pounds or about 200 kilos. Just getting it on the boat would've been a feat on its own. He'd need to butcher it in the water.

I convinced Jimmy to stop by telling him the blood would attract sharks and send them into a feeding frenzy. They'd much prefer to eat him than a hard shelled reptile. Our hunter gatherer soon changed his attitude as he contemplated his possible fate; the turtle was spared, to splodge another day!

We still had enough dried food to survive but that incident made me realise how desperate they thought things were. I searched the boat for something to make a hook and found some large safety pins in the first aid box. I soldered two together to make a grappling type hook.

I pushed down the prongs to the shaft and held them in place with a small ring which I tied to the shaft and line. The idea was that the prongs would spring up as the fish took the device and pulled the ring clear of the points. It was the world's first spring-loaded fishing hook.

If we'd had any flying fish, I'd have trimmed the carcasses and made a flapper. They're usually slices of mackerel. The shiny skin reflects sunlight as it's dragged through the water imitating an injured fish. It's much the same as a metal lure or 'spoon'.

Anything bright moving through the water will attract predators.

If it's moving slow enough, they'll snap at it. I'd proved this to my son on the River Tees by catching a pike on an NGK spark plug key ring and a treble hook.

I didn't want to wait until more flying fish jumped on deck. I cut some ribbons of red, blue and yellow canvass and tied them together on the device as a lure.

My crew thought I'd been smoking too much as I trailed the apparatus sixty metres behind and tied it to the push-pit.

When I checked two hours later, I'd hooked a big juicy amberjack. It must have been fighting for some time as it took no pulling in despite weighing over ten kilos.

Their faces lit up as it came on board. I pretended it was nothing but I was chuffed to bits. I cut half into steaks and steamed them with garlic, chilli and lime juice. It was restaurant quality, the most beautiful, succulent fish I'd ever had. I was definitely the hero of the hour.

We were sick of the sight of fish within a week. My device worked so well we actually looked forward to reconstituted beans and rice.

CHAPTER TEN

THE DOLDRUMS: FROM ONE EXTREME TO ANOTHER

Supplies were getting sparse and after three weeks we weren't getting very far. We were approaching the Azores, but we had to stay away because of our cargo. In that area, there's sometimes a weather system known as an inter-tropical convergence zone where conditions can change rapidly. However, at that time of year, it tended to be mostly 'dead calm' and a total nightmare for sailing boats.

They could be stuck in the Doldrums for weeks or months at a time. What little wind there was would shift endlessly and force round the clock adjustment to the sails and steering. Many sailors died of thirst or starvation in the Doldrums; some took their own lives, desperate to escape the misery on board.

The doldrums were described in Samuel Taylor Coleridge's Rime of the Ancient Mariner:

> *All in a hot and copper sky,*
> *The bloody Sun, at noon,*
> *Right up above the mast did stand,*
> *No bigger than the Moon.*

> *Day after day, day after day,*
> *We stuck, nor breath nor motion;*
> *As idle as a painted ship*
> *Upon a painted ocean.*

Water, water, every where,
And all the boards did shrink;
Water, water, every where,
Nor any drop to drink.

And there we were. A painted ship, bobbing about, frustrated, no wind, engine, power, water or morale. A week passed, during which time we sailed the fantastic distance of forty miles. We were at each other's throats, devoid of humour and spirit until I spotted a ship on the horizon. And it was heading our way.

It was a small freighter, not much bigger than our supply ship. She was a scruffy looking heap flying a Cypriot flag. I put out a 'pan pan' call on our VHF, which is an urgency signal that the captain is obliged to answer. He'd be duty bound to answer a Mayday.

I gave enough bullshit to make the captain stop his vessel. As far as he was aware, we'd been adrift for three weeks and had no water or food. My crew paddled across in the crippled dingy and collected some supplies.

They returned with two dirty twenty five litre drums of water, some frozen bread and two cases of tinned hotdog sausages. Hardly a bounty but hey, how could I complain? We thanked them and asked them to pass a message to the UK, updating them of our situation and ETA.

That night we had sausage sandwiches which were a welcome change from fish, pasta, beans or rice. We'd run out of almost everything else like tea, coffee, sauces or anything with flavour. However, that incident gave us hope. At least we were going to be okay. Sick as pigs, but okay. From that day, our mission was to spot another ship and do the same thing; only this time, we hoped we'd stop one with better stores. The Doldrums and our broken engine were good enough reasons for any captain to take pity on us. All we needed was another target.

The scrounged sausages were quite vile but made good bait. We caught a couple of unidentified fish which were passed as edible after the crew tested them; well, there's no point in killing off the captain, is there? I knew morale was becoming a serious problem. I tried all sorts to raise it including singing, telling jokes in turn, knife throwing, shove ha'penny and mini basket ball, anything to take the edge off the boredom.

Order was breaking down; we nearly came to blows a number of times. Jimmy was bullying Graham at every opportunity and I could see it turning nasty. It was also affecting the performance of the boat which needed constant attention and teamwork just to keep moving in the right direction. Then we spotted another ship.

The Noble Star 13 was a nearly new, medium-sized container ship, chartered to the United States of America's Navy. She was heading for Hamburg in Germany but believe it or not, was calling at Brixham where the Mable E Holland was berthed.

She was fully loaded and judging by her bow wave, she was doing nearly 20 knots. I called up the captain using a Pan Pan again and explained our predicament, asking first for water. He could hardly refuse, even though the cost of stopping such a ship would run into thousands of dollars.

He sounded like a great guy. We chatted while the ship stopped and I told him we were okay for food for a while as we'd broken into the life raft's emergency rations. I sent Jimmy and Graham over in the dingy... a spectacle I'll never forget.

They had to paddle because I'd robbed parts from the outboard motor to bodge the generator. Neither of them had bothered to fix the floor which was now flapping open at the bow like the sole hanging off a shoe.

It was inflatable so there was no chance of it sinking but with water lapping about the floor, it was very slow progress and it wouldn't go in a straight line.

The ship was a mile away but looked closer because it was so big. It took them more than an hour to reach her. I could hear them shouting at each other as they veered off course. It was as hilarious as it was embarrassing.

What little air flow there was must have been deflecting off the ship and produced enough breeze to start our boat moving. We'd actually dropped the sails because the flapping was driving us nuts. I raised the foresail and slowly tacked behind the dingy.

They were paddling against the current and sweating like hell in the searing midday sun. The air was blue as they cursed each other. Jimmy spat his dummy out a couple of times and refused to soldier on.

Finally, despite the fun, I couldn't watch them suffer anymore. I was conscious of the cost of this huge ship stopping for us. I shouted at them to lift the outboard motor up on its bracket to reduce the drag. It worked and they were alongside in no time.

The crew lowered box after box until the raft could carry no more. It took thirty minutes as the typical over-the-top Americans took photographs and videos. I remember thinking we could be splashed all over the media.

They returned to the Diamond White with a bounty of goodies Santa Claus would've been proud of. We expected only bottled water, not Jack Daniels, beer, coca cola, fruit juices, chocolate bars, frozen steaks, hams, 2,000 Winston cigarettes and God knows what else. We could have hosted a Christmas party for twenty people.

I thanked them via the VHF and promised to write to all the yachting magazines with the story. The Captain replied with something like, "You guys are so lucky… we only changed course to avoid Hurricane Chris."

"What?" I said.

"You guys ain't heard about Hurricane Chris?"

"No… what about it?"

"Well, it's coming this way! You better get ready for it; we have to go now, sorry!"

I asked him to pass an immediate message for us to the UK. When he confirmed it had been received, I switched off the radio to save power.

Our joy was certainly short-lived. Typical! Weeks without wind, now a hurricane! I have to admit that my arse was twitching. We were too far from the safety of land even if we had an engine to reach it.

Our cargo presented a serious problem; it was a positively dangerous situation to have so much loose weight flying about. We hadn't anticipated a hurricane when we stashed it. I cooked a cracking meal from our bonanza before we set about Operation Survival.

I remembered reading a magazine story on board about a reporter who flew to the Azores to meet the legendary Robin Knox Johnston and sail his little 32 foot ketch Suhaili back to the UK with him. They were caught in a hurricane and the article described in detail how they survived.

The first and most important mission was to find that article! I've done more miles in more boats than the vast majority of sail boat owners and crew, but Johnston is a God of the seas. His little boat was nothing, compared to the multi-million pound projects that followed in his wake and broke his records. Any advice I could glean from that man was worth its weight in gold.

I searched frantically for a couple of hours and finally found the magazine. There wasn't too much I didn't already know but to have it all described in detail, plus a few new tricks, was a great comfort. At least we'd have the best chance possible. The five Ps are: preparation prevents piss poor performance. But I prefer the three Ps: preparation, preparation, preparation. And for twenty eight hours solid that's exactly what we did.

We broke down the sacks of gear and stashed slabs as low as possible in every conceivable space from stem to stern. We needed the centre of gravity as low as it could be and the balance to be 'Cock Knacker' perfect.

The waterline, which was still visible, is used as a reference. If it's the same all round the hull, the balance is as near as damn it.

We tied all the sails down apart from the storm jib (a very strong small foresail) and a few square yards of mainsail. Anything and everything was tied, jammed or fastened down twice.

Every long line we had, including those already in use for sail handling, were knotted for extra drag and made ready to deploy along with a number of makeshift sea anchors.

We'd only just finished our third inspection and sat down for grub, when the wind started to pick up. I fired up the generator then the radar.

At the forty eight miles setting, I could see the main storm coming directly for us from the east. I decided to take it as it came and not put up more canvass; we couldn't risk not being able to get it down again. A hurricane follows a path but can veer miles north or south in the blink of an eye. If you're lucky... you're lucky! We braced ourselves.

I couldn't resist winding the guys up. I told them to write a goodbye letter to their loved ones and seal it in the yellow waterproof flare container, like a message in bottle, should we go down. The silly buggers went for it and then I thought maybe it wasn't such a bad idea. I placed our ship's log in it, just for safe keeping. They looked like it was their turn on death row; chain smoking and staring down at the floor.

I gave them a pep talk. They had to follow orders. It was no good freezing and locking the hatch as they'd done before. They donned life jackets, harnesses and ran safety lines fore and aft. I put on an oil rigger's immersion suit as I'd be in the cockpit alone. I worried that they were highly likely to let me down!

The wind speed rose to thirty five knots propelling us along at a respectable nine knots in minimal sail area. I made ready the sea anchors and long lines which trail and stop the vessel veering off course or going beam-on as she gets tossed about.

Sometimes they get tangled but still have the same effect; in any case, they were better in than out and certainly weren't going to be a problem for the propeller. I had total confidence in the rigging as it'd carried full sail in the storm off the Canary Islands, when she was blown almost flat while my shitty-arsed crew lost their bottle.

It started to get dark, even with the sun still high in the sky. I knew I was about to be tested and have to admit to asking for a bit of help from any God that was listening... and of course my trusty spirit guide.

Hurricane Chris came steadily towards us. It built at a constant rate until it howled through the rigging like an out of tune harmonica. The ocean built up and slewed us about. I could hold course surprisingly well as she crashed along at ten to eleven knots. The wind speed picked up to sixty knots and held steady for nearly an hour. By my calculations, the tide would soon flow against the wind, significantly altering the sea state.

Ocean sailing is not as bad as sailing in a choppy sea close to land, but when it does build up high, it can be quite scary, especially if you get it wrong. It's vitally important to maintain course at all costs. Going beam-on to a big breaker will capsize or knock a yacht down.

The extra low weight was helping us, but made her a bit unresponsive. The waves built higher and became more erratic with the tide as I fought with the wheel to keep her nose up.

Graham came up once for less than a minute while Jimmy took a photograph. No doubt the story would grow in time and they'd be holding court in the bar about how they rode out Hurricane Chris!

The first hour passed without incident and I began to wonder what all the fuss was about. Hurricanes can fizzle out or build at any time. I reckoned we'd been lucky as I'd not seen the wind speed go above seventy knots and could see sunshine through the clouds twenty miles ahead. I kicked at the hatch and told Graham to do me a joint and a large Jack Daniels!

I'd gulped the drink and got half way down the joint when the heavens opened, lashing me with sharp, sandy rain. It was impossible to see anything. They ran below but I shouted for a diving mask as the boat veered off course, causing the sails and rigging to bang and clatter. A wave broke over the port side and knocked me down.

Luckily, I was still clipped on as the second wave flooded the cockpit, picked me up and tried to throw me out as she heeled right over to starboard. The next wave hit the sail. All that stopped a total knockdown was the extra weight down below. Saved by cannabis!

I had to correct the course; the last thing we needed was the sea anchors jamming the rudder. This meant we had to go beam-on to the waves again and risk a possible knock down. It was a no brainer, but luckily she came round okay after I managed to get a mask on and see what I was doing.

I still couldn't see ahead or anywhere further than the boat. At least I could open my eyes. I could only steer a course by looking at the wind direction indicator in front of me. In all the panic, I hadn't noticed, but the same instrument was now showing a speed of eighty five knots gusting to one hundred and showing no sign of letting up.

I remember chastising myself, "Typical of me... just when I needed to be at my very best, I was drinking Jack and smoking dope. What a dick!" Twenty five frightening minutes later, we sailed into sunshine as the wind and sea calmed. I'd heard about the eye of the storm and concluded we'd been in it. Graham took the wheel while I went for a much needed shit! Down below, the adrenaline hit me very hard like a Class A drug rush. My head was bursting with it.

I'd been awake more than forty hours. The effect of a spliff and Jack Daniels seemed to be multiplied now that the pressure was off. I gorged myself on chocolate and high protein goodies until I levelled out, ready for the next bout. But by the time I emerged, psyched up and ready to resume battle with the elements, the sky ahead had cleared and we could see no sign of any heavy shit.

I know it makes no sense, but that's how it was. It was over! What a relief! From that day on, we knew our vessel could take anything the Atlantic Ocean or Mother Nature could throw at us. Well, that's what I thought at the time!

We were soon north of the 'separating zone' between the weather systems in light winds. It seemed like we were racing along after weeks of boredom. I'm sure our bonanza from the Noble Star 13 made all the difference. The time for decision making was looming. We would soon be at the rendezvous point.

It was approaching the end of August and we'd been at sea for ten weeks including the few days spent in various ports. We had a litre of petrol left for our makeshift generator as we neared the 'secret' co-ordinates. The transfer could only be done at night, so we kept twenty miles away until the sun started to fade.

I could see a vessel's navigation lights four miles off our portside. We fired up the generator, GPS, radio and radar. The GPS confirmed that our position was correct but radar showed the boat was heading away. Clearly, she was not the Mable E Holland.

Next, we used the VHF radio to call out the secret call sign:

"Bonny Lass, Bonny Lass, Bonny Lass, this is Dirty Dancer, Dirty Dancer. Are you receiving? Over…"

Then we waited for the secret response which was: "Dirty Dancer, Dirty Dancer; this is Shark Snatcher. Shark Snatcher, receiving. Over." None of these names had been uttered verbally in person or by telephone. For security, they were written down and passed from person to person.

We called out the same, once every thirty minutes until 1am before sailing away to return the next night. The ship four miles away seemed to be trawling in a square or box. Being short on petrol and power meant we couldn't use the radar unless absolutely necessary.

As dawn broke, the wind dropped and we were engulfed in thick fog. We still managed four knots but lurking in the shipping lanes was a bit hairy. It was necessary as we'd attract attention unless we looked like we were heading somewhere. We had no choice but to use precious petrol for the radar to check regularly if anything was on collision course.

Unfortunately, this strategy didn't take into account a container ship belting along at more than twenty knots that missed us by only three hundred metres. It hadn't shown up the last time we checked. It left us in shock, as we didn't even hear it approach. It was mid-afternoon before the fog cleared and we headed for the rendezvous point.

Again, there was a large vessel in the vicinity; it was too big to be the Mable E Holland and far too big to be waiting for us. It continued to steam around in a box. According to our pilot book, there were some seasonal fishing grounds nearby so we thought nothing of it.

Again we hailed on the VHF and again there was no response. We were dumfounded, gutted and ever more desperate as the petrol barely covered the bottom of the tank. We knew this because the generator began to falter when the boat rolled.

It was a critical situation.

Without power, we'd be screwed. Something was badly wrong. The relayed messages to the UK had been confirmed as received.

We were in the right place at the right time but the only ship within miles seemed to be trawling.

We sailed away into the night. Any hopes of an end to this God Almighty nightmare faded that night along with the dream of a hot bath! We were a hundred miles from the UK, but it may as well have been a thousand.

I had to make a decision and fast. I racked my brain all night. Why was there was no boat to meet us? We had a shit load of gear worth millions. Why would they leave us here?

I knew my phone would work up to ten miles from shore but the battery was almost flat and we'd be inside territorial waters and subject to scrutiny, especially on the south coast. I thought long and hard about dumping the gear overboard and even discussed the idea with the crew in what was supposed to be a brainstorming session. Fat chance of that with my crew!

Eventually I decided to put it to the vote. I didn't need to cast my vote because Jim and Graham pitched up straight away that they wanted to take it in to port! They were motivated purely by greed. They'd recruited themselves against my orders and wanted paying. Plain and simple, they didn't have the brains to calculate the risks. Maybe they thought I was bullshitting about why I'd become involved.

CHAPTER ELEVEN

SMUGGLERS' CREEK

I agonised over our situation as we neared the UK coast. I made half a dozen plans. I could only guess why nobody had met us, but it seemed highly likely that given past experiences with the Firm it was down to pure incompetence.

The truth would be irrelevant; the blame would be laid on those without guns! In short, our lives were worth Jack Shit compared to the cargo. Whichever useless bastard was responsible for the cock up, would murder us rather than accept responsibility for the loss. All things considered, dumping it was not an option.

One of the pilot books gave detailed descriptions of every port, marina, river, inlet and anchorage on the south coast. I identified the Helford Passage near Falmouth as suitable place to slip into – hopefully undetected.

It seemed perfect with only fifty residents in a small village upstream called Durgan. There were only limited yacht facilities, but I was looking for the least populated inlet with high banks and minimal access on foot. That seemed ideal and I set a course.

I wanted to arrive at night so we farted about in the channel, hoping to blend in with the WAFA's (wind assisted flipping arseholes) or recreational sailors who never leave sight of land.

I was a bit paranoid. We seemed to be getting shadowed by various craft but as we weren't following any particular course, it was impossible to tell without radar. We only had enough petrol for navigation lights and maybe charging a mobile phone. Things were pretty desperate really.

We sailed close to the Lizard and got a phone signal. I called

Dawn on the secure line. She was surprisingly co-operative after she'd refused to help us escape from Dakar; obviously, she thought we were due a big pay day. I told her everything was okay and that we just needed some money bringing to Durgan. The phone went flat before I had time to explain that the gear hadn't been transferred or that I needed spares and fuel.

We rounded the Lizard as night began to fall and switched on the navigation lights; the last thing we wanted was to draw attention by sailing with no lights. In Falmouth Bay, the wind dropped to almost nothing. It did fall to nothing as we closed on the Helford Passage. Worse still, we were against the tide and struggling, tacking back and forth, trying to get closer.

It took us seven hours to do a couple of miles. The batteries were totally flat after only three hours. We were completely dead in the water with less than a mile to go; it was tragic.

We were getting pretty desperate at 4am as it would soon be getting light. We even put the dinghy in and tried to tow the boat, paddling like hell for an hour. But to no avail. Another yacht came into view; miraculously she was going to the same place. The Whitbread was a charter ketch, bigger than us and she had a full complement of young guests on board.

She sailed close enough to hear our plea for help. I made it clear we were not in danger and there'd be no salvage claim, only a crate of beer the next day. All we wanted was a tow into the river where we would drop anchor until later that morning. She came around and took our line. Within half an hour, we were far enough in for good cover. I slipped the line and thanked the skipper before we laid our anchor near a shoal beach.

It was pitch black, just like I planned it. The banks surrounding the passage were high. There was no moon. I saw the odd light go on and off quickly, but in different places every time. I also noticed navigation lights up river, again only for very short periods. I hadn't expected to see any craft, but after the yacht towed us in, I concluded our pilot book was well out of date and maybe the Helford Passage had evolved. Also, it was still the busy school holidays; I didn't give it much thought.

It'd been twelve hours since I'd called Dawn. I told Jimmy to pack a bag including the injector pump and some clothes. After giving Graham instructions, we jumped onto the shore and set a small anchor up on the bank. All we had was a little torch, my phone, Jimmy's bag and ten tons of adrenaline each.

We set off on the footpath up river. It was so dark we could only just make out the path and we didn't want to use up the torch battery or draw attention. The path wasn't well beaten, which fitted with my mental image of the place. We stumbled and struggled a few times, but it began to get better.

After nearly twenty minutes, I estimated we were a half mile from Durgan as we walked across a small clearing near a landing area. Suddenly four silhouetted figures came out of the dark, just five metres away.

As they moved across to pass us, I mustered up my best fake Cornish accent and said, "Morning." As I was speaking, the yellow high viz material on their jumpers lit up and two huge German Shepherd dogs came into view.

My heart stopped dead. I swear it. We continued to walk at the same pace. After ten metres, my heart pounded back to life while my head felt like it was going to explode. I don't know if Jim was doing the same, but I was instinctively holding my breath.

Another twenty metres and we were almost at the edge of the clearing and into the foliage again, when our worlds fell apart. Someone said, "Hang on a minute lads, can we just have a word please?" A bright torch dazzled us.

I looked at Jim and said quietly, "Don't you run," before starting to walk towards them. Jim followed close behind as I practised my version of a Cornish accent in my head.

"What's the problem? Bloody hell," I gasped, as one of the dogs lurched forward and I saw two MP5 sub-machine guns.

"Can you tell us where you've come from, lads?"

"We've just come off the back of the Whitbread," I said.

They must've already seen her coming up river. To be honest, I knew the wheel had come off and the chances of escape were minimal.

"What are your names?" asked one.

"Show us some ID," said the other.

The third stood back and brought his MP5 to waist level, flicking off what I assumed to be the safety catch. The fourth was looking at poor quality photos of us.

The dogs, alerted to the adrenaline in the air, immediately pulled on their chokers.

"Phil Berriman and James Ritchie," I blurted out, as Jimmy looked at me like I'd just grassed him up, the daft bastard!

We were caught. No ifs or buts about it. I wasn't about to make a drama of it and get my arse ripped out or worse still a bullet from a nervous copper. Coppers love to set their dogs on crooks. Who could blame them?

Everything suddenly made sense. The mysterious lights in a supposedly deserted creek at 5am, police on the river bank with submachine guns and attack dogs; they'd been waiting for us.

I dropped my phone on the grass, put my hands on my head and gestured to Jim to do the same. Immediately, they started to freak out, shouting and bawling orders above each other. The dogs barking like hell!

I'd like to think this was part of their training to disorientate and confuse their victims, but they seemed pretty scared... despite the fact they had the guns.

"Get down on your knees! Look at me! Get up! Look at me! Hands up! Get down! Get up! Turn round! Look at me! Get down! Get up! Hands on your head!" and so on. The guns were twitching up and down as they changed stance every couple of seconds.

As soon as I'd seen the first gun, I'd made up my mind to do nothing! I just stood still with my hands on my head, looking away. Jim followed my lead, much to their annoyance!

After thirty seconds of pure adrenaline-fuelled chaos, we weren't reacting as planned; the coppers paused and calmed the dogs. The two gunmen stood back, still training their weapons on us.

One of them was clearly shaking. I remained cool and Jim did the same. I figured they were actually scared of us and shouted at what looked like the boss, "You need to get those two twats under control mate. Who the hell gave them guns?"

"Now calm down and get the cuffs on, before someone gets hurt!"

"I'm in charge!" he said.

"No? Really?" I retorted, as I nodded at the two gunmen. "Take charge of these dickheads then!"

I wanted to be arrested, cautioned and in lawful custody as soon as possible. Anything that happens before that (unless of course you are in Stockton Police Station) falls into a different category of enquiry. All they had to say was we were resisting arrest and who wouldn't believe them?

Guns, dogs, villains and coppers full of adrenaline in the dark are a very dangerous cocktail. The vast majority of Armed Response coppers only dream of a live situation, and I felt in real danger. After a few more heated exchanges, we were finally cuffed, searched, arrested, cautioned and marched about three hundred metres along the path, to a gravel road and a clearing.

By now, there was no need for the blackout. The riverbanks were lit up like a Christmas tree as dozens of vehicles came to life and headed our way, waking up every household in the once sleepy creek. They must have thought they'd been invaded.

We were bundled into a dog cage inside a minibus and left there for a few minutes. I struggled to retrieve and eat a list of numbers taped inside my belt; these numbers would've incriminated half a dozen people. I knew from experience that it's no good crying over spilt milk. You have to keep your head together; there's going to be plenty of time to feel like shit later on!

They drove us a short distance to a small car park packed with vans and cars and at least a hundred people in groups, some armed and some with dogs. They all looked pretty pleased with themselves. More were arriving every minute. They must have had the whole valley swarming and now they wanted to see the prize.

A traffic car turned up, followed by Dawn's car driven by a copper. They stopped nearby and both Dawn and Jimmy's partner Trish were led out in handcuffs; I was mortified!

They were both dressed up to the nines, high heels, hair done, the lot! It was a pretty devastating sight, and I'll never forget it. The coppers put them back in the car and proudly paraded us to their colleagues before loading us into a van which had not been designed to carry dogs.

The convoy arrived at the main police station at Camborne just as it was getting light. Graham was led out first, followed by the girls. We were last. I recognised a CID bobby I knew from Middlesbrough called Bill McBungle; he was looking pretty pleased as he identified himself as being from the North East Regional Crime Squad. Customs were present throughout the proceedings; it was clearly a joint effort, pardon the pun, and they took great pains to be equally involved.

Finally, the cell door shut behind me. What a relief! It may sound mad, but I felt safe for the first time in a very long time. My family was safe! Whatever had happened, I'd done everything possible, against all odds to fulfil the orders. I knew I was looking at fourteen years, but I'd have died for my kids, and that's the truth of the matter!

From the minute I was arrested, my brain raced through every option and scenario possible. We were headed to jail, no doubt about it. As far as I was aware at that time, Dawn had been my faithful partner, supporting me throughout the nightmare. I would do anything to get her free, even agree to an interview. Normally, until I had all the information necessary to negate any charges, my reply had been, "No comment."

Although Dawn was in the information loop, I foolishly believed Trish had no idea what Jimmy was up to. We spent the whole day waiting to be interviewed. Obviously they'd be searching the boat and preparing themselves with all relevant documents. This suited me, because it gave me a chance to rest and prepare myself.

Our pleas for decent food and a hot shower fell on deaf ears; we hadn't even washed in fresh water since Dakar, let alone a hot shower! In typical British fashion, we were treated worse than terrorists; what difference would a little hot water have made to them?

Of course, given what I knew about Cordite and his gang, I'd always believed in the possibility that we'd get nicked. It was just a better option than me or mine getting shot, kidnapped or tortured. I'd prepared a few things in advance.

The ship's log would be exhibit number one. Unbeknown to my crew, I'd been entering subtle references to our terrible predicament for weeks. Anyone who read it carefully would be able to ascertain that we were acting under duress. It'd be no good asking a judge to consider duress as mitigation without something to back it up.

Also, I'd programmed the GPS and plotted a course to a place in Holland called Ijmuiden I knew from a yacht race as a kid. I thought this would demonstrate there was no intention to import the cannabis into the UK, but into a country where the likely sentences were much shorter. In actual fact, I probably would've taken her to Holland had we been able.

I knew Graham would say nothing as instructed. He was easily led, even he accepted that. Jimmy was another matter. I remembered an incident many years before when he was caught using a stolen credit card. When threatened with remand, he grassed on a guy called Kev Smith who worked for me. Kev found a wallet in the street; Jimmy begged him not to hand it in and promised him a pair of nice shoes. Kev gave him the card, but instead of the shoes, he got his door kicked in by cops and a criminal record to boot.

Of course, I knew Jimmy couldn't talk his way out of this one, but faced with a long stretch, he'd stand on us both for an extra blanket. If I'd learned anything about him, it was that he couldn't be trusted.

Luckily, he didn't have the arse to implicate Peter Cordite and Co, so I knew he'd be more interested in feathering his own nest.

When the cell door finally opened, the custody sergeant seemed a bit put out when I said, "Piss off! I've no intentions of co-operating before I've had a nice hot shower, some decent food and two cups of strong hot tea with full fat milk and one sugar! Shut the door behind you, dickhead." My attitude was a measured response to the way they'd left us all day with nothing!

His face was a picture, but I knew the visiting Crime Squad and Customs wouldn't be very happy with them if they missed the chance to talk to us. Sure enough, all my demands were met almost immediately. It was my first genuine Cornish Pasty. Lush!

Detective Bill McBungle and Customs Officer Tom Burper were my interviewers. Bill was tanned. Not nearly as tanned as me, but brown enough for me to comment as soon as I sat down.

His reply was very significant, "We've been flying around Tenerife looking for you lot."

The original destination had only changed when we picked up Miguel in Casablanca; this was the first indication of an informer in Cordite's gang.

Introduction and small talk over, the tape was switched on. Their faces were a picture when I started answering their questions and co-operating. McBungle, from Middlesbrough, knew my reputation and had been expecting the standard, "No comment." But I answered almost everything. They couldn't shut me up long enough to ask the next question. I had their heads battered.

I knew exactly what I wanted to do and how best I could do it. There was no point in denying we'd just sailed up the river with a humongous cargo of hashish; the news said about fifteen million quid at first. The only thing we could do was try and mitigate as much as possible.

I used my fast talking best North East accent and deliberately repeated myself. I padded out my answers with dozens of irrelevant points knowing full well it would take many hours to type up.

Also, the investigating team analysing the recording would struggle to understand my motive for rabbiting on like I'd had a gram of Speed.

During the first interview, I slipped in the whole story from John Hannibal the Cannibal attacking me in the club to the point of getting arrested but refused to name anyone! All they really wanted was a confession. I confessed and took the blame for everybody else who was arrested, insisting they had no choice.

I slipped in the bare bones of how much pressure I was under but it didn't seem to register with them.

I knew sometime in the near future I may need to demonstrate the same to a judge who would take this into consideration when sentencing me. "No comment" is what professional villains say, not affluent businessmen like me who had no choice but to comply with the demands of lunatic gangsters capable of absolutely anything. I would be able to pick out all the relevant detail from the reams of drivel in my interview while I was awaiting the judge.

The investigating team wouldn't have the time to unravel it because the overtime clock was ticking. But I'd admitted my part in the caper and said I'd duped the others. I wanted to keep talking to mask my hidden agenda.

I told them after the first day that I'd be prepared to be interviewed again when they let the girls out. They bailed them and I got to meet Dawn in the charge room alone for five minutes before she went to face the cameras outside.

I knew fine well the charge room would have its video going and made damn sure it'd be useful to me later! I didn't give her any chance to talk and incriminate herself; I just apologised profusely over and over again and said I was scared for my kids.

The bastards on the monitor watching knew it wasn't doing them any good and cut short the time we had. But if they charged Dawn or Trish for that matter, the recording would've been the get out of jail card for her and helped me!

I was interviewed three times until they were sick of hearing the same thing. They had questions about items found at my house and paperwork. I'd never have anything at home or anywhere else that would incriminate anyone else. I answered everything honestly. We were charged and remanded for a week!

CHAPTER TWELVE

SAFE IN PRISON

We arrived in Exeter Category B prison as our story hit the news. We made the front page of all the tabloids.

It was the largest ever seizure of cannabis on a private vessel! And I was not the first person to identify Helford Passage as the perfect place for a smuggling operation. French smugglers and locals had been using it for hundreds of years.

In fact, Daphne de Maurier wrote a book, "Frenchman's Creek", which over the years had evolved to "Smugglers' Creek".

And so the headlines read: "SMUGGLERS' CREEK: RECORD CANNABIS SEIZURE". Our pictures were splashed everywhere as the media had a field day. We were famous as far as the inmates were concerned; cannabis is a valuable currency in jail, as we quickly found out.

A 'red band', a trusted inmate, often a cleaner or cook, passed me a tiny package as a gift at reception. He told me it was a phone card deal. When I came to smoke it, it was ninety per cent wrapping – a tiny piece not big enough for a decent joint.

I remember this as a stark reality check as days earlier we'd thrown much bigger chunks out of the hatch as dog ends.

Exeter was an old dump of a jail, two to a cell and only a bucket for a toilet. I 'padded up' with Jimmy while Graham was a couple of doors up with a frequent visitor called Alex, who'd been locked up the same day as us. He wanted to be seen with us and jumped at the chance to share a cell with Graham. It was a big mistake!

During the night, we'd heard some commotion but couldn't quite work out what was going on. Since our arrest, Graham had shat constantly. I've never seen or heard of anything so bad. A doctor looked at him in the police station, but as he was in a cell with a toilet, it wasn't much of a problem.

After our first night, the screw unlocked the door at 7.30am for 'slop out' (emptying buckets). We watched as he opened Graham's cell and recoiled as the stench hit him, cracking his head on the door post.

Bloody hell! We were in bits. Alex was standing on the bed sucking fresh air through the small window. His bags were packed; he jumped down, grabbed them, pushed past us and started pleading with the officer, "Boss, boss. I can't stay in there, boss. Please boss, move me, boss!

Graham was lying half comatose on his bunk; both buckets were overflowing with liquid shit! Long out of bog roll, and with nowhere else to go, he'd just messed his pants and laid in it! At that moment, I realised why people always say they're 'shitting themselves' when they're scared.

The screw was balking as I told him Graham needed to go to the hospital. "Boss, it's the third day and he's had nothing to eat." Graham lost two stones in a week before he could hold food down for more than an hour. He couldn't have lost more with surgery. He really was scared shitless!

I did feel sorry for him. This was why I'd kept him in the dark about everything. He wasn't even streetwise, let alone capable of handling something of this magnitude. I have to give him credit for his "No comment" stance which he maintained throughout the interviews. He could be a good hand; he just needed telling exactly what to do.

Jimmy had taken advantage of Graham's compliant nature. He was a devious bastard, and to be honest, I should have known better than to leave the two of them together in Gibraltar. After two months of listening to his new mate's rhetoric, here was Graham charged with the biggest private cannabis importation in history.

They seemed to enjoy the big fish status, but I didn't want to be a jail celebrity. Far from it; I wanted to blend in so I could find a way out of the conspiracy that'd transformed my playboy lifestyle into a never ending nightmare!

I looked forward to sleep as an escape. It's the same way someone who's mourning a loved one can find some peace from the grief. But, just like them, I had to face the reality all over again every morning. "Bugger me, I've just woke up. Thank God, it's all a bad dream."

Seconds later, the stink of the foisty blankets wafts in and the cream, graffiti-covered walls come into focus. The humdrum buzz of a hundred trapped souls, trailing buckets of shit along the landings becomes a roar; you start to panic and knots grip your stomach!

Soon, a familiar clunk churns over the lock. The big steel door swings in to present a screw, grinning like the Joker from Batman. He knows just what you're thinking as he shouts, "Berriman, Ritchie… Slop out!" That's when you know it's no dream.

I'd already got my head around the fact that we'd be in for some time but as long as there was hope, I'd be doing everything in my power to minimise the damage at home.

I felt strangely tranquil, which was also quite disturbing. For the first time in many months, I felt safe. In the face of utter adversity, I'd done my absolute best to get the cargo back to the UK; nobody could say different. Consequently, nobody was going after my family or me, although it would've been a lot different if we'd dumped it.

So the risk of prison was a soft option! At least we were all safe from the gangsters, the ocean and the weather. Dawn and Trish were free; I had a lot to be thankful for.

I managed a couple of phone calls and discovered my father had been in Gibraltar looking for me and was due back any day. There was some sort of panic going on at my business premises, but no one was answering and mum could shed no light!

Aware that anybody I called would be looked at severely by the cops and Customs, I kept my calls and phone conversations to an absolute minimum. For sure they'd be recording every word.

I finally managed to speak with Dawn. She put on a hysterical voice, said our house had been ransacked, and she'd moved to her mother's. More to the point, she wanted nothing more to do with me.

Strange that. When she thought I'd landed a boat full of dope, she'd dashed three hundred miles through the night done up like a £500 hooker!

The fact I'd been living a lie with a gold digger came as no shock. She was heavily involved with a manager at Jav's club before me. People warned me off, but after a tumultuous couple of years, I thought we'd proved everybody wrong. Anyway, I had more pressing problems than worrying about a rat jumping off a sinking ship.

We buckled down to some menial jobs in the workshops; making gate latches, stripping and soldering wire ends. The first week raced away before we were due back in court for a bail hearing.

We only had the clothes we were arrested in. We were taken down to reception looking like three beach bums with fantastic tans. The officers picked to escort us to Truro Magistrates' court didn't look happy at all. We were cuffed up and loaded into the van before heading through the gate.

CHAPTER THIRTEEN

THE DEVIL'S CONVOY

Outside, we were shocked to see there'd been a major incident. There were a dozen or so police Range Rovers, vans, cars and motorcycles and a helicopter and light aircraft overhead. Coppers were hanging out of vehicles with their MP5 sub machine guns. It was all happening – or had just happened. We assumed someone had escaped and asked our guards what'd happened. They refused to answer.

To our horror, they formed a convoy ahead and behind us before screaming off in dramatic style. In all, there were fifteen vehicles. It was hard to take in but after the initial shock all we could do was pretend to laugh and hang on for dear life.

It was an hour of wailing sirens and stage-managed bullshit.

Still bewildered, we arrived at the court to find it surrounded by more armed police plus cameras and reporters, pushing and shoving to get close to us. They dragged us inside through a corridor of armed coppers in full body armour with stun grenades. What a farce! Once in the holding cells, we managed a quick word with the duty solicitor who'd turned up after our arrest.

He was very nervous and seemed scared of us. I demanded to know what the hell was going on. Reluctantly, he said he'd heard that Devon and Cornwall Police had received credible information from Cleveland Police that a gang of armed, ex-Special Forces mercenaries planned to spring us from custody en route to court.

You could've knocked me down with a feather! And the reason seventy armed police were waiting for us at the Helford Passage was that they were told we had the boat rigged with explosives and were heavily armed.

Jesus Christ alive. I'd never heard anything more ridiculous in my life. "We had cannabis, not frigging Semtex!" I laughed.

He said there would be little point in asking for bail.

No shit, Sherlock?

We were pulled upstairs followed by a copper who didn't look old enough to drive, let alone carry the MP5. The poor lad tripped and fell on his face still clutching the gun across his body armour.

"Bugger me, son, do you want a hand with that?" I laughed as the door opened and we were in the dock, still chuckling.

The courtroom was packed; I counted six machine guns. What a circus! Anyone would think we'd shot the prime minister and blown up the Houses of Parliament. We spoke only to confirm our names and were remanded for a further twenty eight days.

Downstairs, I was allowed a short visit from my father, who was clearly traumatised by the farce. I placated him as much as I could and he could see I was in good spirits. He thought I'd be devastated by his news. First, Dawn had deserted me. I just smiled and told him I already knew. Next, my home, my workshops and my business premises had been stripped bare. It was difficult to take in. At first, I assumed he meant the police and Customs had gone through everything, but it was far worse than that.

My salvage yard was completely decimated. Everything had gone by the time he returned from Gibraltar. Hundreds of thousands of pounds of stock had been disposed of; even the huge steel railway sheds had been cut up for scrap.

All that remained were the brick built offices, toilet block and concrete slabs where the sheds had been. My home and personal workshops had also been stripped bare by a frenzy of vultures. I didn't want to know anymore, especially as the conversation was being recorded.

Even though I was devastated, I laughed it off. But there was more. The Michelle Louise had been seized by the Admiralty Marshall in Gibraltar on behalf of the owner of the Melanie who was claiming her through breach of contract. "Bloody hell, dad, have you got any more good news?" I laughed as my stomach wrenched.

All too soon they pushed him out. He'd travelled three hundred miles for fifteen minutes with me, bless him, I was the apple of his eye. He liked nothing better than me popping in the Malleable Working Men's Club for a couple of pints with him. His mates would ask about the supercar outside. In there, I was just one of the lads without airs and graces.

I really felt for him because he thought he could've done more if he hadn't been in Gibraltar when I was nicked. He did say that he'd done some research on cannabis, and that he was aware it wasn't considered bad by the majority of the public! That really made me feel a lot better considering he'd always berated me for smoking it!

I did learn something massively significant from his visit. Despite him sailing the Michelle Louise, owning it on paper and co-signing for the possession of the Melanie in Gibraltar, he hadn't been arrested, or even interviewed!

There could only be one reason for this. They must have had an informant so close that he knew my dad wasn't involved. Quite frankly, it was a mistake not to arrest him; they'd slipped up and given me a large missing piece of the jigsaw.

Graham's brother, my pal Paddy Cavanagh, had also travelled down during the night with his daughter's boyfriend for company. Arriving early, they slept in the car park before being woken with machine guns in their faces then spread-eagled in puddles as frantic coppers searched their car.

The boyfriend said he was terrified, poor lad. It'd been a dramatic day with a lot to take in; I was looking forward to getting back to Exeter for a lie down and a spliff. The convoy set off again with cameramen running alongside the van.

We didn't go direct to jail! Instead we arrived at the police headquarters in Exeter. We stopped and the support vehicles circled us like a wagon train waiting for the Apaches to attack.

Of course, they wouldn't tell us anything and we waited there an hour before setting off again. Sixty minutes of high speed lunacy later we were in Bristol. Typically, as soon as they slowed down, the coppers were hanging out of the windows, posing for the public and toting their guns. Bunch of tossers!

We pulled into HMP Horefield Bristol and were unloaded with great ceremony into the reception. The screws in Bristol were well nervous of us. The Principal Officer said, "Bloody hell, what's this? The Devil's Convoy?"

We were still surrounded by ten screws when Principal Officer Greenslade said he had some bad news for us. "I'm afraid you've been made up to Category A Status," he said, expecting a reaction.

As it was my first and only time inside, I had no idea what difference it made. I just shrugged my shoulders and said; "Does that mean I get a cell on my own, away from this grumpy bastard?"

We got our red card with our names on and a big A, before being led up to the top landing of a block, where all eight 'A cats' were housed.

Some food was brought up a few minutes later as we'd missed 'dinner'. No sooner had I finished, when four screws arrived to escort me downstairs to see Mr Greenslade again. He said he had more very bad news; I thought my old dad had suffered a heart attack or had an accident going home; my stomach knotted in anticipation. Could this day get any worse?

"I'm sorry to tell you that you've been made up again, to Double A Category, High Risk!" he said with a grimace.

Relieved, I shrugged my shoulders and said, "So what? Jail is jail, mate. What's the difference? I still can't go home."

He started telling me something about visitors and regulations, but I couldn't be arsed listening. I took my new blue card with AA High Risk on it, before being taken back to the same cell. Little did I know that I was the only Double A, in the whole prison!

The cell was a big improvement from the shit hole in Exeter, especially as it had a toilet and wash basin; there was even a polished stainless steel plate I could use as a mirror. How very quaint.

In the morning, the screw unlocked and opened the door very gently. There was no grin, shouting or anything else that might upset the 'lunatic, Double A, high risk remand inmate'. I was still just the same Phil Berriman but a blue card slotted in the frame outside my cell said I'd transformed overnight into a dangerous master criminal. What utter shite.

"Morning, Mr Berriman… if you want breakfast, you need to head downstairs and join the queue." I didn't make him feel any easier by just glaring at him; I hadn't quite worked out what was going on or how to take advantage of a bad situation.

Every cloud has a silver lining, glass is half full, take a positive out of negative, wait until the dust settles and so on had been ringing in my head since the Devil's Convoy. And I still hadn't got round to worrying about my business and house.

I waited for Jimmy and Graham to be unlocked before we sauntered down to the canteen, starkly aware that everyone was trying to get a look at us while trying even harder not to stare.

Of course, they had no idea that our status was a farce; the word had gone through the wing like wildfire. The queue went quiet then parted near to the serving hatch. We were ushered in by two red bands, and without saying a word, received extra portions along with a respectful nod.

I remember thinking of the cult movie Stir Crazy with Richard Pryor and Gene Wilder as we ate a decent breakfast while trying to act like we'd done more jail than Nelson Mandela. Maybe this elevated status bullshit wasn't so bad after all.

Wrong! It soon became obvious why I should've been upset about my new found status. HMP Horefield was mostly Cat C and B prisoners, but it was rated high enough for Cat As but not Double As.

One of the restrictions imposed by my captors was enough to make my piss boil! I couldn't have any visitors or phone calls to anybody who was not cleared by the prosecution. This move was normally only imposed on terrorists.

This visitor process started with a written application to the prison which went to the police, who then arranged a home visit to the applicant by two police officers briefed by the people in charge of my case. They would report back before any approval was given. The whole procedure, if successful, took a minimum of two months.

I know this sounds ridiculous and draconian, but the fact remains that the filthy bastards had fixed it so I couldn't see or call my own children! My God, I was enraged! I didn't even believe they could legally do it! What were they up to? Why was it so important to cut me off from the outside world? I was on remand! Innocent until proved guilty! The plot thickened.

I suspected that the Crown Prosecution Service or Customs' legal people had scrutinised my interviews and ship's log and realised that my apparently full and frank admissions were far more complex than they first thought and perhaps, contained a route out! They were obviously furious about something. Why else would they make up such vile shit, costing the tax payer a bloody fortune for the security circus alone?

In this category, normal rules don't apply. In law, an accused man has a right to private legal consultation. Regardless of what they say, all visits and communications are recorded and passed over. Nothing, repeat nothing, is private when you have a double A High Risk status.

This is known as "Abuse of Process" and if proved can result in a charge being thrown out of court. In reality, 'the system' knows it goes on. The guidelines are that it happens only in exceptional circumstances where there is concern for national security.

And I would agree. It would be stupid to allow a terrorist bomber to have any secret conversations. But to abuse these provisions as they were with me is nothing short of shameful.

I'm here to tell you that the British Justice system is definitely not as fair as you've been led to believe.

I wasn't allowed the gym or a job; they said they didn't have the manpower to watch me. This meant twenty-three hours a day solitary confinement apart from two hours 'association' twice a week.

I did get to walk in the yard an hour a day with Jimmy and Graham, but that was my lot. I was furious and started writing letters of complaint to all and sundry. There's no point in kicking off, they're only doing as instructed. But, it's illegal all the same.

A remand prisoner, according to the prison inspectorate, should be allowed out of the cell for ten or more hours each day; a study in 2002 showed only seven per cent of the prison population achieved this figure.

Twenty-three hours a day solitary 'bang up' for an un-convicted prisoner on remand is barbaric. People plead guilty even though they're innocent because they're going mad being banged up on remand. They know things get so much better once they're sentenced and enter the rehabilitation programme.

I wrote to my father and asked him to send me some music urgently as I badly needed a distraction. A couple of days later, I was notified that a parcel arrived, but it would take some time to be cleared. A week later I got a Realistic mono tape player/recorder (no radio) and two tapes with "Keep the Home Fires Burning" and other such wartime classics. Bless him; he must have got them from the collection in the old folks' home he ran.

I was devastated and wrote back explaining I needed a radio/cassette to keep up with news, current affairs and modern music. He obviously wasn't thinking straight, but this was to be the most significant screw up he ever made!

I did get a radio cassette ten days later but by mistake, they left the first machine with me. Usually they don't allow more than one in case it's used for trading.

During the limited association, we met some other 'Cat A' prisoners who became our prison buddies. They were remanded on similar charges. The firm of smugglers including Graham Bozormany (known as Boris) and Nick Hammer 'The Captain' were awaiting trial for an importation of cannabis on board a vessel known as Abundance.

They'd allegedly had one good load into the Bristol Channel, but success and cash had gone to their heads. They soon attracted the attention of Customs around Poole Harbour with their designer clothes and flash motors parked alongside the scruffy old ex-fishing vessel now sporting a £25,000 sea-crane and a big RHIB on deck. Alarm bells had certainly been ringing.

The Captain, Nick, was about sixty. He'd no intentions of

smuggling again and had settled down. But once you ride the tiger, it's very hard to dismount! The gang, under threat from the big boss in Spain, had all but kidnapped him to sail again.

He, allegedly, was Big Ron, the father of another of the gang, Tyroni, who was being held in another jail. The intended customer for the next load was none other than the infamous Curly Warner, who they'd nicknamed the Black Death. In short, there was a job on and to say "No" wasn't an option!

They'd loaded off the coast of Morocco and were in the English Channel at night near the Isle of Wight when Customs swooped, surrounding the boat with launches and observation from an aeroplane. Clearly they had intelligence and were out in force. The weather was foul; it was impossible to board so they directed and escorted her into harbour.

En route, a launch developed a problem and had to make for safety. The Customs' men were all violently sea sick as chaos ensued. The big old Abundance could handle the swell no problem, chugging along at six or seven knots. The Customs' launches, designed for speed, were bouncing about like corks, trying to hold formation.

Soon, the flotilla lost formation and the desperate crew seized the opportunity; nothing to lose, they began to throw the bales of hashish one by one into the boiling sea without being seen or photographed.

The plane had to circle leaving a blind spot on the starboard side. Each time the plane was on the port side and the vessel pitched down and starboard in the swell, a bale of cannabis of about 35 kilos would be thrown over before they were in view again.

Incredibly, the Customs officers, sea sick as pigs, eventually gave up and dashed for land, relying on the plane to keep the Abundance monitored. They believed the cannabis would be cleverly concealed somewhere in the ship.

This wasn't the case. Nick and his crew had smoked copious amounts of very high grade hashish, not the commercial product they were transporting. Luckily for them, the best laid plans had gone awry in the hazy blue wheelhouse. Even after a week at sea, the stash was easily accessible, as they'd all been too stoned to hide it.

Nick and Boris couldn't believe their luck. They pointed the Abundance at the Customs' boats and jumped ship as they entered the harbour. But only after more than a ton of quality product had been jettisoned to Davy Jones locker. Allegedly.

Nick, a heavy smoker, was soon caught. Boris, in his twenties and not long out of the navy as a submariner, managed to get a mile away, but for some strange reason known only to himself, went back to rescue his Captain and was promptly captured. He'd been watching too many movies.

He wasn't the sharpest tool in the box, but it demonstrated his character to me and I liked him.

While they waited on remand, Customs had tried everything to recover the stash but found nothing! They used experts in storm tide prediction, oceanography based estimated positions, even sub-sea search and recovery teams. The vicious storm surge had created unmapped currents around the Isle of Wight which scattered every bale of precious evidence far and wide.

One bale was hauled up by a fishing boat some months later but there was no way to tell if it came from their boat as it didn't match the crumbs of cannabis they found in the carpet of the wheelhouse. Clearly the lads had their own stash for personal use.

The case against them was tenuous to say the least, although one of crew had confessed to that and the previous shipment.

The rest of the gang stuck to their guns with the standard, "No comment". The guy who confessed would have to plead guilty and he and his testimony would be dropped from the trial, leaving the rest to take their chances in court. The jury would never know any details about the guilty man. I read their depositions many times and helped their case quite a lot. I knew it off by heart.

They both smoked hashish and had a little supply chain organised which we subscribed to. Boris was the son of an ex-chief constable and quite posh. Both were quite funny and we exchanged many stories. Nick showed me how to spice up a 'pot noodle' with ingredients bought from the canteen. He taught us most of what we needed to know inside as they'd been there a year and had a good idea how to go on.

I couldn't understand how these guys were also Cat A but soon, a pattern began to emerge. If there's any doubt of a conviction being achieved at court, the Customs in particular will push for the status so that the security measures will scare the jury.

It was said that once a person was made up to my status, it was virtually unknown to be acquitted. Now things started to make more sense. I couldn't imagine a juror voting not guilty or a judge taking the intimidation into consideration after witnessing the security circus. Let's be honest, things weren't looking too good for me!

I kept complaining to various offices about my human rights and they finally eased off. Only my father was allowed to visit. Also, I used the library once a week. When everyone else was locked up, two screws would unlock and escort me down the stairs to exit the wing into the yard.

Two more screws with dogs would meet us at the door. Me, handcuffed, four screws and two dogs would walk thirty metres to the library Portakabin where I was given five minutes to choose two books. I invariably chose law books and almanacs namely Archibald which I studied diligently.

I was waiting for my depositions to arrive... usually five to six weeks after being charged. I had a number of defence tactics and wanted to explore every possibility. If we couldn't get off, I wanted to receive the absolute minimum term; all my time was spent working on our case.

Finally the 'Deps' arrived and I spent a week reading every word over and over again. Some of it was hard to believe. In the evidence bundle, there was a copy of the note I'd brought back from Istanbul and given to the Cordite firm; the evidence log stated it was found during the search of my home in my bureau.

I knew this was impossible. Also, during my interviews, anything significant was faxed down to the police station and I was questioned about it. If such a document had been found, it would've been extremely important and worthy of more questions.

The document (page 86) was damning. It related to the price of various types of cannabis per kilo, including bribes paid from the Turkish undercover officers who'd tried to set me up. Worse still, it was in my handwriting. I was devastated, it looked bad.

More importantly, I had to find out how on earth they got their hands on it. I'd folded and hidden it in the handle of my hand luggage and never let it go until I passed it to them with instructions to destroy it afterwards.

I was flummoxed; no way had I left it in my house. I racked my brain. Had the Turks taken an impression from the next page of the pad I'd written on and created a document? The alternative to this was very serious indeed!

There was a copy of a letter that Jimmy had written to his partner Trish while he was sailing out of Gib. He'd never posted it, and despite my explicit instructions in the English Channel to burn any incriminating documents and photos, the daft twat had it on him when he was arrested. He also had photos in his camera of him posing with me and Peter Cordite in France when he and Dawn drove over with his passport.

He'd told Trish everything and even referred to "this job" and all the money he was going to make. He claimed he had scurvy from being at sea so long, when actually, he'd been out four days on a failed run and the scabs were from a filthy slut he was licking out at a coke party on the Melanie. What a tosser.

I also discovered they'd been searched by Gibraltar Customs because they tried to enter port without lights. Passport details of the first skipper and crew were all there with statements from interviews. I was fuming, wondering why they hadn't told me.

To cap it all off, it transpired from the property logs that the stupid, thieving, slippery, slimy toad, had twenty kilos of the product in his kit bag when we were arrested.

I decided to keep quiet. He wouldn't read his deps and probably hoped it wouldn't be mentioned. Let's face it; it was hardly relevant compared to 3.7 tons. Jimmy had put us all in danger of a severe kicking – or worse – by helping himself.

All of the above was making the preparation of any defence very difficult. Even the solicitor was allowed only one hour with me. Clearly the prison was pandering to the Customs' directions.

I couldn't even speak freely with the brief. They always put me in the same room for the legal visit where the smoke alarm had two cables running to it; in every other room, there was only one. These smoke alarm/bugs/cameras could be bought for £100, even back then. The solicitor was useless and clearly out of his depth, but I did manage to pass a few messages back and forth.

One such message that came back was a significant game changer; Peter Cordite had been arrested at Malaga airport about two weeks before us. He was awaiting extradition for the kidnap and torture of Billy the Boiler and escaping from custody.

My mind racing, I went back to my cell and pored over every document in my bundle. I'd read something that made no sense but had dismissed it. Eventually, I found it in the 'observations' section.

A huge contingent of police and Customs had been waiting along the south coast, quite a few in the vicinity of Brixham where the Mable E Holland was berthed. Clearly, they'd known the plan! They were on station from the earliest time we could have arrived until they were stood down some three weeks later.

They obviously thought that we'd gone elsewhere, contrary to their intelligence source. Significantly, Cordite was arrested in Spain the day after they'd given up waiting. Even more significantly, everybody was ordered back on station, the day after his arrest.

I discovered that observations on the Melanie commenced the day after I'd told Geoff Burge and Cordite that she was in Ceuta. The next morning, a Customs officer called Wayne Right had flown from Manchester to Malaga, hired a car and boarded a ferry. I remembered the guy in the shell suit. It was him.

I recalled the meeting with Cordite the day before he'd accused us of completing a job and not telling him. He forced me to disclose the name and location of the vessel to prove we hadn't double-crossed him.

I'd put it down to paranoia on his part. But, was it a clever way to get the information? Maybe he'd told someone on the phone and it was bugged. He was by far the least security conscious gangster I'd ever come across.

Wayne Right had watched until the night we got him drunk and we slipped out in blanket fog. They'd lost us after that until Cordite was arrested. Then we'd had an RAF Nimrod looking for us; the same aircraft we'd waved at after changing the name and disguising the boat.

Another bombshell added to the mystery; our secret co-ordinates for the meeting had been passed to the Customs' vessel named HMCC Searcher. This was the same vessel that had been on station four miles from the meeting point. We'd assumed she was trawling.

Only Burge, Cordite and I had these co-ordinates when we left. Cordite would've passed them onto someone else if Burge hadn't turned up. One mystery was solved though; why nobody had been there to unload us at the meeting point.

Cordite, Burge and Gary Parkin were top of the list now; Burge had been a day late in Gibraltar and disappeared again while I went to meet Cordite. Parkin hadn't turned up at all after being arrested at Dover with a stolen outboard motor.

Had he turned informer and then turned Burge, his mate? Had Burge told them about the Melanie and that my own crew had sailed her, or that Cordite said he would've made me sail it, if he hadn't turned up?

This was exactly what happened when he disappeared. Of course, he could have been acting under instructions from Cordite. Only he and Burge knew where the boat was the day before observations began on her. All the others who knew were charged!

My head was battered trying to work out the possibilities. I needed a system. I got some highlighter pens, post-it notes, sticky tape and paper from the visiting canteen/shop. I covered the wall with blank paper and set about making a timeline chart.

It took two weeks at sixteen hours a day to load everything that'd happened and cross reference the observations, statements and evidence bundle with everything I could remember. Eventually I could lay on my bunk with a joint and study the whole case going back to November 1990 with John Hannibal and why I got involved with Cordite and Co. I could access all relevant documents in an instant.

The others thought I was mad and that there was no way out. But I wouldn't give up. I couldn't sit about and do nothing while my children were missing their dad. I began to see things in a different light; was I the target all along? Who were their sources of information? Was it a set up from the beginning?

Was Cordite's arrest for kidnapping the 'spanner in the works' that ruined the elaborate setup with the Turks? Was his escape really facilitated and was it so they could continue the plot?

In the observations, there were photographs of us arriving at the Michelle Louise in Torquay with Cordite. Everybody was identified apart from him, the most wanted man in Britain. Days later, and his new passport arrived in his own name. Was he their informant or a tool in an elaborate setup?

It all sounded very farfetched; surely they didn't want me more than him? Did they think he'd double crossed them and arrested him because we hadn't turned up? Maybe it was someone very close to Cordite who was he meeting at the airport when he was arrested?

Did that person set him up to be arrested? Did they know where he was all along? Who relayed that we were still at sea prompting the return of the seventy strong surveillance team the day after he was arrested?

I had to tread very carefully. Was my bizarre High Risk status an attempt to keep the lid on to protect high level informants or their handlers? Who'd stuck their necks out?

Was turning a blind eye to the serious crimes and facilitating the escape part of the deal to nail their targets at any cost?

Inspector Dick Heed came to mind; he was very cosy with the Home Secretary and always on the news. The Home Secretary of course was in charge of the prisons and had the power to order the high-risk prison truck to be replaced by a civilian minibus and dictate the route! The plot thickened, or was I paranoid?

CHAPTER FOURTEEN

THE DANGEROUS BROTHERS

In early November, two older guys arrived into the exercise yard; they too had both been graded as Double A High Risk, the same as me. John Short and Tony White said they were ex-bank robbers from South London. Both had been arrested on drug smuggling charges concerning 20 kilos of cocaine hidden in a VW minibus, 140 kilos of cannabis in a truck spare wheel and 500 kilos of cannabis in a camper.

We introduced ourselves. I was so shocked that they knew so much about our case that I first thought they were undercover. They knew things we hadn't even disclosed in interview including information about our supply ship and the fact they'd taken our food and not fuelled us up.

I was pretty convinced they knew more than they let on, but without doubt, they were pukka and we soon became pals.

Tony White was famous for the biggest robbery to date, the Brinks Matt gold heist back in 1984. Although he was acquitted, it was no secret he was a lead figure in the robbery.

His acquittal came as a result of bent coppers trying too hard to convict him by producing false evidence of an interview that never happened; this common occurrence was known as 'verballing' and was largely the reason that PACE (Police and Criminal Evidence act) was brought into UK law.

Before PACE, coppers would 'verbal' someone by saying they admitted the crime but wouldn't sign the statement. The classic line used in magistrates' court by the arresting bobby was, "The accused said, 'It's a fair cop, governor'." This evolved to them writing up a questions and answers record of the interview, swearing that it was a true record, but that the accused refused to sign it.

The magistrates generally took the side of the so-called honest policemen. The jury in Crown Court usually did the same, unless there was compelling evidence to the contrary. This practice is largely responsible for the shameful number of miscarriages of justice in the UK.

Tony White wouldn't even come out of his cell to be interviewed. After two days, the custody records showed he was moved for forty five minutes while his cell was cleaned.

The police claimed he was interviewed during this time and produced an unsigned questions and answers document as evidence. In court a year later, the bobby was challenged to re-write the document in the same forty five minutes (without pauses). After one and a half hours, he had to accept he couldn't do it in the allocated time.

Tony was acquitted of the crime, but shortly after I met him, he was sued by the insurance company and agreed to pay a settlement.

The full true story of that robbery is fascinating. I heard it first-hand. The gang had no idea the gold bullion was there. They were working on inside information from (believe it or not) Tony Black, Tony White's brother in law, who worked at the facility near the airport.

The target was the vault and £1.6 million in used notes that had been returned by some bureaus de change in the USA.

An employee trusted with one half of the combination was doused with water and petrol and although he believed he was about to be set on fire, his mind went blank. He couldn't remember his numbers.

The gang was about to give up when they decided to break open one of the many wooden crates stacked outside of the vault. This crate – and the rest – were full of gold bullion.

By all accounts, an aircraft transporting the gold to Saudi had developed a technical fault and rather than leave the crates on the plane overnight, Brinks Matt was asked to store them. Even the staff had no idea what was inside.

Faced with a massive logistics problem, the gang worked all night loading any vehicle they could get their hands on, including a white Hillman Avenger Estate owned by Tony's wife. Twenty seven million pounds later, they found themselves responsible for the biggest robbery ever!

Much like the Great Train Robbery, the Met pulled out all the stops to find the gang, who now had a huge problem; laundering the haul. The rest is history and has been told a number of different ways in various books.

If they'd only taken their original target of the banknotes, they may well have remained undetected. As it turned out, people were still getting killed over missing money twenty years later.

I trusted Tony and John. Both had done some serious bird (time in jail) in the past and I found it quite amusing that John would be giving me advice about smuggling and staying one step ahead of the law when he'd already served eighteen years and was looking at more.

Both men were wealthy with accountable assets and massive respect in the higher echelons of the criminal world.

They didn't explain fully how they knew about our fiasco out at sea, other than some of the people involved with the load on the mother ship were their business associates. They said it was no secret that we were treated very badly and hinted that it was widely believed that we were sailing directly to jail.

I learned a hell of a lot about the smuggling trade from "The Dangerous Brothers" as we affectionately nicknamed them.

The supply ship was already on top long before we got there. Everybody in the business had given it a wide berth. That's why it was drifting without supplies for months, waiting for some daft bastards to take the risk.

The story of a broken engine and the wait for spares was part of the con; remember how they steamed towards us after radar contact?

The operation, far from being the fruit of a well-organised firm of tight-lipped, professional smugglers, had been abandoned and passed about like a parcel of unstable dynamite at a terrorist convention.

The firm had more leaks than the rusty old tub we'd met off the Gambia. Maybe a deal had been done somewhere, to let someone off a charge or pay them huge sums on the condition that the large seizures were credited to the UK agencies.

Enter Cordite and Co who'd welcomed the opportunity with open arms. Well, why wouldn't he? He didn't have more than a couple of thousand pesatas in petrol and other trifling expenses in the whole operation; he was already on the run and didn't even need to risk his own men.

If he was working as a paid informer, he'd be paid a shed load of reward money for us, and the load. If he wasn't – and we'd got through – he'd have a massive windfall with no risk.

Remember that this load should have been off Ireland, then Tenerife. Clearly it was safer for all concerned for her to stay two hundred miles off Africa. I had to accept we'd been mugged and forced into an almost suicidal mission. Even without the grasses in Cordite's firm, the chances of us getting back free and clear had been non-existent.

After explaining more or less everything that had gone on, the Dangerous Brothers seemed quite keen to help out. I don't know if it was guilt, embarrassment, sympathy or a combination of all three.

I didn't expect them to tell tales on any of their associates; they were clearly 'old school' with a reputation to uphold.

Tony had the same solicitor he'd used back in 1984, Henry Milner based in London. He was now a high flyer with his own successful company. He asked him to take on our case as a favour.

I spoke to Jimmy and Graham who, to my surprise, decided to engage their own solicitors but still maintained we would all stick together. I suspect now, it had something to do with the twenty kilos Jimmy had stolen, or they were both going to take advantage of what I said in interview about them having no choice once they were at sea.

I didn't mind them blaming me. That was the plan in interview anyway; there was no point in all of us getting heavy time if it could be avoided.

When I was taking the blame for them, I'd no idea they'd already been pulled and searched on the Melanie, pretended it was theirs, kept incriminating letters and photos, or that Jim was caught with the twenty kilos he'd swiped.

Had they told me everything, my interviews would have followed a slightly different path. As it was, they'd made a right twat out of me and my statements.

Having studied every avenue open to us in the Archibald law books, I would still insist the plan had been to take the load to Holland and that the Helford Passage was merely a 'pit stop' because of the problems.

It was pretty easy to prove this with the ship's log. It wasn't going to get us off but we could hope for a lighter sentence. In Holland, such an importation would more likely attract three to six years, not the fourteen our captors would try and stick up my arse.

Another option was to prove there were 'agents provocateur' involved, acting on behalf of UK police and Customs. Of course the Turks would've been an easier option to prove, but that was a separate importation.

I didn't know for sure who was involved in transforming me from salvage and boat dealer to a drug smuggling king-pin. Anyway, I was only the captain! If I sell a fast car to a known or suspected bank robber, it doesn't make me part of the gang.

Even if they proved I knew what they wanted the boat for, the sentence would be a lot less than the masterminds of such an operation would normally get.

My biggest problem was that I was the most senior person in the operation to be charged and they were going to try very hard indeed to stick it right up me. On such a large consignment, someone would have to get seriously heavy bird!

Much like the Great Train Robbery or the Brinks Matt, the sentencing would reflect the value of the load and not the actual crime. Tony told me about an old guy who'd no idea what was going on in 1984. He was just there to make the tea, but was sentenced to eight years!

I was only driving the boat, but sure as shit sticks to a blanket, they'd be nailing me up as the main man. Yet another good reason for my farcical Double A status.

If I could prove the police and Customs had used agents provocateur to entrap me, we could all walk free. The fact that Cordite was awaiting trial put him at the bottom of the list of suspects. So I worked on the assumption that Burge and Parkin were the most likely culprits. I came up with a plan.

I would find where they lived and get a mate to act as a CPS official with dodgy ID, a recording device and a chauffeur-driven car, to visit them saying I was going to name them in court and the CPS wanted to apply for PII (Public Interest Immunity) to stop me doing so.

All they needed to do was make a short statement to the judge regarding what they did, and why they didn't want it made public, swear it and sign it. Bingo! I'd have signed statements from agent provocateurs. It was a long shot, but it could work.

One factor I had on my side was duress. I'd honestly been under extreme pressure since Cordite had sorted out Hannibal the Cannibal and his cronies a couple of years before.

In English law, any crime other than murder can be absolved by proving duress. Apart from duress in a marriage or relationship, it usually involves the taking of a hostage. There'd been examples of gangs holding a bank-manager's wife, while he helps rob his own bank.

Duress is more usually used as mitigation to reduce a sentence after a guilty plea. Such as, "I only robbed my employer because of my drug debt and the dealer's threats to harm me." But this is not a full defence because, if the defendant hadn't taken the drugs and got into debt with his supplier in the first place, he wouldn't owe the money!

For duress to qualify as a full defence, four requirements must be met:

1. The threat must be of serious bodily harm or death.

2. The threatened harm must be greater than the harm caused by the crime.

3. The threat must be immediate and inescapable.

4. The defendant must have become involved in the situation through no fault of his or her own.

A person may also raise a duress defence when force or violence is used to compel him to enter into a contract, or to discharge one.

Over the three interviews in the police station after our arrest in Camborne, I had effectively told the full story from November 1990 to our arrest in 1994 albeit slipping bits in here and there without naming anybody, or making a big thing of it.

My interviewers were quite happy as long as I wasn't denying what we'd done. They didn't realise that the bare bones of a full duress defence was hidden amongst the pages and pages of drivel, and was even backed up with Exhibit Number 1, the ship's log.

Had the penny dropped, they would've tried to negate it. I was sure my farcical status was partly because they'd realised this in the first week when their legal people got to read the interviews and view the exhibits.

Along with the ship's log, there was the recording in the custody suit when I spoke to Dawn before she left the police station. Before my first meeting with Henry Milner, I studied my wall until I knew everything backwards.

For the first time in two months, hope had morphed into self belief. In my mind, I was working towards acquittal and nothing would convince me otherwise. I prepared to pitch it to Henry and was confident I had answers to any questions he'd throw at me.

I decided to grow my hair and beard to portray myself as a gentle, placid, hippy type victim, rather than the fearless playboy portrayed in the press. A jury would need a lot of convincing to acquit us of such a huge smuggling operation.

I'd do anything for the sympathy vote. The odds were stacked against us. My appearance was only the start; I'd work on my accent, vocabulary and presentation, anything at all to improve our chances.

I met Mr Milner and told my story with a passion, laying it on thick and fast. I was a victim, in fear of my life and that of my family and friends. No one was safe. Even though I'd done my best, the gangsters still blamed me. My house and business had been stripped bare after my arrest.

He hardly said anything until the last fifteen minutes. Then he bombarded me with awkward questions as though he was the prosecuting barrister. I fired back the retorts without a pause. He was surprised and impressed and while warning me that it wouldn't be easy, he agreed to take on my case, and we would plead not guilty. I was ecstatic; here I had a top bloke, who thought we stood a chance.

I couldn't wait to tell the lads that we had a chance of beating the wrap. They didn't seem too excited, even our new friends pissed on my bonfire. I suppose I could see their point of view, but I'd convinced myself that there was a chance, however small, and I would concentrate my total belief in it. If the shit hit the fan at trial, and I was sent down for a long time, I'd deal with it then, and only then, rather than the negative drudgery that was consuming the others.

Prison wasn't going to beat me, even if I had to do ten years out of fourteen. I wouldn't become an institutionalised robot. For now, I was an innocent victim fighting for freedom! Damn the rest of the doom and gloomers! Positive mental attitude would protect my mental health and keep me strong.

My father was a regular visitor, although I quite often got the impression he was humouring me; he usually did what I asked. It was a long journey from Teesside to Bristol, but he never batted an eyelid. He always went away in a better mood than when he arrived; I made damn sure of that.

I managed to sneak him a copy of my interviews for Jock Smith, who'd scarpered after my arrest and hadn't been seen since. I managed this, even though a prison officer (screw) was sat with us. We exchanged so many irrelevant documents, he stopped checking them and read his book.

Jock had a nice camper van that he and his lovely wife Joan, often drove to Italy. I guessed he was away in it. They also had many friends and some property in Scotland. Just like my dad and Graham, my co-accused, I'd kept him in the dark to protect him. But he was far from daft; he knew more than he let on, but wouldn't ask questions. Rather he'd nod, wink and smile – all at the same time – and I'd do the same back. It was a type of understanding that only good friends can have.

Even though he was thirty years my senior, I rated him as a top man. The last thing I wanted was him arrested. I'd done my best to negate every second of his involvement; a copy of my interviews and depositions would seriously help him when he got a pull. He was a paid hand, innocent of any crime, I'd told him nothing!

The copies were handed over to Jock by his son at a rendezvous at Scotch Corner on the A1. After studying them word for word, they returned home and waited for plod. It was Bill McBungle, the guy who'd interviewed me that went to his house and arrested him.

Bill said to him that his answers were so accurate that anybody would think he'd had a look at my interviews.

Jock replied, "Well that just shows you, we must be telling the truth then." He became a 'cleared visitor' and often accompanied my dad.

Against all of his principles, dad paid someone in Bristol who had the means to get cannabis to me. It helped me concentrate at a deeper level. While I was lightly stoned, I could block out the relentless buzz from hundreds of neighbours.

During one association, an ounce of beautiful 'Soft Black' arrived. Before I could share it with the members of our co-operative, a 'landing rat' told me of a plan to rob me that evening during lock up.

I tipped the scrote a couple of joints worth and set about dismantling part of my steel bed. Arming myself with two feet of box section hidden down my trousers, I descended the stairs to the lair of Leroy, the gang leader of the fashionable Afro Caribbean community that lurked on the ground floor with their jeans falling half way down their arses.

Not wishing to enter into their slang, like "rasclart & bumbaclart", I spoke in broad Teesside, "Have this, Sunshine!" Boom.

After a few sharp blows to his head, I held the bar across his throat telling him, "I'll get my firm to find out where your family live, and burn their house down, with them in it! Why do you think I'm Double A? Dickhead!"

The brazen assault, coupled with the AA card outside my cell door, obviously gave credibility to my ridiculous threats; they never bothered us again. They even showed us respect.

After that incident, Jimmy really took advantage; he'd push to the front of the queue for the telephone and chalk our names at the top of the board for the pool tables. He was a good actor and would scowl at them, spouting such things like, "Oh dear, looks like the white boys are first. Any of you black bastards got a problem with that?" Amazingly, we got away with it every time, much to the amusement of the screws.

A letter came from Henry Milner, saying that he was too busy to take my case personally, but would supervise it and allocate his star man. I could understand his position. I couldn't pay the sort of money he commanded privately anyway, I was claiming legal aid.

The letter also said that the police had applied to interview me about a firearm found at my house, during the search after my arrest. It was actually a 9mm pistol which fired CS gas; still illegal, but not deadly. I'd got rid of the real guns, as soon as my life wasn't being threatened by Hannibal and his agents.

I thought it a bit pointless considering the charges I was already facing, and mentioned it to the Dangerous Brothers. Tony quickly educated me about a widespread practice. Apparently, when a high level criminal is caught bang to rights and looking at heavy time, the police – especially the crime squads – attempt to incite them to turn informer and grass on other criminal enterprises.

If the information proves useful, the newly-converted grass gets a letter passed to the judge, which results in leniency when sentenced.

He said that ten years before, they were allegedly involved in a William and Glyn's bank robbery in London. Police visited a co-accused and offered to put a word in with the judge (who just happened to be a golf buddy of the senior officer) if he named some of the bent coppers in the Flying Squad, who were taking bribes.

The villain taped the meeting and it was played in court. The judge stopped the case and threw it out, rather than it become public knowledge that such things went on. Tony advised me to try and tape the forthcoming interviews.

This was another route... another chance. I was well excited. I asked dad to send me the smallest tape recorder he could find, even a Dictaphone would do. Unfortunately it was refused at reception and I spent the next week or so trying to find a foreigner who had one for translation purposes. I failed again as the interview was looming in two days, on 29th November 1994.

I had to try and make do with what I had. The Realistic tape player/recording machine my dad sent me was still in my cell. I confided in Boris, who donated a four inch thick ream of his defence depositions for the cause. The machine would fit within the A4 papers. I sat up all night, carving out a compartment with the blade from a disposable razor. The sides were only half an inch thick, so I stiffened them with coat after coat of diluted toothpaste, drying it on the big old radiator, until it held its shape.

The machine fitted quite nicely. A few perforated sheets above the microphone would make the recording clearer. I practiced slipping my fingers in to press the play/record and stop buttons until I could do it blindfold in less than two seconds every time. The longest tape I had was forty five minutes. I tested it with the file closed and open, to determine the proximity and adjustment needed to capture the best sound quality. I couldn't believe how well it worked. God bless my dad!

The door swung open at 10am. The two screws were there to escort me to a 'legal visit'. If they were honest and said it was a police visit, a lot of inmates would refuse to leave their cell.

I picked up my defence file as always and followed them to the search facility at the visit block. A usual strip search includes a clothes' change with my kit going into an x-ray box.

One screw asked about the file. "It's my defence file... it's a legal visit and I take it everywhere." Another one nodded to him, confirming what I said was true. As I walked to the room, turning on the recorder, my heart was thumping.

A uniformed chief inspector was waiting. I'd never met him before. Imagine my disappointment when he said he'd come to investigate a complaint I'd made dating back six months. I was devastated! The complaint related to an accident with my old Porsche, which was hit by a truck. The police got involved and messed up the insurance claim by falsely stating it couldn't have happened as I'd stated.

The ensuing conversation was so damming against police that had I been able to produce the recording; I would have won any case. Clearly that wasn't an option, because it would've blown my plan. I had much bigger fish to fry.

I went through the same security procedure returning to my cell. The screws knew I'd been with a cop so there was little chance of me smuggling contraband. The search was minimal. I checked the quality of the recording and it was good. I wondered if I could pull it off again. Talk about stress! I didn't dare have a joint; I needed to be razor sharp.

My big chance came again within hours. Luckily, the same screws were still on search duty after lunch and again, they knew I was meeting cops. I stripped off, changed in a hurry and waltzed through, switching the tape on before entering the room. My heart was pounding again, and I was praying very hard to my spirit guide. Believe me!

I instantly recognised Bill McBungle from the regional crime squad, who'd interviewed me after my arrest; the other guy was a sergeant Heinz Kitchup from Durham.

I'd thought long and hard about how I was going to wind them up. I knew what I needed and only had forty five minutes tape time in which to get it. The last thing I wanted to hear was my file on the table 'clunking' as the tape ran out. That would blow it completely.

Although I hoped the tape would be played in court a lot of what I said was bait to provoke a reaction. I had to wind them up to get what I wanted. I have highlighted and numbered what I considered to be significant in the annex.

CHAPTER FIFTEEN

THE GOLDFISH BOWL

I went into jail owning a £250,000 yacht, a luxury home, workshops and yard, a Porsche 911 Turbo and other toys. I had the trophy woman and a playboy lifestyle. It was all funded by the best auto salvage yard in the North East. From nothing, I was a self-made man, pocketing £5,000 a week.

Within a week of my incarceration and a very realistic prospect of a long jail sentence, my house and workshops were stripped of everything and my huge steel sheds which had been filled with hundreds of thousands of pounds worth of stock were reduced down to the concrete.

Paul Daniels and the rest of the magic circle couldn't have made it disappear any faster!

The locusts and vultures responsible for this atrocity were not the gangsters or police and Customs. The diabolical vaporisation of my life was a feeding frenzy of greed and shame by so-called mates, staff and even family.

The very people who lived off me were the biggest culprits. I'd never hear from most of them again. Those horrible bastards know who they are.

There was supposedly some misconstrued rumour that police and Customs would seize everything I had. Nobody yet understood the new Proceeds of Crime legislation. Each thief had asserted they would "keep safe" the proceeds to return to me. Yeah!

At least a dozen parasites valiantly fought each other for 'custody' of my every belonging. My car and vehicle stock were apparently sold for peanuts. Everyone had a windfall. They know who they are too; I bet it was one hell of a fire sale, lads!

I took the news very well, which surprised my father who relayed the stories. By the time he'd finished telling me, I'd already taken a big positive out of it; I could use it in court, claiming that in fact the gangsters had robbed me of everything as soon as I was arrested and people were too scared of them to call the police and report it.

The greedy, selfish, low life bastards had no idea how much they helped me! What use is money if I was doing fourteen years? Let's face it: Gangsters or robbing bastards, there's not much between the low life bastards. I could state all this in court without the prosecution being able to disprove it.

I barely had time to thank Tony White for suggesting I make the recording before they were ghosted out; I wondered if I'd ever see them again. A couple of weeks later Jimmy was mysteriously ghosted to Oxen, a low category cushy jail. I knew it wouldn't be long before he'd be co-operating to feather his own nest.

I'd been complaining constantly about restrictions because of my AA status and it wasn't long before I too would be moving, but it wouldn't be to a lower security jail. Oh no, there was no chance of me shitting on my mates for an extra blanket.

Transfer day was ever so funny. I'd managed to stash a small amount of cannabis resin and was having a smoke when I heard the rattle of keys in my door. I was used to the twice weekly 'spins' where three or four screws would come in and search everything in fine detail. Such was my status.

This morning was different. "Pack your bags, Berriman," I was told. "You're leaving."

I had twenty minutes to pack up everything into three plastic bags which would be sealed before transport to my new mystery home.

Ghosting is a term used when the prison service want to move someone they suspect could have the contacts and the organisational skills to arrange an escape. Nobody has advance notice so there's no chance of tipping anyone off. You come out for lunch and your pals have gone!

I now had three lumps of cannabis to hide or bin. Getting caught with this while on remand for 3.7 tons is not going to make much difference and they could hardly make my life any worse; I was already in jail. I just didn't want to lose it.

I was pretty sure I was heading for Belmarsh SSU where the only other AAs, Tony White and John Short, had been sent. Everything would be x-rayed.

The only possible solution was to swallow the cannabis or 'bot' it. I've never been one to have anything shoved up my arse, even during drunken sex with a one-night stand. If a finger so much as touched my sphincter muscle, my hard-on was gone.

Swallowing was not an option either; I'd heard horror stories about that. I could hear the screws coming back up the stairs so, without further ado, I squeezed out a little Johnson's wanking lotion and violated myself for the first and last time in my life.

The trip to London was low key. I was really enjoying the run out in the minibus with four screws. I was still cuffed in a cage, but hey, no sirens, no drama and no stress. It was absolutely great to get out of that shit hole.

After an hour, my arse started to bubble! Not because I was scared of going to the SSU. Tony White had put me in the picture; I was actually looking forward to getting out of the cell for more than the fourteen hours a week I'd endured in Bristol.

My arse was bubbling because I hadn't realised the cannabis had to be wrapped up watertight!

Half an ounce of good quality 'Paki Black' was slowly dissolving in my arse and creating an ever increasing back pressure. No wonder I was having a nice trip; I was stoned because it was entering my bloodstream. It felt like I badly needed a shit but the chances of them stopping for me were zero.

Eventually, too stoned to care, it was really shit or bust. Luckily for them, I farted, long and loud! The van reeked of scrambled eggs and ganja! I couldn't pull myself together.

"Bloody hell," the screws shouted, "what the hell, have you been eating?"

"Nothing," I said honestly. "Just the eggs you bastards gave me this morning. I don't cook it, you do. Serves you right." Tears of laughter were streaming down my face.

By the time we reached Belmarsh, I was a right mess; taking the piss out of everyone and laughing at my own daft jokes. Everything was hilarious to me. The strip search saw me accuse the Belmarsh screws of being queers. Eventually they put me in a holding cell over lunch.

I pushed out the three pieces, which had reduced to half their original size. They were like washed pebbles, all smooth and rounded. After rinsing them in the wash basin and cleaning up as best I could, I collapsed on the bed in a giggling heap until the screws came back.

I was taken into the special secure unit block and was about to be taken into spur one of four, when I demanded my property bags. There is a system and rules regarding a prisoner's property. The bags are sealed with numbered tags in just the same way as evidence is bagged and tagged at a crime scene. On arrival at a new place, a prisoner would sign for the bags after checking the seals were intact.

I wanted my defence file, which for the first time since my incarceration had left my side. They refused to bring my bags, so I refused to enter the spur. The Bristol screws, who knew me well, actually agreed. They were responsible for the handover and knew fine well that a prisoner's property had to be accounted for first.

"Win, lose or draw, lads, I'm not going in there without my defence file. If you want a fight, ring an ambulance first, because at least one of you is going to hospital!" The Bristol lot knew I was serious; I'd battered a couple of the 'hard case Rasta men' who thought they ran the wing.

It was agreed they'd get my bags. Nobody wanted the paperwork and with the screws from two prisons present, it wasn't worth the hassle; we all knew this.

My bags arrived; they were open without any seals. The rules had been broken and I kicked off, screaming and shouting. The screws looked dumfounded and tried to calm me down. Eventually, I was told to retrieve my defence file as the rest had to go through the x-ray machine.

Incredibly, my defence file was the only thing missing from the bags. "You dirty bastards!" I yelled.

They jumped me and bundled me into the spur, trying to calm me down. "We'll find it," they said.

Two hours of stoned oblivion later, my defence file was brought to me.

Everyone was locked inside the spur. There were twelve cells in each of the four spurs making up the special secure unit or SSU. As the doors opened, I was pleasantly surprised to see the 'Dangerous Brothers', John and Tony.

Next door to me was allegedly the highest ranked Italian Mafia Godfather and hit-man ever locked up in the UK. Francesco Di Carlo, known as Frankie the Strangler, was in his fifties and had been inside for ten years already for a huge drugs' haul.

My other neighbour was Frank la Pero Soto, allegedly the highest ranking member of the Columbian Cali cartel. He was on remand for a coke importation and in the process of claiming duress as a full defence. Amazingly, his solicitor was Henry Milner.

These guys were to become friends and I'd learn so much first-hand information, I would become quite an authority on international drug trafficking. It was a mistake to make me up to the farcical status of Double A. The people I mixed with had a wealth of information and experience and I wanted to understand everything.

I started a hunger strike because of the missing defence file which had obviously been copied. My protest was widely reported by the media. My dad wrote to my MP, the late Frank Cook (God bless you, sir) who arranged to come to the unit to see me after ten days of starving myself. He promised an investigation and managed to get the prison ombudsman involved. His report concluded that they had indeed stolen my file to copy for the prosecution.

Amazingly, in the forthcoming hearings, the judges wouldn't allow any mention of this disgraceful incident. This sort of abuse of process is commonplace in high profile cases. The law in England purportedly requires a person's defence files and legal meetings to be private. Cases have been thrown out for just such an abuse of process.

Not so, it seems in an SSU, especially Belmarsh with its hidden cameras and microphones. The screws do as they're told and are bound by the Official Secrets Act.

After the hunger strike, I settled down to a much better environment. I was no longer in solitary for twenty three hours a day. It was mid-December. They even allowed me to call my children, something the filthy, dirty bastards hadn't allowed since my arrest on the September 5th.

They only cleared me for phone calls to my family when I arrived at Belmarsh on December 18th. Don't be fooled by what the newspapers say. The Home Office and Prison Service can, and do, treat people very badly at the behest of the Customs, and sometimes the police. You have no real human rights in these places, whether you're convicted or awaiting trial.

Once you're sentenced, you get downgraded, get a job, visitors and can mix with others.

I met Tyronio Donattelli after two weeks there. He came in from Winchester having been a Category A remand prisoner, but was upgraded to Double A for no reason other than his trial was coming up. The Customs, in fear of losing the case because none of the load was recovered, wanted the jury to see the armed police convoys, arriving, guarding and leaving the court.

The jury would be frightened into thinking their lives were in danger and welcome the company of Customs and police as chaperons who were basically just jury nobblers for the prosecution.

It was said that once they made you high-risk, the chances of acquittal are virtually nil! It was a very expensive exercise, but effective. They'd invented intelligence that Tyronio was also planning to escape and ghosted him off to Belmarsh. Six foot four inches in his early twenties, he was shitting himself; this had come as quite a shock.

I introduced myself and told him I knew his co-accused in Bristol and all about his case. It was at least two days before he believed who I was. Completely paranoid, he thought I was an undercover plant until I repeated confidential details of the conversations I'd had with his crew.

Through Christmas, we spent time not getting captured for smoking weed while I helped him with his case. He was ghosted to Bristol for trial in February and was cleared as I expected, despite the high risk circus orchestrated by Customs.

I considered Tyronio a friend and promised to meet up with him when the nightmare ended. He was getting cannabis resin sent to me inside CD cases which were passing through security; when he left, he gifted me his CD player. The scam was working well, until Vera Lynn became involved.

Rather than buy up to date CDs, my dear dad was robbing them from his old people's residential home. Unfortunately the security department couldn't comprehend my taste of music and looked harder than usual when they saw the WWII Armed Forces' Favourite medley, with my name on it.

Up in front of Governor 5 Bob Carol, I denied all knowledge and informed them that the CDs were coming from Tyronio in Bristol prison. They let me off thinking I'd grassed him up and passed on the info to Bristol, only to discover he'd been acquitted. So I made a mistake; what the hell were they going to do? Lock me up?

Although the prosecution now had my complete defence file, they knew nothing of the tape recording; I wouldn't even talk about it in the spur, never mind on the phone. I knew they had details about my plan to dupe Burge and Parkin, the two suspected grasses, so with nothing to lose, I got my brief to fire off interrogatories regarding them. Interrogatories are questions that are agreed or denied to save time in court.

The answers came as quite a shock, revealing that Burge had been sentenced to five years in Malaga, having been caught red-handed on a drug run just after he disappeared from Gibraltar. Gary Parkin was on remand having been caught with Lancashire Frank and others on a ship at sea called the Woodleigh with a few tons on board.

Oh dear! It seemed like everyone involved with Cordite and Co was set up and locked up. All apart from Dale Gordon, that is.

Cordite had been extradited and given high risk status like me. Mittener had also been re-captured. Surprisingly, Henry Fiction passed the interviews and became a cleared visitor. He handed me a copy of a document Davy Mittener had written in Winston Green Prison.

It said he wanted special treatment and that he'd been a paid informant since 1992. He was recruited after being arrested for a revenge attack against the gangs who took over the rave in Teesside.

He'd been getting paid for relaying information about Cordite and other villains' crime sprees. He admitted various shootings and implicated many others. The document was to be used against him as he'd simply gone too far while on the run. It was seized in the prison and the governor passed it on to be tendered as evidence.

It wasn't bullshit! Cordite and Mittener had grown up together. They were very close and I started to believe they'd been so pivotal in the elaborate Turkish set-up, they were allowed to get out of jail. Escape was the only way; if they'd been bailed, alarm bells would've been ringing across the north of England and nobody would deal with them again.

I still didn't know if Cordite was an accessory or a target, but it seemed someone was going to a lot of trouble to get me. Inspector Richard Heed was at the top of my list of suspects. Many of the mysteries started to make sense with at least one, very high level informant confirmed. I'd still be hunting more pieces of the jigsaw for years to come.

More of Tony and John's associates turned up in the same spur; there'd allegedly been an ongoing conspiracy to bring 330 kilos of cocaine by catamaran from the Caribbean. Some of the gang realised after they were nicked for three different importations that they were all on top, meaning everything they were connected to was very likely to fail. Word had been passed out to abort the operation! Abort, repeat, abort!

Unfortunately for a large number of the firm, it seemed the principals at large had spent a lot of the collective funds on very high-profile and lavish lifestyles. Having duped the Columbians to accept worthless bearer bonds as security for the consignment instead of cash, the pair from Scotland, Benny the Todger and Billy the Beard, were living like rock stars while the agencies followed and watched them. Maybe the cocaine job had to go ahead or the money would have to be accounted for.

Outgoings, mentioned in the depositions included a 55 foot luxury Sunseeker yacht in St Tropez, pallets of high quality champagne, a Mercedes gifted to a prostitute and gold Rolex for all of one family. In all, about twenty-five villains in Operations Stealer 1, Stealer 2, Splinter 1, Splinter 2 and Splinter 3 were nicked and awaiting trial. All because the advice from inside had been ignored, allegedly.

I read all the depositions and knew the cases off by heart. Tony had walls covered in timelines like mine. They worked tirelessly and I learned an awful lot about the London underworld, the various agencies and their methods, but also, how to pull apart a conspiracy, the depositions and apply for unused evidence.

Later, they'd all be convicted in Bristol, but not after the prosecuting team had refused to continue in the first trial because the Customs' reams of observations were blatantly false. Tony had found discrepancies in them. Even though they all knew each other, it was not enough to prove a conspiracy.

Disgracefully, the judge ordered a new trial, where Customs were allowed to re-write their notebooks – minus times and dates – and present them to a new jury that knew nothing of the previous trial.

This diabolical farce of a trial was held in a private court. There were no witnesses to this miscarriage of justice perpetrated by the Crown. It would be four years before this wrong was put right at the appeal court. But it was still better than the twenty odd years they were given.

If Tony had been more of an academic at school, he would've made a good solicitor. Perhaps he'd learned from the best legal teams money could buy. Who knows? I took it all in... I needed to. Tony told me there was always something wrong in the depositions. And he was right.

In the SSU, we had gym, table tennis, volleyball and even cable TV. But I still did eight hours a day on my case and legals, especially while banged up behind the door.

I practised my story on anyone who'd listen. They had volunteers trying to recruit us into church that counselled and 'reached out' to us. I had them devastated by the time I'd learned to present my version of events; one guy broke down in tears, feeling so sorry for me.

I always tried to get on with the screws and had a number of them convinced I was innocent. They had a table tennis league and I have to admit, I was shit hot at it. They would bring their top players in from the main prison to challenge me. At home, during parties, I challenged and beat all comers, even when drunk or stoned. It was a well-needed distraction.

The SSU is known as the Goldfish Bowl because for every twelve prisoners in a spur, there are four guards behind the glass wall into their office and three or four guards mixing with us or sat at a table, dealing with our requests. Every single thing you do is recorded and reported in your file.

We had our own showers, phone, Sky TV with recorder, pool or table tennis table, kettle, toaster and an endless supply of toast, butter, jam, boiled eggs, milk and cereal. Although we had to share the gym and yard with the other thirty six men in the unit, it wasn't at all bad, compared to Bristol.

It sounds reasonable, but bear in mind all forty eight of us couldn't work or mix with anyone else. We had nothing to look at but a wall. If we managed to get over it, we'd still be in prison. The only time we saw daylight was an hour a day in the yard. Double A is shit; make no mistake!

They supply the perks to ease the tension. The screws were chosen because they had a good attitude; if we got a jobsworth being a bastard, a complaint would be made and they'd be back to the main prison the same day. The SSU was a tinderbox, full of powerful people and the clever screws were rightfully wary.

My pal, Frankie 'the Strangler' Di Carlo, had been told by his own doctor that he had high cholesterol and needed a special diet, which the governor refused; I went with him to the office to help translate as he requested.

We had to explain that if Frank died of a heart attack, and it was known to the family that the governor had refused to allow what his doctor had ordered, it was highly likely they'd blame him for the death of their Mafia Godfather.

Given that Frank was a chief suspect in a number of high profile murders, including that of 'God's banker', the top man in the Vatican's bank, Governor 5 Carol's face was a picture I'll never forget. I can still see it today as the penny dropped. Frank the Strangler had brown rice and chicken that night.

The SSU gave me the opportunity to practice my defence of duress. The more screws I convinced, the more wanted to hear it for themselves; I'd done the same in Bristol, resulting in less onerous security attitudes toward me. If I'd not been nice to them, the copies of the deps would never have reached Jock, and the recording of the cops wouldn't have happened.

I met my appointed barrister, Trevor Burke. He was a nice enough bloke, but I could tell he was just going through the motions and didn't really believe I had any chance of acquittal. In fear of being recorded, we'd communicate important matters by note or letter passed between us. He dismissed my recording, saying we could never get it admitted as evidence as it was made after I'd been charged. I disagreed and told him so.

I asked how far I could go in court with regards to Cordite and his gang without them getting charged. The answer was a revelation of significant magnitude; I could say what the hell I wanted. Nothing I said in court while charged, giving evidence or being cross examined, could be used against anybody else. So I could get details of Cordite's cases to show the jury, and even name him in court.

As a result, we applied for all of Cordite's depositions including kidnap, torture, guns, ammunition, stolen goods and the escape. Strangely, we were refused this material on the grounds that such disclosure was too sensitive and not in the interest of the public. How about that for a turn up for the books? We were clearly onto something.

We had to postpone our trial date so that a Public Interest Immunity hearing could take place. My barrister told the judge and the prosecution what we needed and why we needed it. The judge decided what, if anything, was too embarrassing or dangerous for the agencies and for any informants involved.

The hearing took three days. We were refused hundreds of documents; they really did have something to hide. But we did get what I really wanted – details of the kidnap, torture, escape and guns. All of this had been in the media in one form or another, so the judge, however biased, had no choice but to give us it.

Rather than try to convince a jury that I was scared of an anonymous gangster who the prosecution would say was fiction, I could reveal who and what he was. I had photos of the arsenal of guns and ammunition found in safe houses along with scary allegations of kidnap and torture. What a result!

Shortly after this, as a direct result of my defence strategy being disclosed to the judge at the PII hearing, both Dawn and Jock were arrested for aiding and abetting an escaped prisoner. I was interviewed under caution and admitted taking Cordite across the sea, but I said I'd only done so in fear of my life. I assured them that no other person knew who he was at that time.

My barrister was present throughout; police and Customs expressed disbelief and asked me three times, "Are you really going to tell the truth?"

I assured them I had nothing to fear because the rules of extradition prevented the police from interviewing Cordite on new charges. His extradition was granted on the specific grounds of escaping lawful custody while awaiting charges of kidnap and torture, not cannabis smuggling.

I knew that Mittener at least was a paid informant. So they knew everything anyway. That's why everyone concerned with them was locked up. If they could have, and wanted to connect him to me, they would have at least interviewed him about it, and they hadn't.

They asked how I knew about Mittener being an informant. I couldn't tell them it was through Henry Fiction. Then they offered me a deal to plead guilty and a six year sentence, meaning I could be out in two with time already served factored in. My hard work and dedication was clearly paying off; fourteen down to six and we weren't even at court yet.

"No thanks," I said. "I'm going to be walking down the front steps."

Even my barrister thought I was a bit hasty, but their faces gave me renewed confidence. I could see they'd come to do a deal at all costs; they were worried!

I said, "Meeting over, gentlemen. I have work to do. Good day." I asked Trevor for a word in private.

I told him that Mittener had been wreaking havoc with guns before and more importantly, after the kidnap and escape from custody; he'd been a paid informer for more than two years on a gun rampage with his new found impunity, but his handlers were not allowed to turn a blind eye and would be in deep shit already… even deeper if details of any investigations fell into our hands.

Now they had him back in custody, he'd be threatening to expose the escape plot and screw up any on going cases if he was charged. I was guessing but it made sense to us both. Mittener was the type who'd use anything to get a better deal; heads would roll if the public knew for certain what many suspected about the escape.

It was at this point that Trevor became interested. He said he'd do his best to find out what they were scared of; he'd seen their faces too. I gave him a list of further things to do, including checking airline manifestos for any familiar names on certain days to Malaga and Gibraltar. I had a feeling we'd find something important.

Back in my cell, I was ecstatic; I stayed up late making adjustments to my wall charts corresponding to my interpretations of what'd been said. I was ready for court now; bring it on! Henry Fiction visited again to ask about the rumours. I told him how it was:

1. Due to Cordite's lieutenant David Mittener having been feeding the police information for years, I was hardly grassing anybody; they photographed him getting on my boat, sent him a new passport and let him escape the country for God's sake! Helloooo! They'd also arrested everybody involved in his transport to Spain.

2. Cordite was never and will never be interviewed about the cannabis, despite Detective Bill McBungle naming him in my interviews, and me refusing to confirm it.

3. Cordite's extradition was applied for and granted on the grounds of the specified crimes he was charged with, plus the escape from custody.

Henry went back a much wiser bloke, but the rumour mill was working overtime back home. Cordite would be trying to negate the fact that half the North East underworld knew that Mittener was a grass and all of Cordite and Co's hashish crews were in jail. The underworld was worried.

Meanwhile Cordite had his own problems. He was ashamed his childhood friend was the reason so many investors had lost so much money. His trial was scheduled at the same time as ours a couple of months away in October, but three hundred miles apart.

Cordite's intended meteoric rise to the top of the hashish business on the Costa del Sol had resulted in three separate crews and more than six tons of drugs being nicked. Maybe jail was the best place for him.

As expected, I was ghosted back to Bristol; the trial judge in Exeter had refused to allow us a QC as it would mean someone more senior than him in the court. They refused to move the trial to Woolwich Crown Court, which would have meant only a short hop through the tunnel connecting it to Belmarsh prison.

Instead, we were housed in Bristol and had to make the eighty five mile high-risk Devil's Convoy circus twice a day, five days a week, so everybody would see three ruthless, master criminals surrounded by MP5 machine guns and some terrible acting.

I met up with Jimmy and Graham again. They didn't want much to do with me as I tried to get them in my cell for a last minute briefing; I was buzzing with anticipation and assured them we were going home. Despite looking a bit sheepish, they still insisted they intended to follow me and my barrister's lead.

I briefly saw Lancashire Frank on the landing heading for his second long sentence; I had his depositions and discovered that Gary Parkin was arrested by police and Customs in the North West, but he requested to see Peter Hollier from Leeds Customs North East headquarters. Hollier arrived and signed him out of the custody suite for several hours.

Who is Peter Hollier? The very man in charge of my own case! Seems Parkin hadn't earned enough brownie points. He was charged along with the rest... good enough for the dodgy bastard.

The day finally came when we were woken, fed early and taken to the courtyard for what was to be our last ride together. Our day of reckoning was upon us!

CHAPTER SIXTEEN

UP FROM THE DUNGEONS

The Devil's Convoy roared through Bristol bringing chaos to the rush hour. Police motorcycles cleared junctions a mile ahead so our speed never fell below 50 mph in the city. It was a bit scary at times but we had other things on our mind.

After a 100 mph belt down the motorway, we arrived at the crown court housed in the Castle complete with battlements. It was actually still a royal seat of power. The scene was worse than at Truro when we were first arrested. Talk about pushing the flipping boat out!

TV satellite link trucks, a media scrum, dozens of coppers, MP5s and full body armour, crowd control... the most ludicrous acting I'd ever seen. It was completely stage managed; everyone assumed a menacing stance, bringing their weapons up as the cameras rolled and flashed.

Granted, it was the biggest stash found on a private vessel and a huge haul by any standards. But the level of security for three bullied unarmed sailors with no criminal record was truly obscene!

Inside the gate, cops were up on the roof and hiding behind trees, four more on the door. What the hell were they expecting? The squad outside trotted in like a pack of circus display ponies before fanning out to surround the building. Jesus!

The portcullis gates were locked behind the convoy, obviously in case a company of highly trained ex-Special Forces mercenaries managed to hijack some tanks and a helicopter gunship to break us out.

I wonder how many of the brave bobbies would put their lives in danger or die to stop me escaping; not many I wager. I was hardly Francesco Di Carlo. Most of the two faced twats close to me had helped themselves to everything I had. They were hardly going to get a team up to break me out, were they? Ridiculous!

Inside was no better; ushers and even security staff were cowering as we were led down into the dungeons. We split up to talk to our respective legal teams.

We walked into the packed bustling courtroom as it fell silent; everyone glaring at us like we were extra terrestrials. Dad was with his old mate Brian Wolsey who was clearly shocked at the circus. I smiled from ear to ear at them and then at the Customs' team to my left. The noise picked back up until a door knock heralded the judge was about to enter. Here we go then; fourteen months to get here, let's have it. Bring it on.

Introductions over, we were given the usual warnings; should we be found guilty, our sentences would be greater than if we changed our pleas now to guilty. It's a fair comment; you get a discount for saving the court's time and money. I'd heard it all before and yawned, just as Jimmy and Graham's barristers jumped up together. What the hell?

I couldn't get my chin off my chest or my tongue back in my mouth as I listened to them both pleading guilty. There was no discussion or direction; I quickly noticed their legal team had hardly any papers compared to mine. They'd all known well in advance what was going to happen. Maybe ever since Jimmy had been moved to his cushy prison.

The judge congratulated them on their wise move, and while glaring straight at me, sent them down to await the end of my trial when they'd be sentenced. All they said as they walked past was, "Sorry, Phil, you know the score."

It was like a knife gutting me. Treachery! They'd been promised a deal. That much was obvious. I'd have little time to change my strategy. They'd left gaps in my defence I couldn't fill. I was even devastated for them, regardless of the stunt they'd pulled; they'd probably been mugged by the same team that'd offered me a deal.

Then another request rocked my boat even more. "My clients ask that the judge order that they be kept separated from Mr Berriman from now on, in case of retribution, your honour."

"Granted, see to it," he said as he nodded at his clerk then glared at me again, like I was Cordite himself.

Mutiny. Mutiny! I'd been working my arse off for us all to be walking down the front steps. All this time they'd planned to mutiny and leave me alone to face the enemy!

I missed half of what was said after that bombshell, but it was just legal drivel. The jury would be in tomorrow; that's when it really started. I was devastated by the prosecution's first punch below the belt. The team across the room couldn't help glancing over and giggling to each other. I couldn't hide my shock and disappointment.

I had ten minutes with Trevor before the Devil's Convoy resumed. He said, "You have a better chance without them. Trust me." I couldn't see it. I had a plan for every point we could lose. Jimmy and Graham could've filled the gaps, but they jumped from the sinking ship like rats. I had to pull my head out of my arse and get on with it.

Back at Bristol at 7pm, I was moved from my cell into another wing full of the noisy arseholes, who shouted until after midnight. A cold lasagne was all they could give me as everything was closed down. When the noise finally subsided, the screws came past every half an hour and rattled my hatch until they could see me wake up.

At 3am, I warned the screw I'd wake the whole wing up next time he did it. The anonymous bastard just laughed. Twenty minutes later he rattled it again. I put my radio on full belt and bashed my bin against the door, shouting like hell until the wing descended into a frenzy of door bashing and screaming lasting forty five minutes. The cons and screws would all be on edge tomorrow as a result. People get grumpy when they're tired. The screws would have their work cut out.

In the morning, I complained and threatened to do it again if I wasn't allowed to sleep. O'Brien, the wing governor, said it was orders to check on me and he'd put me down on the block, so nobody would hear me.

I said, "Try it; I won't go to court and you'll get blamed. Sir!"

The convoy was an expensive affair, and he knew I meant business.

Another nightmare journey and I found myself in the castle dungeon completely knackered and starving, having set off before breakfast. I was convinced it was orchestrated to grind me down; it went on for three days. The wing was almost in riot stage, as I kept them awake too.

On the fourth day, I insisted my barrister speak to the judge in open court and tell him I wouldn't be attending again unless I had decent food and sleep. The judge had no choice but to speak to the principal officer in charge of my escort and insist on the matter being regulated.

I looked like a bag of shit. Surprisingly, there were three nice-looking girls in the jury. But the rest were a mixed bunch of various ages and backgrounds. I tried hard to get eye contact as soon as possible, but it'd been hard without proper food and sleep. I had a pony tail, beard, flared suit and a kipper tie. I had intended to look like a bit of a hippy, but after four days without sleep, I resembled a crack addict.

The security circus had spooked them. Occasionally I would catch one staring at me but only for a second. As the prosecution revealed more and more exhibits and observations, I could see they were puzzled as to what the hell was I doing pleading not guilty, when even an idiot could see that I'd done it.

That's the point of a genuine duress defence. You don't deny doing the crime; you have to prove that you had no choice but to do it.

The jury had heard my interviews in which I readily admitted the crime. The prosecution said that Cordite was fiction or not involved and that I was the main man. It went on day after day; the tactic was just to drum my guilt and apparent wealth, into the jury.

Shit like "…and there you can see Mr Berriman in his big red Porsche 911 Turbo with his personalised plate, parked by his luxury motor yacht…" I began to hate that car. I was sick of hearing about it.

In the third week, part of my plan came into play in the form of a bewildered witness named Atwat Bashir, a Customs man. He'd followed my father from my house to a friend's house in Billingham near Stockton. That was it. His deposition meant nothing, because my father wasn't charged.

But we could dispute it and Atwat could be called by us as a witness.

He was bewildered; he'd no idea why we wanted to discredit a pointless observation. But we'd unearthed a manifesto regarding a flight from Manchester to Malaga shortly before we were nicked; I had a copy of it in front of me.

On my specific instructions, Trevor Burke asked him to read his signed and dated notebook aloud in the court. He did and there was nothing untoward. Our legal foe looked confused. Trevor asked Bashir to turn over the page and read the notes about events of the next day. My counsel turned his copy, pretending he too, had that same page in front of him.

Bashir froze. The Customs team were swinging their heads at each other like a bunch of meerkats; the jury noticed and perked up. The judge twice urged him to get on with it. "For goodness sake, Mr Bashir, read it out! Read it out, man!"

"Eerrrr… sent to Manchester Airport to sit next to Dale Gordon on flight xxxx to Malaga en route to meet Peter Cordite. Your honour."

Trevor jumped on the revelation in case any of the now very attentive jury had missed it.

"Well well. Isn't this the people who the prosecution claim do not exist in this case?"

"I don't know, sir. I just do as I'm told."

"Sit down, Mr Bashir; I'm finished with you, thank you."

As Trevor and the jury turned toward me, they saw the biggest grin I could muster. The cat was well and truly out of the bastard bag!

The Customs' team was visibly flustered, wondering how the hell we'd been given the next page of his note book. The prosecution hadn't finished yet, and we'd already demonstrated to the jury that they were lying.

Of course we hadn't a copy of his notebook entry; we'd found Atwat Bashir and Dale Gordon were sitting next to each other on one of the airline manifestos we'd studied. They called an immediate adjournment (more like a crisis meeting) after they'd blown the trust of the jury.

Tony White… God bless you, sir: "There's always something wrong in the depositions."

They called the Customs' officer who I'd met in Burger King, Hemel Hampstead after Cordite's arrest. It was the meeting when I'd grassed up their own undercover men to negate my involvement in their attempted setup in Turkey.

John McIdyot tried hard to dismiss the meeting but had to admit I'd travelled two hundred miles to give them the two purported heroin smugglers and refused to name the firm who sent me to look at a boat.

I was trying to show the jury that I was against them smuggling heroin and quite rightly wanted to help. The jury would never know they were undercover, because McIdyot wasn't about to explain it to them, ever!

When he was quizzed about what became of the information I'd provided, he said it wasn't taken seriously, and nobody acted on it.

The next day the newspaper headlines read: "Super Grass offer in Burger Bar". Had the media missed the point, sensationalised it, or acted under instruction? I had a tape of the meeting, but releasing it would've done more harm than good.

All I wanted to do at that time was negate the Istanbul trip. I didn't know I'd be grasping at straws, charged with another importation.

Imagine a genuine informant reading that headline? Informing on crime would seem very dangerous indeed, risking exposure in open court. The truth is, they wouldn't do it to a genuine informant.

There was no mention of Super Grass; it was a mobile phone number (one of theirs) and the first names of two undercover Customs' officers posing as drug smugglers, trying to set me up in Istanbul.

This dirty trick put me in danger; the majority of criminals haven't the mental capacity to work out what goes on, and if the tabloids say it happened, it must be true, even though none of them trust the agencies. This was the first indication that the gloves were off.

Next, Jim Garlic, the prosecutor approached the bench almost three weeks into the trial, just as his team had no more shit to throw. The judge allowed a late statement from Detective Bill McBungle. It should never have been allowed in as evidence at that late stage, and would have been grounds for appeal, if it hadn't been the pivotal part of my plan.

It stated that on November 29th 1994, he and Kitchup interviewed me about a CS gas gun and that I'd supplied information about the North East gangsters to get my sentence reduced. Jimmy Garlic said it hadn't been their intention to make it public, as it might put me in danger. However, after recent events, they needed to show the jury that I wasn't afraid of reprisals because I'd freely given information about them. My heart raced, the moment he started to read it.

Trevor called an adjournment to discuss the revelation. We met in the dungeon. He was furious. "Why didn't you tell me you wanted a deal, you've made me look like a twat!" he said in a low volume scream.

"It's the same meeting I secretly taped, and told you about months ago," I retorted. "It proves the opposite of what they claim; I wouldn't tell them where there was a bird's nest!"

I went on to explain that because the prosecution introduced a statement about the visit, we could introduce the tape as evidence of rebuttal. As the judge allowed the late statement, he must accept the rebuttal.

When the penny dropped, he said: "Bloody hell! You have been doing your homework. This is just the break I've been waiting for; we could win this, Phil my friend." His face filled with joy, while his mind was doing what it should have been doing long ago.

"No shit, Sherlock?" I said. "I've been trying to tell you this for ten months."

We went up and called an adjournment for two days without disclosing why. We also called Det Sgt Bill McBungle, the author of the statement, as a witness. It took some doing, but Trevor wanted his own transcript of the tape, rather than trust mine; the cheeky sausage.

My plan was working perfectly. I couldn't hide my joy; everyone thought I'd lost the plot.

"What is this man taking to be this happy?" asked one of the screws.

I was on adrenaline, but I could say nothing. Not yet! I could hardly sleep despite being knackered; I worked every spare hour until I dropped.

Finally… judgement day! Trevor had a crafty grin on his face as he passed me a copy of the 'official' transcript of the recording, compiled by no fewer than four people in his offices. It didn't have the same detail as my own because of the speed and delivery of my questions, not to mention my accent.

In only forty five minutes, I'd manipulated and disorientated the cops to draw out what I needed from them. It must've been hard for the London girls to understand my dialect. But now it was typed up for easy reading, and it was dynamite!

Up the stairs, I took my seat with a friendly screw. There were always at least four with me, plus a principal officer. Jim Garlic called Det Sgt Bill McBungle to the witness box. It'd been almost a year since I'd seen him; he'd bought a new, blue, three piece suit for the occasion.

This was his case. He was my interviewer and the man who charged me; the TV cameras would see him at his best. The hero of the hour looked like he was getting married.

Jim Garlic led the witness to explain that I alone requested the meeting and asked for him personally and that I readily offered and provided information without being pressed. He also said I'd offered to do the same in Camborne after my arrest and that he'd refused. (As if, with only the crew charged). Bill was a decorated officer with twenty years in the force and would not lie, he assured the court.

He was up for less than fifteen minutes for the prosecution before he was handed to Trevor for cross examination.

Trevor called him a liar in the first sentence, a very strong statement against a cop in court. Usually counsel would say, "You're mistaken officer."

The judge wasn't happy and said, "Be careful Mr Burke... I won't have that in my courtroom."

Bill stood his ground for three full hours of cross examination. Trevor had dozens of questions. I think he'd been preparing all night.

"Mr Berriman says you arranged the meeting through his solicitor, under the pretence of interviewing him about a CS gun, and that you said the gun was just an excuse to get in and see him."

"Mr Berriman says you offered him a deal and said the judge would get a letter in a plain brown envelope if he helped you. Instead of maybe twelve or fourteen years, he could get six."

"Mr Berriman says he refused to help you, being in fear of the gang and retribution."

"Mr Berriman says you told him you knew Peter Cordite was behind the job, but that he refused to confirm it."

"Mr Berriman says you confirmed that you knew that he was terrified!"

"Mr Berriman says you referred to Camborne and his interviews and reminded him that you'd said if he changed his mind and decided to inform, he'd be better dealing with you, rather than the Customs, as they were the ones who were having a conspiracy against him."

"Mr Berriman says you confirmed this high risk AA security circus was the result of spurious information tendered by a policeman in Stockton-on-Tees who you could not even name, despite being in charge of this case."

"Mr Berriman says, you then said, it was Customs who'd conspired to upgrade his security status, and that you, the police, had nothing to do with it."

"Mr Berriman says you offered to get the security downgraded to Category B, if he helped you."

"Mr Berriman says he showed you the disputed document (page 88 in your bundle there) and that you read part of it out; then confirmed you'd never seen it, then suggested the Customs had planted it after the search."

"Did you bring a brown envelope for the judge? No."

And on it went. McBungle denied everything at least three times even after being reminded about the laws of perjury. The judge thought we were just suggesting things we couldn't prove to the jury. But Trevor went so far, I worried they might realise that we actually had something.

Trevor finally said the words I'd been waiting a year for, "What if I told you Mr Berriman had a tape recorder secreted about his person? Would you change your mind Officer McBungle?"

I was trying very hard, and I mean very hard, not to laugh. The Customs' team smiled and chuckled as the judge coughed and gestured dismissively.

All of them knew the dance; nothing gets through a Double A high risk search procedure. Nothing!

Bill also smiled. I'm sure he was thinking like the rest of them, that this was a bluff, or that I'd got two old lags to help me compile a fake muffled recording which I would swear was real and hope it created some doubt. After all, I was Phil the Fish, who wriggled out of everything!

My heart was in my mouth as I waited for Billy the Liar to fall into the hole that Trevor had meticulously and painstakingly dug for him. "Come on, Bill, come on."

"I would say exactly the same. I'm a decorated officer in the North East Regional Crime Squad with twenty years service and I would never lie on oath." He smiled again as he delivered it like a staunch politician on TV.

Trevor went on. "Well, my client did have a tape recorder and I need a short recess in order to set up the equipment. Your Honour, Detective McBungle will have to remain on the stand as he is still under oath, and we do not want him conferring with his team."

The judge actually yawned and tried to hold back a smile, saying, "Yes… yes, Mr Burke. Let's get on with it."

I was led downstairs and made a point of letting the jury see and hear me say, "Nice one, Billy lad, I knew I could rely on you."

He just smiled, brimming with confidence.

Fifteen minutes later, the jury and I were back. And Billy McBungle was still standing firm in his new crisp blue suit while the Customs' legal team were giggling in expectation of some half-baked attempt to pervert the course of justice.

Trevor rose and with great ceremony offered him the chance to change his mind, much to the amusement of our adversaries. Even the judge guffawed at the jury. A couple of them smiled as though they too thought it was bullshit. No doubt the prosecution's jury nobblers had made light of our claims in advance.

At this point, I was almost crying with relief and happiness. The screw cuffed to me kept asking what was wrong, so I gave him a copy of the transcript. I could see he was blown away by the size of the document and it dawned on him that the shit was about to hit the fan! He was one of the search officers on duty the day of the secret recording.

Trevor Burke had watched many courtroom dramas on TV and wondered if he'd ever get the chance to pull such a stunt good enough for the famous "Ironsides" series. But he'd dine out on this one for years to come. He knew it and relished it with great drama and ceremony.

"If you're absolutely sure then?" After a long dramatic pause, he swished his arm around the room and pointed at the machine like the conductor of a famous orchestra, before nodding at the operator; his brother Greg pushed the button as the court waited with baited breath… for the amusement to start.

The jury hadn't heard me speak before this, as the defence had not even started. My voice boomed clearly through the court's own sound system as they heard me say hello and exchange pleasantries before saying, "So, I thought you'd come about the gun?"

Nobody seemed worried until the unmistakable Geordie-tinged, low gravel voice of Det Sgt Bill McBungle, boomed back, clear as a bell! "Nah, that was just an excuse to get in to see ya!"

After I'd gorged myself on the bonanza banquet of horrified expressions, I screamed with victorious delight! I watched the blood drain from McBungle's face as his career and reputation flashed before him. His suit no longer fitted, his head and shoulders went down, he put his hands on the desk to support himself and every member of the jury looked at him in utter disgust!

"Now you're screwed, Bill," I blurted out, as the judge threatened to have me thrown down into the dungeon. "Sorry, Your Honour, but I can't help it." Tears streamed down my face. I held my head up high and glared at the whole Customs' team, who were frantically trying to find a way of stopping the spectacle.

The release of emotion after keeping the secret for almost a year was too much. I couldn't stop crying. Against phenomenal odds, I'd pulled it off! I was half way home! And I knew it.

Greg paused and rewound the tape while I pulled myself together and everyone who had one, shuffled their copy of the transcript and locked onto it.

The prosecutor looked to the judge for a miracle but to no avail. Even the biased wig could do nothing to save McBungle; he'd shit in his bed. Now he had to lie in it until he was stood down.

The tape went on for forty five minutes. Lie after lie after lie was exposed. The audio was hard to understand for the residents of Exeter, but with a written record to follow, the jury was enthralled.

When the security circus was exposed as a farce, the jury looked violated and glared at the armed police in court who stared at the floor. They'd been very afraid, and why not? That was the plan all along!

The prosecution team began mumbling to each other behind their hands until Trevor went across and scolded them, "Quiet please! There are some in here that find the truth refreshing!"

I was still in bits… quiet but shaking like a road drill. I was trying to contain my glee, tears still rolling down my face.

This drama helped the jury see the magnitude of the deceit. I could have controlled myself, but it was working a treat.

"Mr. Berriman! I won't tell you again," shouted the judge. He could see what I was doing, but by trying to stop me, he was drawing even more attention to me. I apologised and pretended to try.

My old dad was buzzing and joining in the drama by glaring at the devious bastards who'd put my life in danger by calling me a grass in a public court. Now the truth would come out.

McBungle was unsteady and shaking twenty minutes into it. Eventually, after the Double A farce was exposed, 'Judge Dreading' told old Billy to sit down and directed an usher to bring him a chair. I was nodding and pointing, shaking my head and looking extremely angry, as every point McBungle had lied about was laid bare. "Dirty, filthy, blatant lies," as my new mate Trevor, put it later.

So much was riding on that scenario rolling out as I'd planned. I'll remember it vividly for as long as I have a hole in my arse! It was the most audacious coup I'd ever pulled off. When I started to plan it, I thought 10,000 to 1 was a fair bet that my tape would get to court. To sit there listening to it, and watching the bastards squirm, was better than winning the bloody lottery.

When Bill McBungle's torture finally stopped, he was a broken man. Six inches shorter than he was forty five minutes before. He looked like he'd had a stroke. Later, I actually had some sympathy for the man; he was only doing what he was told.

As a respected ground level crime squad officer, I'd never heard anything bad about him. But he was in a position to help secure a conviction. He hadn't planned or wanted to do it, or we would have had notice of it beforehand. The conspiracy to perjure came about after the disclosure that Atwat Bashir and Dale Gordon had travelled together to Malaga on an aeroplane.

It was not McBungle's idea; rather it was those sat to my left, now shitting themselves and wondering how far uphill the shit storm for this catastrophe would travel.

Trevor was silently swirling about in his robe gesturing to the jury, doing his best Shakespeare impersonation, wringing his hands, looking confused, shaking his head. The pause for dramatic effect went on, too long, then at last, "Well, well well, Detective McBungle. Do you still maintain you were telling the truth this morning?"

McBungle looked to his team as all but one looked down. Jim Garlic nodded his head and gullible Billy said, "Yes." Further pause for dramatic effect before Trevor removed the imaginary skewers and allowed him to leave the stand.

The judge stopped him, demanded the other copper, Heinz Kitchup, be there in the morning, and warned McBungle, our star witness, not to speak to him about anything… or else! After making sure we had a copy, he also demanded the tape be taken to the forensic laboratory in Harrogate to be examined for authenticity. Again, he warned the police against any more skulduggery.

"We're finished for today." He nodded to the clerk who said, "All rise."

Home early for tea that night. But not before speaking to my dad. He couldn't quite get his head around the significance of what I'd pulled off, and told me not to get my hopes up too much. What a day! I needed some serious joints to get any sleep that night.

I tuned into the news on the radio but for the first time since the start, there was no mention of the show trial in Exeter.

The next morning, I was surprised to still have the Devil's Convoy. But I deduced they still had their public image to consider. The cost, embarrassment and effect on the jury of abruptly ceasing the circus would have ramifications all the way back to Parliament. They would at least reduce it slowly.

In court, Heinz Kitchup got up and was briefed in a clearly stage-managed and rehearsed manner by Mr Garlic, before Trevor's turn.

"You've been told, haven't you, Sergeant Kitchup?"

"I don't know what you're talking about, sir."

"Didn't you have breakfast with Detective Sergeant McBungle in his hotel this morning, against the specific instructions of the judge?" Trevor said.

"Errm… Errm. I did have breakfast with him this morning but, errrm I haven't been told."

"What, haven't you been told, Sergeant Kitchup?"

"Errm… Errm… Errm. I don't know what you mean."

"You said, 'But I haven't been told' and I am asking, what is it that you haven't been told?"

"Errm… eeeerm."

"Sit down, Sergeant Kitchup. You're no use to me."

The judge was furious. More so because McBungle had met Kitchup for breakfast in a public place, after he'd warned him in front of the jury not to speak to him. The jury had just witnessed yet another conspiracy to pervert the course of justice. We were well in front and he knew it. My old dad was in the same hotel as McBungle; Cheers Pop, I love you. RIP x

Both McBungle and Kitchup were arrested on the orders of the judge and charged with perjury. Of course the jury would never know this, nor would the public for some time. The Judge issued a gagging order on the press.

A lot of people still won't know such powers exist, but a judge can stop any reporting of any part of a trial or hearing, for as long as the reason for doing so is valid.

In this case, his reasoning related to the charges against the two perjuring plod and the potential public fury at them for being caught red handed; not only lying through their teeth to get a conviction, but also putting my life in danger in the process.

He said if it was made immediately public, the bent cops wouldn't be able to get a fair trial as it would be hard to find a jury who hadn't heard about it.

A recent case had involved Gillian Taylforth's (Cathy Beal in Eastenders) boyfriend, who'd been charged with assault. His case was dismissed because the papers gave details of the alleged incident. His defence also argued that an impartial jury was impossible to find.

Obviously, in my opinion, the judge was biased and didn't want the jury to know the plods had been arrested and certainly didn't want it laying bare to the public in such a highly publicised case.

There'd have been a public enquiry into the team behind it and possibly into the judge's decision to allow a statement three weeks into the trial. This trial stank to high heaven. It wasn't just perjury; it was a conspiracy to pervert the course of justice and conspiracy to endanger life.

CHAPTER SEVENTEEN

FROM DEDUNGEON TO DEFENCE, MY FINEST HOUR

I spent the weekend planning what I would do first on my release. After the spectacle the jury had witnessed, I expected the prosecution to give up, or the judge to throw it out.

Up early, raring to go, I waited downstairs for the circus parade to arrive. After an hour, there seemed to be some confusion before they took me back to my cell. As usual, I was told nothing.

At noon, I was taken back to the gate yard, where instead of the usual Avon and Somerset Propaganda Brigade, the Devon and Cornwall Amateur Dramatic Armed Response Convoy was waiting. Oh yes, these guys looked extremely serious. Clearly, this was a rare major job. There was an abundance of senior officers present.

We finally reached court. I'd convinced myself the delay was down to legal arguments about dismissing the case, or that the jury had been directed to find me not guilty. I couldn't wait to see Trevor.

My hopes of an immediate end to the trial were dashed; it would be left to the jury to decide the significance of the explosive revelations in the recording. They'd arrested the perjuring pair and leaked it to the jury, thereby distancing the wholesome and honest prosecution team from the corruption. Yeah right!

However, the day was not without its bounty; the whole firearms squad of the Avon and Somerset Force had been suspended after two officers had been shot! Yes... two shot! Not by my crack force of ruthless mercenaries, waiting at sea to bust me out, but by one of their own men.

Unfortunately for them, my dear old dad was in court, when the reason for my absence was discussed. He slipped out to call Tyne Tees TV reporters and local radio. Before it could be suppressed, the news carried far and wide.

It appeared the squad was messing about in the station yard while waiting to set off. It got a bit boisterous and a machine gun discharged, shooting the bearer through his own leg and dropping another of the squad.

The Devil's Convoy circus was now the subject of intense scrutiny by the media. The judge and the prosecution team were livid. The jury already knew it was a farce and now the media was reaching the same conclusion.

Councillors and MPs were demanding to know details and costs. It was a good job they hadn't heard the tape recording! Meanwhile PCs Tin Tin and Tonto were still in hospital, but would recover.

In a blatant abuse of his position and as a direct punishment for notifying the media, the judge banned my dad's companion, Brian Wolsey, from the court for apparently staring at the jury as they walked in. One of the court officers noticed it and told the prosecution. What bollocks.

Brian was in his sixties and a respected hotelier from Torquay. He was originally a coach company owner up north, straight as a die and not much over five feet tall. He was a lovely man by any standards, but was hauled before the judge and expelled from the castle by armed officers. What a sad, sad farce.

Clearly the prosecution was rattled and planning something very dirty; this would be only the start. My father was reassured by Trevor that it was a good sign; they were worried.

Trevor rose for his opening defence speech. After recent events, the jury was very attentive. I had regular eye contact with all three fanciable girls by now. My my, how things had changed. They'd no idea of the difficulties I'd faced to get the recording into court. Nevertheless, I'd still gone way up in their estimations, and now they were very keen to hear my side of the story.

Trevor explained the law of duress and what was expected of them. He told them to imagine someone using nothing but fear to control them and their actions, absolutely, and totally.

First he offered the documents and photos regarding Cordite and Co's recent high- profile reign of terror. "This is real; make no mistake, members of the jury," he said. "These are the Crown's own allegations and documents. This cache of guns and ammunition recovered by police is enough to start a small revolution."

I noticed a distinct increase in eye contact from the jury and the rest in the court. Until now the prosecution had not even admitted that these people existed. Tales of vicious gangsters feuding for control of a city's crime – guns, kidnaps, torture, prison breaks and multi-million pound drug deals – were the stuff of Hollywood, not Exeter. They were transfixed. They would never forget this tour of jury duty.

I took to the stand wearing the same brown suit as day one. People at home would've had trouble recognising me with my long hair and full beard. I was clearly a broken man compared to the flash bastard I'd been before. Did I look like a master criminal?

Trevor led me for three hours from the violent attempts to disfigure me in 1990 to the vaporisation of my life's assets and business after my arrest. I also told them that I'd changed my appearance so I wouldn't be recognised as I was still in fear for my life.

Trevor had been very worried about my delivery to the jury, only having heard me on the tape and during prison meetings. The judge had even quipped, "Next we will hear from Mr Berriman, that is, if we can understand him, ha." The cheeky biased twit.

I was starkly aware that I'd have to slow down, smooth my accent and use the Queen's English, if I was to be understood. I'd practised my story in condensed form many times during my remand. I was brilliant! Clear as a bell! I could see the relief on Trevor's face, and the clouds darkening over the enemy camp.

I gave the jury details of various charitable things I'd done, including one which made front page of the Teesside evening paper. It was shown to the jury.

A young girl in Acklam, Middlesbrough, who was twelve, the same age as my daughter, had been kidnapped through an open window at home and sexually assaulted on a path. The pervert had lost his watch at the scene. Police were getting nowhere until I offered £1,000 reward for information leading to successful prosecution. The perv's own wife grassed him up. Happy days! The jury loved it.

The prosecution couldn't cross examine me while the jury was still stunned by what I'd been through. Not without a long break. As if I'd squirted the three young women with a secret pheromone, they began to flirt outrageously. I swear it! Court adjourned. Home early with plenty of time to swot: Great day.

I couldn't consult with anyone after being sworn in. The battle was only warming up. I had cross examination to face; this was what I'd studied for. Despite my cowardly crew deserting our sinking ship, I'd plugged the holes and pumped enough water out to stand a chance! This day would be 'shit or bust' for at least the next ten years.

The screws were late collecting me. I don't know why. We cleared all the gates and arrived at the gate house twenty minutes after the Devil's Convoy had arrived. I was laughing with my escorts as we went through the door.

"You're late!" bawled a principle officer I'd never seen before. PO Bootstrap had been a military policeman or Regimental Sergeant Major; that much was obvious from his appearance. He almost stood to attention with his cap peak on his nose.

"Nothing to do with me, mate," I said. "I think you'll find I don't have a set of keys mate." I grinned.

"I'm not your mate!" he said. "You are my prisoner and you will not talk to me like that!"

"Pull yourself together, you dickhead. Who do you think you're talking too?"

He said, "Right, you're on a charge of insubordination! Do you hear me, Berriman?"

"Yes, sir. Sir... sorry, sir! Now pull yourself together you dickhead. There's people waiting out there, I've got more important matters than your ego, dickhead!"

He was seething, even squaring up, like he wanted a go.

"Go on then, dickhead," I said. "I dare you!"

The screws were trying not to laugh. Clearly this twat had been imported. He certainly wasn't a Bristol bloke. We climbed into the minibus and I was side-on in the cage, handcuffed. Bootstrap 'the dickhead' perched on a pull-down seat at the rear. The next thing that pissed him off was that he wasn't in charge anymore.

The police circus co-ordinator was always in charge from the moment we left the gates. Nobody would even acknowledge the dickhead on his radio. His face was red as beetroot as he fumed all the way through Bristol in pouring rain; this time, in a convoy of only six vehicles and no motorcycles.

The Devil's Convoy entered the slip road onto the motorway, but without the motorcycles to clear the way, the leading Range Rover screeched to a halt to avoid being crushed by a truck in the inside lane. It was rush hour; what the hell did they expect?

Our van's brakes were no match for the Range Rover. As we hit it, Bootstrap was flung forward violently. Only restrained by a lap belt, his nose hit the briefcase on his knees and broke, spurting claret about. It was so funny; I didn't even notice the pain in my soon-to-be badly bruised shoulder.

As if that wasn't enough, he was still leaning forward holding his smashed nose when the Range Rover behind slammed into us, catapulting him backwards.

His dinky pull-down seat didn't have a head rest. He smashed back into the middle of the two doors' locking bolts with such force, that one came out of the re-enforced bracket.

He was almost unconscious and groaned loudly as the biggest 'head egg' I've ever seen sprouted on his bonce. It was like a scene from Tom and Jerry. "See lads, I told you God would get him back." What a laugh.

The scene outside was chaos. Cops were showing off when they came to the junction. But imagine the embarrassment of our twenty heroes, no seat belts, hanging out of the windows with sub machine guns, all coming to a very abrupt stop.

The pileup turned into a panorama of injured cops, broken guns and five write off vehicles. Not to mention the arch criminal in the van, at risk of escaping!

After a couple of minutes, the walking wounded wandered about helping clear up the scene. Bootstrap was conscious but dazed. He thought it was a breakout and screamed for everyone to take cover. Then he was on the floor using his phone to call the police, or who knows, maybe an air strike!

"Ow Egghead, the cops are here. Egghead, Egghead, the cops are here; it was an accident! Helloooo, an accident!" I was enjoying this very much.

The cops opened the doors with guns up. "Who's in charge here?"

"Egghead is. On the floor here, boss," I shouted before anyone else.

"Oh Jesus! You need an ambulance, mate," said the copper.

"He's not your mate," I bawled in Egghead's unmistakable tone.

The screws shook their heads at me and had to turn away to laugh. Oh joy!

More and more police traffic cars surrounded us in a rolling motorcade, until we arrived at a police station car park, which was quickly fortified by the armed response squad.

As they blocked the access, every vehicle took a place circling our damaged minibus like a cowboy wagon-train expecting Red Indians. Oh, please stop this bullshit! It was like a never-ending bad movie! Where was Roy Rogers?

We waited while a new convoy was assembled, this time complete with six motorcycles and helicopter support. Two hours later, we were on the road again. It was hardly worth it by the time we got there but, it'd definitely been fun. The Devil's Convoy had come back and bitten them in the arse twice now. I could only hope there'd be more.

The rumour mill had taken over the castle. Trevor seemed very worried until I assured him that it was just a stupid accident. The Queen's own jury nobblers were fuelling rumours of a possible attempted breakout; thwarted by brave policemen who'd been injured in the line of duty. Piss off!

Now it was just me and Jimmy Garlic, Her Majesty's Customs' star prosecutor. I gave only three hours of evidence to explain my defence, but a new record was to be set in an English courtroom.

I was cross examined for five full days. A relentless barrage of questions and insinuations all concocted by a prosecution team worthy of recognition, despite being my foe!

But they weren't fighting for the next ten or more years of their lives. They'd see their children, have everyday choices they took for granted, and feel the touch of the opposite sex. I wasn't going to give up those years without a fight; I'd spent fifteen months solid working for this. It was the most important battle of my life!

The walls in my cell were covered with 'trees', routes that any particular line of questioning could follow with every possible answer and the 'ripple effect' they could create. I'd played out every scenario from every question I could imagine, and then charted a route to the best possible answer or direction to take.

Yes, I was up against a bunch of highly intelligent, academic professionals, but I was highly motivated; I had a lot more to lose. They had many cases to deal with; this was my one and only.

I was up to the challenge and fought every single point until I knew the jury had accepted my side of the story. This infuriated Garlic and the judge, who couldn't shut me up until I'd finished my explanation. I refused to continue until I'd put my side of the story and negated his points.

After the third day, he was at his wits' end. I think they wanted to put as much time as possible between the recent shocking revelations, and the closing speeches to give the jury time to forget. Or they were planning another abhorrent scheme.

Garlic had descended into utter drivel. He produced a photo of me, Jimmy the Dip and Cordite posing in Brest, France. It was found in Jim's camera, despite my orders, and his assurance that he'd got rid.

"It doesn't look to me like you're in fear of your life there, Mr Berriman. How do you explain this?"

"The lunatic gangster in the picture was on the run, having escaped while he was facing kidnapping and torture charges! When Peter Cordite tells you to smile, you smile, Mr Garlic," I replied in a serious tone, before grinning and shaking my head at his desperate stupidity.

He continued like it was water off a duck's back. "Here's a photograph of you on board the Melanie. You look like you're enjoying yourself, Mr Berriman. Hardly the actions of a man in fear for his life."

I'd wondered why this photo was in the bundle; it had no relevance until that day.

"The orange suit you see me wearing," I said, "is a helicopter, submersion, survival suit. We were in the middle of Hurricane Chris, fighting for our lives in the mid-Atlantic. At that time, I was bursting with adrenaline, more in fear of Chris, than Peter Cordite. Yet, as you can see, I still managed to smile. Check Exhibit 1, ship's log, page fifty six in your bundle. You'll find details there, Mr Garlic!"

Most of the jurors flicked to the page in search of the words "Hurricane Chris". They ignored Garlic until they'd read all about it, despite him trying to distract them.

Then came by far his most desperate, pathetic attempt. "Ladies and gentlemen of the jury, here we have a page from a notebook seized from the defendant's vessel. Please turn to page twenty-four of the exhibits in your bundle." He paused for dramatic effect, looking intently at the jury as they all found the page.

What the hell?

He finally spoke. "As you can see, Mr Berriman, whose handwriting you can clearly identify, has re-written the words of a song that you will all recognise, as by the brilliant Otis Redding, Sitting on the Dock of the Bay. Can you believe he was in fear of his life, when he did this?" He paused for the jury to contemplate the magnitude of my heinous crime.

"Explain this atrocity then, Mr Berriman!" as he regally waved the document in the air. Well sod me! I hadn't planned for that one. Some clown in their legal team must have jotted that down over a bowl of magic mushrooms. Jesus!

I started to laugh and shake my head.

"Something funny, Mr Berriman?" he sniped.

"Yes, Mr Garlic. I was just thinking how much you're struggling to convince the jury, I should get fourteen years for desecrating your favourite song. We were hundreds of miles from land, no engine, no wind, no food, no water, no power, no lights and no hope! I'm sure Otis would forgive me for trying to raise the moral of my crew."

I could see the jury nodding in agreement, so I cracked on.

"Surely you watch the movies; I was the Captain, it was my job! If that's the best you can come up with, Mr Garlic, I think I should be arranging a taxi home!" Then, I started laughing again, and so, significantly, did the jury.

Old man Garlic was badly wounded. He was angry and glaring at the team of idiots who'd been loading him with ever more ludicrous bullets to fire. He was losing badly and he knew it.

They attacked my apparent wealth; how could I afford such a lifestyle? Why was I not VAT registered? How much did I earn? I was very candid and explained I had numerous registered businesses, all under the same banner, with separate accounts and telephone numbers. I showed them the adverts and accounts that kept each business below the VAT threshold. It may have been a little naughty, but it was legal.

I even had photos of my Porsche being re-built from the damaged shell to it being finished and painted, just as I'd showed the police at the time. I had the bill of sale for my yacht Michelle Louise, showing only £26,000 paid. I'd bought my house cheap with a bridging loan as it needed repair. After survey, I mortgaged it and bought my yard with the balance and a loan from the bank. I was ready for anything and everything they could throw at me, and then some!

It went on until the end of a marathon fifth day, before he finally stood down. Trevor had no need to re-visit anything. I'd done better than anyone could have hoped; even me. I went down to the dungeon where he was waiting, beaming from ear to ear.

It'd been seven days since we'd spoken. His words were, "Philip, well done. Congratulations, you batted him clean out of the ball park on every point. You were marvellous, marvellous, my friend!"

I spoke to my dad and Jock before being whisked back to Bristol absolutely shattered. The prison had done its best to disrupt my sleep again that week, but pure adrenaline can get you through. All they did was drive me to study longer for the next round. By then, I could sleep on a clothes' line; I'd even learned to grab a kip in the Devil's Convoy, and during recesses at the Castle.

I was extremely short of independent witnesses. Dawn, my loyal, delightful, rock of a woman, didn't turn up as promised. Trevor told me she was on the missing list so as not to distract my concentration. He knew something I didn't.

All I knew was that she'd changed her mind from dumping me to supporting me, and then dumped me again. Having promised to give evidence, she'd failed to turn up, leaving me with yet another gap in my defence.

I'd also begged my ex-partner and mother of my children to give evidence about her asking me for a will during the Hannibal saga, and about how I earned my money. She point blank refused; I still have her letter today. When everything I had disappeared, she was up there with the best of them.

She had Simon, a ship's officer who didn't know about Gary, her land-based, married boyfriend. Simon wanted to move to Wales with my kids; I'd refused. She thought I couldn't stop her now and with my business destroyed, what use was I? Especially as I'd be in jail!

Kenny Simcox, a real man, has now sadly passed away. But I'll always remember what he did for me back then. When all around me hid away, scared, selfish, disloyal or malicious, Kenny said he would come and he did, despite being visited and warned by the Teesside branch of Cordite and Co, a week or two before.

Why they wanted me convicted was a mystery. Cordite was on trial three hundred miles away; how could it possibly be of any benefit to him? Kenny, my brother's brother-in-law, was well aware of what happened after my arrest. He drove to Exeter, stood tall and swore what 'they' had done to my house, workshops and yard. He even testified to the threats he'd had, and why others wouldn't come to court.

Asked why he was prepared to risk his own safety, he replied, "Because nobody else has the bottle to do it. Everyone that lived off him has deserted him, and I can't stand by and watch an innocent man go to jail. I'm not made like that, and I'm not scared of anything!"

God bless you, Kenny, you were a bright star on a very dark night! We didn't know each other that well at the time, but we were definitely good friends until you passed. RIP mate, sleep tight x.

Kenny was as hard a man as you would meet, scared of nothing and a legendary electrical engineer. He'd made a fortune in the past, even having his own plane. He stood up and was counted by all that day; I'll forever have him firmly in my memory.

My last witness, believe it or not, was a policeman.

Terry Beevers was the copper who'd witnessed the Hannibal incident and later came to see me. I needed someone to stand up and tell the truth about what happened. Jimmy, Dawn and Trish, who'd all been there, had left me up shit creek without a paddle. Terry was the only man available with first-hand knowledge. He was also a copper, which made what he said, very important to the jury.

He wasn't a willing witness by any means, and had to be summonsed. I'd known for many years he was a mate of Kelvin Donks, the scrap yard bully who was either my friend or my arch enemy behind my back, depending on which way the wind was blowing.

Donks would do anything, even get me locked up, to revive his ailing business. But Terry never stepped over the mark to become a corrupt or bent copper.

I'd noticed this rare phenomenon and decided to gamble on his honesty. Don't get me wrong, he wasn't a dim plod by any standards. He was a crack firearms' man and seconded to some elite squads during his career. He'd have gone further up the promotion ladder, but he had scruples.

I'd already said in my evidence that I wasn't scared of Hannibal the Cannibal, but that the women in my life were terrified. I knew

Terry would be under pressure to help the prosecution. All the same, I bet on him.

Sgt Beevers, with his impeccable references, begrudgingly confirmed the terrible reputation of Hannibal, his previous record, my injuries, the shotgun attack and all the other details which had seemed incredible but now they were under oath, fact!

As expected, he added, "I must say that in my opinion, Phil Berriman was not scared of John Hannibal and his henchman. In fact, he badly hurt both of them in the fight, and even wanted to fight him, one to one."

I'd read him like a book; Trevor had told the jury the exact same thing in the defence speech, and I'd repeated it. Terry Beevers, the only straight copper the jury had heard, only added weight to my integrity.

I was never scared of Hannibal; by getting Smiley to shoot at my house and car, he showed his cowardice and lack of mettle. It was the effect on the women I'd mistakenly believed loved me that'd pushed me to resolve the problem.

Terry, the most unwilling witness ever, had confirmed why I'd become involved with Cordite; it was a huge part of the burden of proof I needed, for my defence of duress.

"Thank you, Sgt Beevers, that will be all, you may step down," said Trevor.

We broke for lunch. Well, they all went to lunch. I had a pasty.

Back for the afternoon session, there was commotion in the courtroom; the legal teams were arguing with each other. Finally, Trevor came to tell me about a very grave problem. Some of the jury had complained that they were being followed before and after court. They were very concerned for their safety.

The Crown's nobblers had got the police involved and now there was going to be a call for a retrial on the grounds of jury interference and intimidation. It was a cynical lie… the lowest depths of deception. Why on earth would I try and intimidate a jury when we were winning hands down?

This stage-managed, diabolical attempt to pervert the course of justice was nearly complete, when a juror stood and demanded to be heard. He was tall, about thirty five and had done nothing but listen for five weeks. Today however, he blasted the corrupt prosecution team with a ballistic missile of biblical might! Even though the judge repeatedly warned him to sit down.

"Your honour, the two men who were following us at lunchtime today, were having breakfast at 07.30 this morning at the Golden Egg Café, with that man over there." He pointed to the leader of the Customs' legal team. "I swear it!"

He sat down. The judge was enraged. Was he part of the thwarted plan or was he just furious that they'd been caught out again?

I booed and jeered as much as I dared. Eventually it was passed off as a misunderstanding and that the Customs' men were covertly guarding the jury so as not to distress them. Bullshit… bullshit… bullshit; it was a filthy, dirty conspiracy to pervert the course of justice, and they'd been caught, red handed!

The closing speeches were due next, but as if by magic, John McIdyot arrived back from Pakistan, only to be allowed to retake the oath and discredit something I'd said in my evidence. It was unprecedented to allow a prosecution witness to end the defence proceedings. But hell! The whole trial was an unprecedented conspiracy!

Trevor could hardly remember what McIdyot had said before that day, and apologised to me later. He'd been getting slaughtered in the hotel bar with my dad and Dave Rennison until the early hours. I was speechless.

I asked my dad what the hell he was up to, getting my barrister slaughtered while I was fighting for the next ten years of my life. I'd enough trouble with the prosecution trying to screw my chances up without him joining in. He was devastated when he realised the magnitude of his own stupidity.

He said he had someone who'd buy my house and an estate agent to handle the sale of my yard. I hit the roof. If he couldn't support me and believe I was walking down the front steps after all he'd seen, then he should piss off back to Teesside and stop pissing on my bonfire.

I was devastated and stormed out of the visitors' room. I

stayed up most of the night, going right through my game plan and marking the wall with points won, lost or dubious. I'd achieved more victories than I'd considered necessary to create a reasonable doubt in all but the most stubborn juror.

I concluded my old man had been pissed or hung over. Either way, he hadn't appreciated my tactics. It turned out however, that Trevor was more of a pessimist than most, and was telling dad not to get his hopes up.

I wouldn't hear of failure until the jury had gone home! A positive mental attitude had got me this far, and nobody but nobody could shake my faith. If it all went tits up at the end, I'd deal with that then; but I would not suffer for something that hadn't been decided.

I'd made deals with God, my spirit guide and any others that may be watching. If they let me win, I promised to change my ways; I'd forgive the vultures of the feeding frenzy; and forgive everyone who'd let me down. I'd never forget it and I'd learn from it, but I'd forgive the vast majority of them.

The closing speeches start with the prosecution, followed by the defence. Then the judge has the opportunity to sway the jury one way or the other, depending on various factors:

1. His own opinion, with the benefit of experience or inside information.

2. His certain knowledge. Often, significant material or information cannot be shown to the jury for legal or reasons of national security and so on.

3. Pressure from above. I maintain that even a democracy like ours, has judges that can be manipulated to protect the public image of the agencies involved. It happens. Get over it!

4. Some belong to groups or not so secret societies, which swear to help fellow members before non-members, whatever the circumstances. If one is asked to do something by a senior, his rise in life could take a turn for the worst if he fails to comply.

All of my opinions expressed about the judiciary and the trial are guesswork; they should not be taken as fact because I have no proof.

The judge needs to be very careful. A judge's summing up is often grounds for an appeal if what is said is considered biased or inaccurate.

These matters are often tested in appeal courts, so there are many precedents.

Consequently, they know just how far to go without looking like a bastard and conceding an appeal.

My problem was that this judge had already crossed that threshold by allowing the late statement. After the diabolical events that we'd all witnessed, it was fairly obvious that the prosecution and the judge would be perfectly happy with a retrial where I wouldn't have the element of surprise on McBungle and Kitchup. More than likely, I'd be convicted.

I had the weekend to contemplate just how much damage the judge could do and concluded there was a real possibility he could ruin everything. The gagging order had worked on the media; there'd been no mention of corrupt coppers or retraction of the super grass headlines.

One factor I thought would prevent him going too far, was the media who had reported almost everything from the police shooting themselves to the pile ups. It had attracted serious attention from some big newspapers.

The judge's gagging order had only infuriated them and brought even more attention. The Observer for example, had their top man on the job. I wondered how far 'His Honour' would go under such scrutiny.

The full story would eventually be told in the press, but only after the courts had dealt with McBungle and Kitchup.

I could sleep, knowing I still had a good chance of watching my kids grow up.

Before I nodded off, a letter of apology from Jimmy and Graham was pushed under the door, probably by a red band or friendly screw. They were in the next wing and the escort screws were keeping them posted on my progress. As things could now go either way, they were trying to make amends.

I'd already forgiven them. This shit was scary shit. If I could forgive the worms at home, I could forgive them. I passed a message back thanking them for the support and kind words.

They were well aware that if I was acquitted, they'd likely get a much shorter sentence and be released on the 'time already served' rule. I'd no idea what deal they'd done to drop me in the shit, but I forgave them anyway.

However, I'd keep the letter in case I was found guilty, and the judge was still under the impression that I'd bullied them into the job. At sentencing, it would be every man for himself.

Even though they'd stolen the lifeboat, jumped off our sinking ship and left me to man the pumps for fifteen months, I'd still throw them a ladder. I'm a bigger man. I'd send them money or look after their family. I was their captain; they, my crew. We were missing in action; I had a duty.

Me (second left) with The Aubriender crew

The Aubriender crew

Airbags

Captain Sullyman

Chilling

Aubriender at auction

Aubriender refitted

Candy

Jimmy The Dip, Big Al and Me

Celebrating a drop

Fast RHIB

Nic and Teddy

Pirate Nicola

Teddy and I Go Karting

Pirate Phil

Teddy and I

St Joost

Melanie Arrested

Me and Nic

Cornish Maiden

Me and Moto sunset

Michelle Louise

RH with sails up

Me on Don Inda

Phil Jnr, Teddy and Nic

Super catch

Salvage Tug Aquarius

In Spain

Running for Teddy

Scattering my father's ashes on the Longscar

The Little Flea

CHAPTER EIGHTEEN

SO NEAR YET SO FAR

Prosecuting counsel tried hard to persuade the jury that they, "Should detach yourselves from the scandalous events of recent weeks and look above them. Forgive the men who've tried to secure a conviction by any means possible. They're victims of their own passion to see justice done. We don't condone it, that would be wrong. But we understand it, that is the point, ladies and gentlemen of the jury."

Photographs of my beautiful yacht, Porsche, motorcycle and house were vilified as the trappings of a master criminal and smuggler, instead of the fruits of a good business model.

In the opening speech, they're allowed to say, "What we will prove is…" Even if, they don't prove it during the trial. In the closing speech, they're allowed – without defence cross examination – to say, "What we have proved is…" This tactic boils my piss.

I could see some of the jury wondering if they'd fallen asleep and missed highly relevant points that Garlic was claiming as victories. "Remember the mobile telephone the defendant dropped at the scene of his arrest? I told you at the start of this trial, it would be a very important piece of evidence, and it was."

Unless they'd been putting magic mushrooms in my Cornish pasty every day, he was talking out of his arse! That telephone had never been mentioned again. I wasn't about to let him get away with it; I had a plan. I often have plans!

I brought out my secret weapon, the silent mime show, something I'd been working on for weeks. I could imitate Garlic quite well, even though I'd only had a mirror for an audience. I had an armoury of funny faces and gestures that I could pull to the jury to convey various points and ridicule the shit which was spewing from his mouth.

The judge caught me a few times, but I continued to entertain the jury behind Jim Garlic's back. I had to moderate it when the naughty young ladies at the front of the jury box started giggling. I wasn't taking the piss in general, only in response to absolute bullshit!

He knew the jury was distracted so he kept acting hurt while repeating himself; it just made matters worse.

Nobody felt sorry for him. He was the sort of guy who could easily have excelled at being a Customs' officer, tax inspector, bailiff, traffic warden or prison governor. He was ruthless!

Promotion depends on results, not customer ratings! The jury, or at least the majority, had turned against him. I'm sure he could've been a nice guy as a defence lawyer, but he'd made his bed here as a sneering, cynical prosecutor. Now he had to lie in it!

There was a lot more riding on my conviction. I knew there was some secret shit going on somewhere and that the sheer size of the operation demanded spectacular results.

And ever since the Billy McBungle and Heinz Kitchup perjury, the pressure to get a conviction at any cost was increasing by the day.

I couldn't see them taking the blame on their own shoulders. They'd been prompted. Perjury means jail. But it would be less of a problem if I was convicted. If you cause a problem for the justice system while you're a convicted prisoner, your standard of living, location and release date can be seriously affected; who could blame them?

If I was facing jail like them, I'd be threatening to expose the informants and any other embarrassing facts, including the names of their puppet masters. But I didn't care about McBungle and Kitchup. I just wanted a fair crack of the whip.

Back in my cell, I was seriously worried about the judge's summing up and directions. But my new pal, Trevor, now knew he wasn't fighting a lost cause. When a rising star smells victory in such a high profile case, I could bet my arse he wouldn't be getting pissed with my old man the night before the final battle.

He'd played it the same as me and had most of the jury liking him. I could see some of the women even fancied him. Compared to the miserable, scowling judge and sneering prosecutor, he was George Clooney. I went to sleep praying to God and my spirit guide that we were in the same movie!

I woke up two hours later in a cold sweat after dreaming that my daughter and son were both prostitute drug addicts who'd been caught throwing smack over the wall of a filthy jail to me. I'd become an old lag who buggered young inmates for one hit deals. The gay boys that got locked up on purpose for petty crime in Bristol were my bitches. I rented them out for blow jobs to the inmates who believe you're only gay if you take it. I'd battered a screw to death; got life imprisonment, never to be released, and my old dad had killed himself in despair. I didn't go back to sleep, in case there was more.

By the time the door opened, I'd pulled myself together but really looked like a bag of shit. The trial had been five weeks of farce. As the Devil's Convoy screamed away from the gates, I found myself wondering if it was it all one nightmare.

I was brought back to reality as I tugged on my ponytail and beard to check they were real. Clearly my mental state was declining. I needed sleep. Sound sleep.

Down in the dungeon, I briefly spoke to Trevor. He was uptight, distant and detached that day.

I feared that those in the corridors of power had ordered the lowly wigs in the Crown Court to fix the verdict. Maybe I'd smoked too much dope and was paranoid, but Trevor was hardly listening to me. "Come on Trevor, for Pete's sake. Pull yourself together!" I pleaded as my cell door shut.

He was the same upstairs; everyone wearing a wig looked deadly serious. I'm sure there are matters discussed behind closed doors in high profile cases. The Bar is their exclusive club; it's not in anybody's interest to betray anything said in confidence.

My hopes of walking down the front steps were fading fast. I was sure there'd be one last diabolical act to top the State conspiracy.

The old judge yawned, trying his best to look uninterested as he introduced Trevor for his closing speech. He put his head down as if marking some school exam papers.

My remaining hope for the next ten years began quietly until he had the full attention of every single juror. Then, suddenly, he changed up a gear. I don't know if there'd been any attempt to nobble him. If so, he was defiant.

Maybe he'd been psyching himself up, getting 'in the zone'. But my fears evaporated as he launched into a dramatic tirade, scathingly abusing the prosecution.

He was careful to exclude the judge from the assault, who warned, "Be careful, Mr. Burke," glaring at him. But Mr Burke had no intentions of being careful; he was an animal I'd never seen before, not even when he destroyed the patsies McBungle and Kitchup.

Trevor Burke showed that day why many were tipping him for the top. He displayed passion, anger and drama. His split-second timing and presentation hypnotised every member of the jury.

Apart from the occasional glance at the bowed heads of the prosecution team, the jury was transfixed, focused on his every word. My own emotions were obvious. Tears filled my swollen eyes. I looked a sorry state. My old dad was following suit. It wasn't planned, it was Trevor's performance. Most of the packed courtroom was feeling sorry for me. I was the broken victim of gangsters, a casualty of crime, not a perpetrator.

In a brilliant delivery, he condensed five weeks of ridiculous farce into a short, napalm packed missile, blasting it straight into the prosecution's camp, burning every molecule of confidence off their sneering, snivelling faces!

He spoke of me as a hero who, despite four years of hell, had fought valiantly for his family, crew and sanity, while risking life, limb and liberty to expose the corruption laid before them.

When he'd finished, even the judge needed to gather his thoughts before he adjourned.

The prosecution attempted to regroup and force a few dismissive smiles. But they all saw that the jury had been stunned into silence. I could see anger in some of the jury members' faces. They'd been misled by the prosecution.

As soon as the gavel comes down, the court is no longer in session and I could do anything I wanted. I quite often took advantage with a bit of drama during the few moments before the jury left, or I was hurried downstairs by my keepers.

This day was no exception; I scowled at the prosecution, shaking my head, mouthing and gesturing with my right arm. "Come on lads, put the kettle on," I laughed at my escorts, as I confidently ushered them down the stairs.

I grabbed and shook Trevor's hand in much the same way as he'd done after my cross examination. He was buzzing. I could see he loved his job. He loved it!

After yet another delightful pasty, I was warned by Trevor to expect the worst from the judge, before being led upstairs by a bunch of Bristol screws who'd become much friendlier as the trial progressed.

They need to believe that everybody, even those on remand, is guilty in order to get any sort of job satisfaction. To treat people like dog shit and lock them up for twenty three hours a day away from their families, only to discover they're innocent, must really screw with their heads. Well, at least any of them who have a soul.

"All rise." The court fell silent. After the usher scanned the room to make sure we were all upright, he knocked the door and opened it with the usual ceremony. I sat back down, just as he walked in. The screw tugged on my cuffs as the daggers pricked me all over. When I had everybody's attention, I begrudgingly got up, smiling as defiantly as I could. I knew what was coming and I wanted to show the jury, that I had zero respect for him.

Of course his summing up would be outrageously biased. He wouldn't give two hoots if I was granted leave to appeal my conviction, as long as there was a conviction! At a retrial, there'd be no surprises; I'd be convicted again anyway. I wanted this jury to know that without a shadow of a doubt, I thought he was a bastard!

He was true to form. I was a self-confessed master criminal who'd admitted discussing having Hannibal killed, admitted buying guns and defrauded the tax man with multiple companies from one address. And I was violent, winning every bare-knuckle fight I'd been in.

He said, how, if I wanted to fight the lunatic Hannibal, could I be scared of Cordite? At this point, I was gesturing that I had a gun in my hand, pulling a stupid face. I became the side show, huffing and puffing, shaking my head, laughing under my breath; I had a face for every line of his blatantly biased shite.

The old fart didn't get it all his own way. Every time he stopped to warn me, it put him off his stride. He was reading his notes slowly before presenting the next paragraph. His tone was menacing, as though he was trying to bully the jury.

At the beginning of the trial, he'd have succeeded; today was different. They saw I wasn't scared of him. They'd witnessed so much bullshit and been scared for weeks for nothing. They seemed to be rebelling; why should they be scared of the circus ring master? It was plainly obvious that at least half the jury took offence at his attitude. Brilliant! He was losing his way in his own court. He was shooting himself in both feet.

I knew fine well I'd really pissed him off. If it all went tits up, I'd be getting the maximum fourteen years. My show of disrespect was a calculated risk. They'd already passed the point where we could appeal the conviction. If I was convicted again, it'd be in front of a different judge who I'd be nice to, or maybe I'd do a deal and plead guilty. I had nothing to lose and everything to gain.

So I did to him as he'd done to me; I made an idiot of him at every opportunity!

His final directions, before he sent the jury to do their duty, were grounds for appeal by themselves.

I dismissed his words one last time by coughing through the scandalous, misleading drivel. He glared at me but, I glared back defiantly. Whatever happened now was up to the jury, not him!

The jury didn't see this as the disruptive behaviour of an idiot.

They saw me fighting back, fighting against an injustice, and defiantly standing my ground. I was sure they liked me.

Trevor's closing speech had left them in no doubt; I was a capable man, afraid of nothing except guns! I'd thought long and hard about how far I could go without alienating any of the jury.

None of my performance was spontaneous; it was a highly charged, fluid situation, during which I continuously evaluated my position and altered my presentation accordingly.

I had most of them in the palm of my hand but I needed them all! I had regular eye contact with all but three poker faced mysteries. They'd showed surprise at the covert tape revelations, but none had showed any emotion since then.

Down in the dungeons by mid afternoon, as the steel door slammed shut, it was over. The poignant end of a battle; I'd done all I could in the courtroom. Now I had to wait and see if it had been enough.

Such overwhelming pressure creates an adrenaline rush or euphoric high. You don't know whether you want a shit, shave, haircut or shampoo! Within half an hour, I was babbling to myself, making deals with God, and even attempting telepathy to the jury, droning "not guilty... not guilty... not guilty!"

My brain raced so fast, it produced extra endorphins that fuelled an insanity cycle until I was buzzing my socks off. But, in much the same way as any class A drug, the two hours flew by.

"Come on, Mr Berriman; let's be having you."

"Oh, it's Mr Berriman now, is it? You've changed your tune, Mr Greenslade."

My heart struggled to stay in beat as the jury took their seats. My arsehole clenched tight as the judge studied a piece of paper. He didn't look happy, but neither did the jury. They didn't look at me. The prosecution team was all pretty sombre. Jesus Christ alive! Had I done it? Was it all over bar the shouting?

"Ladies and Gentlemen of the jury, have you reached your verdict?" I looked up to the roof, holding my breath, mentally chanting: "Not guilty... not guilty... not guilty." "No, we have not, your honour," the foreman replied as nearly all of them stared at me to see my reaction.

It wasn't what I wanted, but I took it as a positive. I'd pre-planned for this moment. I didn't know how the jury was split, but I had to assume it was biased in my favour. Accordingly, I almost fell off the bench in apparent mortified shock. I broke down, my head in my hands.

It was a bit theatrical I know, but no one else in the court had any more say in the result. All I could do was act, and hope it had some sway. Maybe my earlier display of confidence had confused them. I needed to demonstrate fear, total fear!

We'd asked them to believe I was in danger before the trial. But the vicious lies of McBungle – repeated by the media – had made me a target for hardened criminals. I wanted the remaining stubborn bastards to think they could be sending an innocent man, to fourteen years of violence and even death!

To that end I earned my Oscar for 'Best Actor in the Dock'!

As the judge sent them to their hotel for the night, my head was still in my shaking hands until the last one went through the door. I was so convincing even Trevor asked me if I was okay.

It wasn't that hard to do… I was frightened and emotional. Any hard case looking at a long stretch that hasn't shed tears behind the cell door, cares about nothing, and probably deserves to be there.

I, on the other hand, needed two extra votes more than anything else in the world; I didn't give two hoots who saw the tears in my eyes, as long as the jury did.

Downstairs, Trevor said he thought it would end in a re-trial. I knew I'd be convicted at any re-trial and just blanked him; I just wanted to get back to my cell and be on my own. It was a sombre trip back to Bristol. I was absolutely devastated!

I knew the jury would be 'guarded' by the prosecution's best; the rules would be broken, as they'd been from the start. If one more juror could be swayed against me, the judge would declare the dreaded retrial. I could do nothing but make more deals with my God, my spirit guide and my conscience. The adrenaline high was gone. I was suffering badly.

Finally, the sun came up to end another tortuous night. I knew that day's Devil's Convoy would be my last, whatever happened. If convicted they'd throw me in the back of a van like any other convict. They'd have no jury to pervert.

I decided to make the most of it to distract me from the drama ahead. As we arrived in Exeter, a few more vehicles joined the farce for one last dramatic entrance through the gates, which were now besieged by TV cameras and reporters.

The jury saw a harrowed ghost as they entered the packed courtroom; I'd already winked at my dad to let him know I was okay, before turning on the fear. The judge asked them to confirm they'd not discussed the case with anyone else before sending them away again to decide my fate.

A long, lonely, manic wait brought lunchtime. The jury was hauled back before the judge who was furious because they hadn't budged from their original position. Trevor warned me it was almost certainly going to a re-trial. I told him to piss off! I wouldn't hear of it.

The judge and jury only needed one person to convert to 'guilty' and they'd all be discharged home immediately.

At ten votes to two, he should have accepted a majority decision, but he refused and left them in no doubt he was disgusted at the ten. I was afraid his cynicism would be enough for at least one of them to change camps. He held them in the Castle with sandwiches and threatened yet another night in a hotel; shocking!

The pressure was intense for another three hours. At 4.30pm Trevor came to my cell to say the judge had invited him and Jim Garlic to his chambers for a glass or two of wine. It meant that somebody had altered their position and the trial was over; it didn't bode well.

He said a re-trial wouldn't necessarily be bad news.

"Not from where you're standing, matey," I said. "Now piss off unless you have something positive to say. It's not over until the fat lady sings. I'm going home; end of story!"

Back in the dock for my last time, at this trial at least, all I could do as I gazed around, was quietly chant, "It's not guilty... it's not guilty... it's not guilty."

The jury shuffled in without even looking in my direction.

"Not guilty… it's not guilty… it's not guilty."

"All Rise for the Right Horrible Judge Dreadful." (I'm sure that's what he said.)

"Not guilty… not guilty… it's not guilty!"

"Ladies and Gentlemen of the jury, have you been able to reach a verdict?"

"Not guilty… not guilty… not guilty!" My head was busting.

"Yes, we have your honour," blurted the foreman. Everyone in court was stunned, frozen in time, until the penny dropped. I knew that ten jurors weren't about to change their minds. The expected answer was, "No, your honour." Nobody expected the last two to convert simultaneously.

"Well?" groaned the judge.

"Not guilty!" cried the foreman with a grimacing smile, clearly enjoying plunging the blunt verdict into the judge's black heart like a Samurai Sword.

I remained completely stone-faced, while I surveyed the main players in the courtroom.

My dad first: he nearly fell on the floor.

The judge, prosecutors and Customs team: gutted! Priceless!

Trevor and team: beaming from ear to ear; completely outnumbered but victorious!

My escort: gobsmacked.

The media made a big point of this later on by saying: "Mr Berriman remained emotionless, then turned to the jury and said simply, 'Thank you'."

Only two, probably the last to convert, didn't smile or nod in approval. The three lovely ladies were beaming. My head was blowing a gasket, but I wanted to hear the words from the judge himself:

"Mr Berriman, you've been found not guilty by the jury, hence you're free to go," he growled, looking past me, instead of at me.

He didn't deserve a reply; I cocked my head to one side, and grinned as I winked at him.

Many would have jumped over the barrier, down the steps and into a crowd of supporters. But I was six hours from home, and there were a few people there to support my dad.

I followed my escort down to the desk outside my cell door and told them, not asked them, to put the kettle on; it'd been a long day. I drank my tea while taking great pleasure to wind them up. "Well lads, how does it feel now? You've kept an innocent man from his family for fifteen months? Now, you've got to tell everybody; you weren't risking your lives to escort me."

I signed the papers for my property bags before they offered to walk me out. "Like hell you will! I'll walk out on my own, this is my day!"

I followed the exit signs before coming across Jim Garlic. He was taken aback first but looked me straight in the eye, and offered up his hand: "Mr Berriman, I have to say... I've been doing this job for twenty years and never, have I come across a more formidable adversary than you. You deserve to be going home today, well done, Phil, well done!"

I beamed from ear to ear. What a compliment; he was only doing his job after all. I shook his hand saying, "I was fighting for my life, mate, not wages."

Trevor was waiting at the door. He said very seriously, "I've got some very bad news."

"What?" I asked, a little bit worried.

"Flares are out," he laughed, dusting the shoulder of my old brown suit.

"It worked, didn't it?" I smiled as I shook his hand and walked towards the waiting cameras at the gate.

I spent ten minutes answering questions on camera before hugging my old dad who still hadn't got his head round it.

Mike Rennison and his partner Jenny Wedge picked us up in her Range Rover to whisk us away. On the corner, a hundred yards down the road, most of the jury was waiting.

I invited them all for a drink at my dad's hotel. I downed pint after pint until I'd done six in an hour. Adrenaline was coursing through my veins. I hardly felt drunk, even though no alcohol had passed my lips for fifteen months. Both Trevor and I basked in glory and adulation!

The three girls had been playing games by deliberately not

looking at me so I'd think it was guilty. I wasn't that impressed, given my stress levels. They were desperate to supply my first shag and made no secret of it.

They competed against each other until I was offered my pick like a high class brothel. But Pa was knackered and people were waiting. So despite eighteen months of masturbating from memory, I politely and reluctantly refused. However, I did pay £70 for a room for one of my defence team who shall remain nameless, but he deserved it!

We hit the road, arriving back at my parents' house around midnight where a dozen or so people were already pissed.

After hugs and kisses, I broke open a £300 vintage bottle of whisky, and had it beat by four o'clock.

I changed the water twice in the Jacuzzi, trying to wash away the dank, musty, miserable smell of prison. Every bit of clothing went in the bin before I fell unconscious in a real bed. Oh my good God…!

CHAPTER NINETEEN

FISHY BUSINESS

After my sensational trial, both the Customs and police were hot on my heels; they wanted me very badly, especially with two coppers facing perjury charges.

I kept contact with some of the big fish in the underworld; those in the special secure unit knew the truth. I suppose I was under an 'umbrella' of protection and probably still have the ability to call on a ferocious retribution, if it were necessary. It's better of course to let sleeping dogs lay, especially ferocious ones.

I studied hard in prison; I became fascinated with the criminal world. I read thousands of pages of depositions from other double A prisoners, and spent countless hours exchanging stories, gaining an unprecedented understanding of some of the most famous gangsters, and their methods.

I went on remand owning a beautiful yacht, a luxury home, a Porsche 911 turbo and a playboy lifestyle, all funded by the best auto salvage yard in the North East. I was a self-made man, from nothing. Within a week of my incarceration, my house, workshops and business were stripped of hundreds of thousands worth of stock; even the steel warehouses were scrapped. Paul Daniels and the rest of the magic circle couldn't have made it disappear any faster! I was on my arse and in debt… but I was free.

A lot of my more affluent friends let me down quite badly, keeping me at arm's length without actually telling me to piss off. It was a good lesson to find how years of loyalty, generosity and support meant nothing when I needed a leg up. Without the support of these high profile people, my circle of so-called friends diminished significantly, such was the stigma, regardless of the result. I can only wonder what it would've been like if I'd been charged with murder.

I made a point of going out every night, until I got involved with a woman called Sally, and re-launched an ailing town centre pub called 'Martinis'. I designed a beer garden featuring a boat for the kids to play on, painting murals of pirates and seascapes on the walls. I called it 'Smugglers' Creek' after the place I'd been caught. It was a little bit of rebellion, and seemed to be popular. Despite the fact that the vast majority of my former friends, especially those who operated businesses I'd helped and supported over the years, never once turned up, the pub was busy.

The police and Customs never gave me any peace. As far as their profile of me was concerned, they were sure I'd commit crime to regain my lifestyle.

I was still under constant surveillance this whole time, and sometimes the police, and other crooks (expecting something in return) would try and entice me into crime. They really wanted me, and made no secret of it.

One day, John Scott, a dealer I used, said while he was on bail, "My mate's got two hundred kilos of charlie in Amsterdam. He needs 'transport' to the UK, do you know anyone to organise it?"

My reply was simple. "Who buys £4mill of coke, with no plan to smuggle it? Wake up, you dozy bastard."

I don't know if he was part of a plan to tempt me into a plot, or he too, was being set up.

He was forever calling me paranoid, because I was always warning him to stop bragging about his dealings, and he was just plain stupid on the telephone. Eventually they got him again, through just that.

I just kept working on my legitimate business ideas. By 2000, I'd developed the design of the spring-loaded fishing hook I invented while on my fateful voyage in 1994. I turned it into a product and tested it in Thailand with great success. Convinced I had it right, I had some made in Turkey, about £25k worth, and launched them with very surprising results. The fishing community and press tortured me, calling me a 'Northern Barbarian' for inventing such a cruel and heartless device. I went to war on internet forums defending it. Nobody would stock it or allow it to be used in fisheries because of threats of boycott. Undeterred, I went to the annual commercial fishing show in Glasgow and found a company who would take on the design for commercial long lining, if I could find a way to bait it automatically.

By 2002 I set about developing sausages, to use as bait, made from fish processing waste under the name of 'Fish Lab', bringing my son, Philip, into the business. The idea was to band them to the pre-loaded hooks by machine. I went to Inshore Fisheries at Redcar. The owner was very impressed and provided us a refrigerated room as a lab, and anything we wanted, that he had.

We bought a fishing boat called Pisces, an unsinkable ex-ship's lifeboat, and probably the most sea kindly vessel I have ever owned. We spent months going out every night in all weathers, testing various concoctions of fish waste sausages. We even sold the best of them on the internet as 'Megabites' for competition use to pay for research and development.

One day, the owner came into the lab astounded; he'd been fishing from the beach the night before (talk about a busman's holiday) and pulling crabs in that were hanging on to the sausages for grim death. Clearly we'd stumbled onto a recipe the crabs couldn't resist.

I studied the crab and lobster pot bait market, and began testing various methods of presentation. The spring-loaded hooks paled into insignificance when we realised how much fish waste could be recycled into bait, saving millions of undersize fish, helping to replenish stocks. I thought the venture ticked all of the boxes, including recycling and conservation. Surely, grants would be easily available. I set about buying a Ford Cargo truck and fitted refrigeration to half of it, while designing and building a fish waste processing machine into the other half. I powered our 'chopper' with a four cylinder diesel engine, mounted underneath on the chassis.

It was basically a big stainless steel vessel with a pressurised hatch, in which up to a ton of fish waste could be chopped up by rotating blades and pumped out into sausage skins or plastic tubes. Mr Inshore Fisheries was more than impressed. We would collect large quantities from his premises in big 300 litre black polypropylene containers, while developing and testing modifications to the machine.

We travelled up and down the country with free crab bait. Tyronio, a pal I'd met in jail on similar charges, lived in Selsey on the south coast. Selsey is famous for its luscious crabs, which are coveted by people like the QE2 chefs, who would serve nothing else. We spent a couple of days there, negotiating a deal for him to be a distributer when all was finalised.

During the research, we talked to crab fisherman who'd been fishing crabs the same way as their forefathers had for donkeys' years. I identified serious failings in the crab and lobster pots, and decided to improve them. We installed tanks at home to watch them feeding with various pot designs.

We made some pots with separate compartments for the lobsters to hide in, naming them 'Rack and stack, crustacean traps'. RASCT TRAP Funny thing was, every time we gave an operator one to try out, we never ever got it back. We continued to test them ourselves from our trusty boat, Pisces, off Hartlepool with huge success, but they were impossible to patent.

We used to joke that the Pisces was the safest boat in the North East, because every time we put to sea, the coastguard did too. Because we'd no intentions of doing anything illegal, we learned to live with it, and laugh at their mistakes. I'd openly warn anybody who was even slightly 'dodgy', that my phone was probably bugged, and to be careful what they said.

We noticed the Customs and police had stepped up their efforts, probably because they couldn't understand what the hell we were doing, knee deep in fish shit, pissing about in all weathers with a scruffy little boat. My profile was luxury yachts, cars and parties. Clearly they thought I was up to something much more sinister.

We'd had a 'covert spin' at home, which involves a team entering without a search warrant, and searching through everything. My cameras picked up two masked men just as the electric was cut off. The place was exactly as left, nothing was taken, but we had to assume the place was bugged. Then one night, a strange thing happened.

We'd been testing a new pump for the fish processor truck. Each time we finished, we discharged the remaining 'fishy slurry' into the river Tees, monitoring the fish that fed on it. The weather was warm, and the stuff didn't keep too well to say the least.

One hot summer evening, we'd modified it at John Nelson's Porsche workshop in Stockton, when we got a blockage in the output spout of the vessel. Luckily the truck was outside when Carl, a dozy twit I'd employed to handle the fish, tried to resolve the problem.

It was the third day we'd been working with this particular batch, and things were starting to smell pretty bad! Rather than dispose of it sooner, and have to trail over to Redcar to load up again, we kept it as long as we dared. The evil sludge bubbled and fermented as it got warmer, especially after being whipped by the fast rotating blades. We were only experimenting and modifying the machine, the quality and freshness of the sludge was irrelevant, but it still had to be used.

Finding someone with any technical ability to do this job had been very difficult, as you can imagine. Carl was one of those guys who'd do exactly what you said, but you needed to be absolutely specific. If, for one minute you left him to make a decision, then the outcome was pretty much going to be a disaster. He was labour only, not a thinker.

The hapless Carl, rather than ask me what to do next, had opened the main valve to poke something up the spout, without first de-pressurising the vessel!

If only this had been on CCTV, it would have gone viral! We heard a thud, looked round and saw Carl doing a backward somersault, propelled by three hundred and fifty litres of rancid fish waste, under ten bar of pressure.

He scrambled to his feet, and tried to stem the three inch diameter, solid jet of fish shit with his hands and body. He failed miserably, becoming a human muck spreader.

The stinking sludge went everywhere, splattering ten to twenty metres up the road, across the road and all over the walls of the unit. Thirty seconds later, Carl was sitting in a pile of it, covered from head to foot. His jeans, underpants, top and coat were full to bursting where it'd blasted its way in. He must have had twenty kilos in his anorak; it was creeping out of his sleeves.

Nobody could help him; I was borking, while Junior was rolling on the floor, pissing himself laughing.

The scene was horrific; the stench was nothing short of outrageous!

"Stay where you are," I shouted, as he tried to scramble about, slipping and sliding on the road. "You're not coming in here like that."

Poor Carl was coughing and puking, while trying to get the shit out of every orifice.

My son pulled himself together, and with tears streaming down his face, started to hose him down. I found John to apologise, he'd removed himself upwind. I thought he'd go spare; instead I found him on his knees, still crying with laughter.

"Doesn't matter mate," he said. "That's the funniest thing, I've ever seen!" and, I had to agree.

The drains were blocked in minutes, causing the whole area to stink for three weeks at least. We shovelled some of it into the two black polypropylene containers to dump the next day as it was getting late. All through, we couldn't stop laughing. our sides were hurting, and we stunk to high heaven!

We finally got home with the truck, and parked it next to the house. We showered, bathed, had a sauna for an hour, and bathed again; still, we could smell it! The washing machine stunk for a week, even though we hosed down our clothes first. God only knows what Carl smelt like when he got home. We never saw him again. I had to send his wages to his house.

Now, here's the strange bit. The next day, we found the padlock on the roller shutter door of the truck had been cut off. At first, I thought it very strange, as I'd already dealt with the local scroats who knew not to come burgling around our block. I lifted the door expecting to find my power tools and tool box gone, but they were still there, in the middle of the floor.

Any smack head, mooching, burgling bastard, could have sold them for £500 without much trouble.

"They must have been disturbed," said Junior, and I agreed,

"Where have the black drums gone?" I said. "Did we leave them at John's?"

It took a long time for the penny to drop, but the fact was indisputable; they'd been stolen.

Just who would walk past £500 worth of tools, and then steal two plastic drums of stinking fish shit? They were bought for £50 second-hand, and would need a Ford transit sized van to move them at least.

Obviously, curiosity had gotten the better of the agencies, police or Customs, or maybe both. They must have got sick of trying to discover what the hell was occurring, and instructed the men on the ground to get answers. Typically, they hadn't the common sense to take the tools to make it look like a petty burglary.

We joked that this machine could liquidise a human body in ten minutes. Perhaps they took it literally, perhaps they thought it was a mixing vessel for drugs, I don't know, we never found out. We laughed for ages, trying to picture them sifting through the contents of the captured drums. However, as it turned out, this was no laughing matter.

The next time we drove into In-shore Fisheries with the truck, the owner was a completely different person. He wouldn't come out of his office, there was no more waste, and he was too busy to help anymore. He couldn't look at me through the window. I waited around to speak to him, but he was having none of it. I don't know what bullshit the police or Customs told him, but he was petrified.

The next blow was Business Link, where I'd applied for grants.

Again I was shunned, totally ignored. My mails weren't answered, and I could never get to speak to anyone.

To be fair, I can't blame any person, or organisation for acting on spurious or malicious information from agency sources. Who are they going to believe in any case? Not me!

I blamed Customs and the police for their poisonous interference; they just wouldn't let me get on. I'd tried so hard for so long to get back on the map, I'd really had enough of the stigma still following me, and the false, malicious intelligence being circulated by those with a grudge. I had to get away from the horrible vindictive bastards.

Around this time I was also targeted by the local police drug squad. Benny The Bell, a guy who years before worked for me in the salvage business, had become involved in the drugs trade (as so many had). He was as dodgy as they come, and taken to surrounding himself with most of the active crooks and drug dealers in the area. Criminals change their phones like underwear, but don't want their names on the bill. Benny made it easy; he'd supply phones, quite happily take cash and pay their bill over the phone on his 'card'. Half the people he signed up didn't exist, or so it was said. There was always a constant stream of smack heads and petty villains trotting into his shop, where he'd sit like a modern day Fagan, haggling over the price of their newly stolen booty.

One day, he was mortal drunk in the pub, bragging that he'd made a killing that day. As Phil Junior and I approached, he bellowed, "Phil, remember when you were the boyo in Stockton? You could pick up the phone and sort anything out, you were the kiddie then, Phil, but now, I'm the kiddie, I'm the kiddie now, Phil!"

"How's that Benny?" I laughed.

"I can do anything, pick up the phone, it's sorted! I've just made £2,800 in less than an hour," he chortled. "Sold a thousand ecstasies at £2.80 and only bought 'em for a quid, then made a quid each on a thousand Kamagra at £1.50. Not bad, eh?"

Now, let's be clear, criminality fascinates me, but I've never sold drugs for profit in my life, but I know a lot due to my time on remand. At that time, a thousand Kamagra (copy Viagra) could be bought for 40p each, and E's were about 80p on a thousand. They were not like the old days, when one cost £5 or £10 and would allow clubbers to dance all night.

"Who the hell did you sell them to, you robbing bastard?" I asked laughing.

"I hardly know them. I bought some England flags off them. They could be undercover coppers for all I know," he said, laughing back at me.

The whole table laughed, Benny was buying drinks for everybody, so everybody laughed. I tried one more time to help him. "Benny, back then it was car parts mate; I was target number one, and look what happened to me. I never sold drugs to anyone, let alone strangers. Who is going to give you £2.80 on a thousand E? They don't fetch that in tens, mate."

He retorted, "I know what I'm doing. You should get into drugs, you'd be good at it. It'd beat messing about with fish shit, ha ha ha."

The cling-ons all laughed with him. I shook my head looking at Junior, who even at fourteen was shaking his head. We went off to play pool.

Two weeks later, he was on the TV being arrested along with the rest of the gang. Story goes, he was sat in the interview room when the two Reebok he'd sold the pills to walked in with two others.

"Oh shit!" he said. "The bastards haven't got you two as well, have they?"

"No, you daft bastard, we've got you," they laughed.

In court, I watched as the charges and details were read out. Benny and his associates were all charged with conspiracy to supply cocaine. Benny's involvement in this was mostly at arm's length, so the cops had made sure to get him by doing the ecstasy and Kamagra deal face to face. He was charged accordingly.

As the details of the sting were read out, they all remained stone-faced, looking straight ahead, until the prosecution gave details of the cocaine deals, "The undercover officers bought cocaine on numerous occasions starting with a few grams, and later up to half a kilo, ranging from 1% purity to 11% purity at best."

When the penny dropped, everybody in court could see that all of them were shocked by the revelations. Obviously, there'd been a good deal of dancing going on (cutting the drugs). The robbed looked very angry, and the robbers very sheepish. If there'd been any chance of bail by convincing the magistrates that there'd been a mistake, it was gone at that moment!

I was and still am very fond of the wife of one of the gang. I got a set of depositions from her to see if I could help. I was gobsmacked to find dozens of observations on me had been faded out as though covered or tippexed out, but not properly deleted. I'd originally been a prime target during this operation, and as it was me, I'd had a lot of attention. After months of surveillance, finally Reebok had to accept that I was nothing but an occasional customer of the firm, they'd reluctantly dropped me out of the frame.

The entries in the depositions, made it quite clear the cops had done their level best to connect me to this firm's business. They failed, not through inadequacies, or bad luck, they failed because what they found proved the contrary.

Me? I was doubly insulted. One that they thought I was dealing drugs, and two, that they thought I would deal drugs with this bunch of idiots.

I'd warned Benny and co months before, but was ridiculed. He also didn't like that I thought the details of his case hilarious, recounting them in the pub for a laugh. Tough shit, Benny, you're definitely 'the kiddie' now!

In any case, the whole episode demonstrated how keen the police were to tie me into anything dodgy, which I was remotely connected to. This farce seriously contributed to our case for leaving.

I decided to buy another boat and sail off to the Caribbean.

CHAPTER TWENTY

CONCEPTION

By the end of 2003, I'd sold an option on my old salvage yard in Stockton and had a nice few quid coming in every year until the sale went through. I thought small to start with, and bought Kandy, a beautiful, forty two feet, Scottish-built, canoe stern, wooden ex-survey boat, with a new engine and gearbox through eBay. She needed caulking and fitting out, so Phil Junior and I set about the task in my friend Keith's yard. Kandy came with a truckload of high quality wood to finish her.

Customs got wind and sent a number of undercover idiots spouting various cover stories. I always gave them time, and allowed them to think they were clever. In particular, I mentioned I was looking for a new wheelhouse. A week later, one of these guys told me that a friend was breaking a boat in Holyhead in Anglesey, which had a real good aluminium wheelhouse. I played along as we had nothing to fear, and maybe something to gain.

We went to look at the Cornish Maiden in Holyhead marina boatyard by arrangement. Once I saw her, I'd have happily given a grand for the wheelhouse. However, the boat, a 50 foot ex-trinity lighthouse delivery vessel, was by far better than the Kandy. She needed some new planks, re-caulking and a paint job, but she had a very high build specification, second to none. Her price new would have been astronomical.

Incredibly, I was offered her complete for £500, as is where is, and all fees paid up for six months, including a re-launch. If they'd asked for £15k, I'd have said yes. Be very wary of strange men bearing gifts.

When things seem too good to be true, there is always a catch. It didn't take me long to spot which of the bunch were undercover. The group, purportedly divers from Manchester, co-owned her. She'd almost sunk in a blow after a botched repair job failed (so they said). I came back to Teesside and pondered for a couple of days. Whatever they were, I still wanted the boat. I also wondered who and what they were down there watching.

A couple of days later, a pal of mine, Les Graham called in to see me. I was clearing my office out, and gave him some filing cabinets for the office of his wife's dog breeding kennels.

An hour later he called me from a pub in Thornaby. He was sat with some travellers that I'd known since they were kids, tatting for old batteries and scrap. I hadn't seen these guys for a while, but knew their main income was the cigarette business. Les mentioned being at my house, and they all asked him to invite me over.

I walked in to a rapturous welcome; they'd clearly been on the drink for a while. I knew four of them, but two I hadn't seen before. They didn't look like travellers, too much fashionable coordination. One spoke with a Yorkshire accent, the other a Manchurian. They were introduced as gentleman villains, who were big hitters in the smuggling business. They were fascinated when they realised who I was. They took plenty of time to talk to me, while the others were fighting over who was going to buy the 'Turbo', (that's traveller code for cocaine). I deduced they'd called me to impress these guys, and give themselves more credibility.

In no time, it was clear to me that the two I didn't know were undercover. They were simply too switched on to be doing any business with these lads, who were barred out of most pubs in the town because of their propensity for violence, seen by them, as the only way to settle an argument.

In contrast, the two Reebok squad were stylish and intelligent, and given to splashing money about, having gifted jewellery and other stuff to the travellers, who by now thought they were in the first division!

Travellers are notoriously hard to infiltrate. They're not stupid by any means, just pretend to be when it suits them. These two had obviously worked very hard to get in so far as to be sleeping in the guest 'caravan' after a bender. I watched them dodge at least 50% of the alcohol the others had.

Years before, these travellers made a good living from scrap metal, exporting trucks and plant (some of it dodgy) or a bit of road tarmac. They only got drunk, drugs were a big no no! They were tight knit and very careful. Travellers, by their very nature don't like jail! Having a caravan meant they could move at the drop of a hat, when the heat is on.

I made my excuses and left after a couple of hours. Next day I got a call from one of the travellers I'd known the longest.

"My pal from the boozer yesterday wants a meet with you," he said. "Meet him as a favour to me, he wants to ask you something."

I was expecting just that, and wanting to confirm my suspicions, I agreed.

My old pal picked me up in a flash V12 Mercedes, which didn't fool me, we were meeting fifty miles away, yet he only bought three gallon of petrol. It was must have been dodgy, he was just too greedy to have it full of petrol, when they swiped it back.

On route, I questioned him about these men, expressing my concern, but he just wouldn't have it.

"They're my friends," he said. "Look at the ring he gave me. They're both millionaires!"

I asked how long he'd known them, if he'd been to their houses, local pub, and corner shop, met the wife, done any background checks, and did anybody else know them? It was only Leeds that they were purportedly based.

He started to get offended and defensive, as he clearly hadn't. I left it at that. He was a big rough lad, not the best fighter, but thought he was. Nobody wants to fight a traveller; even if you beat one, there'll likely be a few at your door in the morning.

On arrival, a bit of bullshit anti-surveillance drama was conducted to make things look right, before one approached us. The other was huge, clearly on steroids. He was obviously handy, and he needed to be. If anything went wrong with this lot, they'd need to fight their way out. He waited in full view, sitting in a brand new, high spec Range Rover, you know, low profile, not attracting attention.

In any case, the little one said to me, "Do you know anyone in Spain where we can buy solid?" (slang for cannabis resin)

"Yes," I said, "I know people who can take you to them."

"What about charlie?" he asked.

"Same deal. I don't mind my contact pointing you in the right direction, as you're pals with my pal."

"Okay brilliant. We'll pay for everything. We'll be in touch tomorrow."

"Whoa there, no need," I said. "I'm not going anywhere. I'll tell you where to go, and I'll tell him you're coming, you can ask him yourself. I can't get nicked for an introduction, can I?"

I began to walk away as he asked for my number.

I just said, "No thanks, I don't do dodgy numbers. The Customs watch my phone anyway. Ring him (pointing to my pal) when you're ready, and I'll meet him to give him a number."

And I was gone.

Back at the car, my traveller pal said I'd been rude to them.

I tried to explain that, "This approach is a standard agency sting. No self-respecting millionaire smuggler needs me to tell him where to buy drugs in Spain. It's common knowledge, and if they're such successful smugglers, why are they looking for a new supplier through contacts they don't know? What's happened to their old contacts?"

What I couldn't say was, "What the hell are these lads doing with you lot, snorting coke and discussing 'business' in front of strangers? Alarm bells are ringing, mate!" Undercover guys rely on greed, giving the targets the chance to move up a rung, cut out the middle man and buy direct. They think the opportunity just arrived by chance. Drugs make people stupid! I was happy to get clear; I wouldn't have been the first 'friend' he'd attacked.

I was faced with a dilemma; do I butt out, and watch a firm I'd known for many years get roped into a conspiracy, or risk trouble and put a stop to it? It wouldn't take much skullduggery to tie me into them, so I had to consider my own position first. It seemed like somebody in charge who had a score to settle was hell bent on messing me up.

Back home, the more I thought about it, the angrier I got. I was sick to the back teeth of these amateur approaches, and fuming over the interference in my legal business ventures. I was sure it would be something to do with the same team from 1994. Could they really hold a grudge for so long? After much consideration, I rang Peter Hollier, the man in charge of my case at Leeds Customs office, but got a blank. "No Peter Hollier here," they said. I put two and two together, and called the Manchester office; I was put through to him straight away.

"Peter Hollier," I said, "Phil Berriman here. I bet you didn't think you'd hear from me today, did you?"

He was gobsmacked as I laughed and asked if it was him who was onto me, and the travellers in Leeds, and told him how I knew about it.

He said, "No, but I know someone who is."

I told him I wanted to have it out with them, and put a stop to the ridiculous shit that plagued my life, or else I was going public! He agreed, and I was contacted the next day.

I travelled down to Scotch Corner services on the A1 with my son. I was keen to show him I was fighting back. He'd put a lot of time into the Fish Lab project, and he knew how much money I'd spent. I couldn't just let them mess it up and get away with it. My son looked up to me; we were best mates.

A few weeks earlier, after smoking some superb skunk, we were discussing the methods these guys on the 'fag job' were using to get cigarettes into the country. I mooted the idea of selling them in international waters as a joke, but we explored the concept in depth until the wee hours, and all the Jack Daniels had gone.

I was pissed off with the Customs by then anyway, and the subject kept coming back to me time and time again. I'd researched it properly, and could find nothing wrong with the idea.

I'd already seriously contemplated it as a way of boosting funds before our departure, but only in a quiet, low profile way.

At Scotch Corner, we met with two 'Reebok squad', so-called, because most wore jeans, trainers, and fake wax Barbour jackets. Rather than beat about the bush, I blasted their attempts to draw me in, and even told them where they'd gone wrong. They were clearly embarrassed, and obviously had to pull their men out of the traveller's operation.

As the meeting was about to end, I told the two flabbergasted Customs officers straight, "If you continue to harass me, bug me, and interfere in my legal business, apart from going public and suing you, I'm going to start selling fags in international waters, and there's nothing you can do about it! Later, everybody'll be doing it, and then you'll wish you'd left me alone."

Just after that, I got up and left, but not before my last volley. "And, I'll still be buying that boat in Holyhead for £500, or you'll have wasted your time down there on whoever it is you're infiltrating."

Their faces were dumbstruck.

On the way home, I felt much better for venting my anger. I'd put up with that shit for eight years, and got used to knowing my phones were bugged. I used to complain, but never hit back. The idea of the 'Baccy Boat' became a reality.

"They're not going to leave me alone," I said. "Let's do it!"

My son knew I was serious; he'd seen this attitude before. Little Phil was probably the only person who actually believed I was coming home in 1995. Granted he was only six then, but I gave him my word, he believed me above his mother and everybody else, and I didn't let him down.

"Oh shit!" he said. "This is going to be fun, Dad. Does this mean we're going to be pirates?"

"Yes, son," I said, "it does."

"Cool."

I never said a word to the travellers who I'd helped stay out of jail; they wouldn't be able to understand why I'd met with Customs in the first place. We'd had many deals over the years, and I still counted them as pals, but I'd never get the credit for helping them, albeit while helping myself.

I'd had enough of being hounded and victimised, it was time to fight back, if only for my own self respect.

CHAPTER TWENTY ONE

THE CORNISH MAIDEN, HOLYHEAD, A STRANGE PLACE

Holyhead was an island as was Anglesey, until the causeways were built to join them to the mainland. It's a sunny place, as close to Ireland as one can get, but quite windy, and an overcoat colder most of the time. A strange beautiful place, normally only passed through, on route to and from the daily ferry.

It has a huge two and a half mile breakwater protecting it from the sometimes violent weather. Anglesey itself is unspoilt. Half the locals can speak Welsh. Aluminium is the only significant industry there. Holyhead is, and has been for many years, a jewel the locals don't want spoiling.

We travelled the long road, and bought the boat with a grin on my face like a Cheshire cat.

She was perfect for our purpose. Built for Trinity Lighthouse as a delivery vessel, the specification was hugely superb. Thick larch planks on huge oak frames, she was built similar to the traditional Scottish 'canoe stern' fishing boats, except much stronger!

As a kid, I'd been off Hartlepool hundreds of times on all manner of craft, in all weathers, and quite often seen similar boats ploughing through the shitty chop, making easy work of it, while we were usually struggling to make way. The design has a well earned reputation.

I hadn't even heard the huge Gardner 6LXB six cylinder engine running, but knew from just looking at it that it would be fine. I know these engines well, they were the backbone of the fishing fleets before the Caterpillar V8, which being more compact, provided more space for the fish hold.

The Gardner engines run forever, as long as they have oil, water and clean fuel. Gaskets are rarely needed on these beauties, as the engineering tolerances are so small. This particular motor, and indeed the rest of the hull and machinery, had done nothing compared to a fishing trawler, which runs for weeks at a time.

The problem with the Cornish Maiden was blatantly obvious; the deck had been neglected. Rain water ingress had rotted two or three planks down the hull in places, and she needed some caulking doing. She'd been used by a bunch of scuba divers for a few years, and instead of replacing the wood, they'd screwed galvanised steel plates bent at right angles, to cover the rot on the deck, and the adjoining planks of the hull.

A serious storm had ripped off the metal plates, letting the sea flood in. They were shitting bricks all night, sat with their diving gear on, hoping the pumps would hold out. They only got back by the skin of their teeth, and then had her hauled out immediately. So scared after their epic episode, they'd clubbed together to buy an unsinkable Severn class lifeboat that had been damaged in its pen by the Irish ferry. All good news for us, the Cornish Maiden would live to fight another day. We measured up, made lists, and set off back to Teesside.

My first stop was John Nelson. He is by far the best engineer I've met, and he happened to be my best mate. I talked him into coming down to Holyhead and getting involved in the project. Between us, we could pretty much get anything done at mate's rates. He had more tools than the Snap-on van in his workshop, and more so, he knew how to use them.

I'd had a back injury years ago, and lived with quite a bit of pain while walking. Small engine rooms and hard physical work called for copious amounts of marijuana rather than painkillers. John could do the work of two men, and we got on really well. He promised his weekends to me, setting off every Friday, returning Sunday night for a number of months.

The next Friday evening, we pulled onto the marina on Holyhead with a truck full of everything we needed. I already had the timber that came with the Kandy still in Thornaby. The Kandy had been someone's life project; it came lock, stock, the flipping lot. The old owner had acquired everything to finish the boat and more. I brought larch to match the hull and Canadian pine for the decks.

From sleeping bags to Jack Daniels, we had every single thing we needed to set up camp inside the Cornish Maiden and start work. Within two hours of arriving at what could best be described as a derelict boat, we had water, electricity, lights, cooker, kettle, heat, music and somewhere to sleep. A lot of stuff had gone west since I saw her first, including the mahogany wheelhouse door. We had dinner and bedded down for an early night.

Next morning, we got cracking early, ripping the rotten planks from the frames all along the port side. By lunchtime we started to cut and fix new planks. We had to sleep on-board and it wasn't the weather for watching stars. By dark, the planks were on, and ready for caulking.

The locals didn't know what to make of us, they gathered in small groups, some of them venturing over to glean information. Some of the small companies based there came to quote for various services. They were completely flummoxed when we said we had everything covered; the only thing we needed was a stable 220 volt supply. To say they were impressed with our work rate is an understatement. This was not the first boat we'd brought back to life. We knew the only way forward was to attack it, and wait for no one.

Dinner over (I'm known as quite a chef), and after a few large Jack Daniels, we headed for the nearest pub in time-honoured fashion. When we're away, working hard, it's the law! We first went to the yacht club bar close by. The steward there wasn't local, and began to put us in the picture. He already knew as much about us as anybody else there, and greeted us with, "You'll be the lads from Teesside working on the Cornish Maiden then?" He proceeded to tell us what we needed to know about Holyhead.

It seemed we'd already upset some by simply buying the Cornish Maiden. She'd been earmarked by locals as a distressed boat, which normally would be bought for peanuts by someone in the clique. This is a common practice in every marina I've ever been to. The scale and cost of repairs is exaggerated to the point that the owner wants out at any cost, before the fees build up.

Many are sold to recoup berthing or hard standing fees. The people in the clique know the truth about the boat, but a non-local would-be buyer is told a different story. When the boat is finally sold, the missing items materialise back on-board. The price we paid for the Cornish Maiden was so low as to lure us there, but it upset those who had their eye on her. I've bought a number of distressed boats around Europe, and always done very well. The secret is knowing just who to pay.

In any case, we deduced, we'd bypassed the lot of them and pissed off a few who'd been looking forward to a payday. We asked about a decent pool table nearby, and were told the 'Vic' had a good one. "But," he said, "You might not be welcome. They're a queer bunch up there."

I knew he wasn't referring to the sexual preferences of the clientele, and was pretty confident I'd been in enough rough bars to handle a few locals and a game of pool, so off we went, half pissed.

Walking into the Vic's pool room was an experience I'll not forget in a hurry. The opposite of rough, the place was clean, well run and busy with mostly well-dressed middle-aged blokes. John, my son Phil and I worked our way to the bar as the room went deathly quiet. By the time the manager served our drinks, the whispering had started.

Ever the cheeky twat, I took advantage of the quiet, and addressed the thirty or so locals. "Hello everybody, this is John my mate, and Phil my son. My name is Phil and we're here weekends, doing up a boat in the yard. We heard that some of you guys could play a decent game of pool, and we're here to find out if that's true!"

"Put your money down, mister, we'll show you all right," said a bull of a man, getting on sixty, sitting in the middle of four or five men. I'd seen this guy that day in a builder's truck with a huge Rottweiler the size of a pit pony at the boatyard. Here he was, as smart as a dart, and just as drunk as us.

Not wanting to stall the process, I went across and shook his hand. This was, as it turned out, to be a good move. Later, we were to refer to this man as 'Mister Holyhead'. John Walsh clearly had been a handful in his prime, and even then, not someone you'd want to tangle with. He had various business interests including a building company, a work boat, and even the local undertakers. It was to transpire, that this man was without doubt, the most respected man in Anglesey.

With a population of about 12,000, the locals all knew each other. Long before Facebook, they had a gossip system connecting everyone. In my opinion, RAF Valley close by was the perfect location for HRH Prince William to be based at the helicopter search and rescue facility. Any stranger, straying from the ferry road, was immediately scrutinised, and reported on.

This place has almost zero crime; it's not allowed, and people know better. The only graft the police have to deal with is a few stranded passengers from a cancelled ferry occasionally. The people of Holyhead want it to stay that way. Greed isn't a vice held by the vast majority, in fact, it's frowned upon.

If you want to get on in Holyhead, you have to be fair and honest, there's no room for the fast buck, the shirker or the liar. The pace was as laid-back as a mountain village in Spain. There are no homeless people, burglars, drug pushers or perverts blighting the community.

The new road to Holyhead was part of the route to and from Ireland, and that's all. Outsiders found it hard to do business; those who bought property would soon sell it again, if they didn't fit in. I always got the impression there was a sort of 'secret council' operating there, looking after the interests of this really tight knit community. It seemed the authorities in Holyhead, were not really in charge, if you get my drift? Maybe they didn't need to be.

If, there was such an organisation, some of these well-dressed, middle-aged guys in the 'Vic' seemed to fit the bill. A fair few of them were first introduced with the nickname 'carrot', which I eventually found out means; he's part of a bunch of us, brothers or otherwise. Names would come later, when they trusted us.

Being pretty streetwise, I quickly adapted to the banter. We all had a great night, especially when the shots started to flow (John Nelson's fault). Thankfully, such people give plenty of weight to the fact we could get absolutely bladdered, and still behave ourselves. The pool results were pretty even, although they play some mad rules down there.

We staggered out of the pub, and told them to call in for a bacon sandwich in the morning, if they were anywhere near the boatyard.

"Fat chance you'll be up in the morning," they shouted, but we were, and bang at the graft. By the time John Walsh dragged himself down, we'd eaten a full breakfast, and stripped off the rotten timbers from the other side. After working all day, we set off back to Teesside, having gone some way to gaining the respect of the locals.

The next week, we didn't have much to carry so we took a car, and were there in time for the Friday night pool match at the Vic. Another great night followed by another early morning. I'd be passing out hot drinks and bacon sandwiches to the lads in the yard, and any of the Vic crew, up until 1100h. We'd made a good impression, and cooperation was coming our way. Some of the men working in the yard were on the lifeboat crew. As far as I'm concerned, they're on par or better than fire fighters. They have my utter, total respect. A bacon sandwich and a cuppa was the very least a sailor could do.

The mahogany wheelhouse door turned up, as did a list of other stuff taken from her before we arrived. Whereas before we were treated with caution, things changed quite quickly. We'd mixed with and impressed the best. All we had to do was mention, "Mr Walsh sent us," to get discounts and service second to none, wherever we went.

"Would that be John Walsh?" they'd say. "Tell him I was asking after him, will you?"

I don't know who or what the Reebok squad were watching down there, but they visited most weekends, checking on the progress of their new boat. They purportedly went splits on the purchase. The group of four 'divers' from Manchester paid the bills, while a yard operative called Toby organised the work. Of course we don't know for certain, who was and who knew, a lot of the story is coggled out of experience.

How to spot which of them were Customs/agency? Easy, no overalls and no manual work! They socialised with most in the yacht club and boatyard, but kept well away from us. Not once did they cross the yard to see the progress on their old boat, or ever speak to us again in the seven or so months we were there.

Full of drink one night in the Vic, I overheard a bunch of carrots talking about them, and realised that everyone in the village knew what they were. "If, they want to keep splashing money about, let them," was the general opinion. I don't know if Holyhead ever had any smugglers operating there, but if there was, they'd be very, very hard to infiltrate. I got the distinct impression that Holyhead would stay the same for some time to come. It's a special place, with mostly special people.

By Christmas time, the crew in the Vic had fully accepted us. We brought family and friends down some weekends; some worked, some didn't, but always had a good time. We even went on the Christmas party bus bender, with all their families. The Cornish Maiden was a boat again, and not far off ready for the water. However, the plan didn't involve a winter at sea. She could stay where she was until the spring at least. I had a few spare quid coming then.

CHAPTER TWENTY TWO

THE SCHOONER RICH HARVEST

Whilst in the boatyard at Holyhead, we'd noticed a beautiful schooner sitting on a huge makeshift trailer consisting of three wagon frames welded together. She'd clearly been there a few years. Ever the bargain hunter, I'd made enquiries about her a number of times. The yard owner and others in the marina would shake their heads and tell us to stay away, "Nothing but trouble that boat".

I got the feeling there was a lot I wasn't being told, and one night in the Vic, I was enlightened. It transpired that some years before, the owner had run out of fuel on a very calm day while on route to Liverpool. Incredibly, he sent out a mayday – not something a good sailor does lightly, unless persons are in grave danger. The lifeboat towed him into Holyhead, where the Commodore of the yacht club, being very impressed with the schooner, invited him into the club, as a member.

The vessel Rich Harvest, then based there, swung on a mooring set down by the club. Every year the club changes the strops, and any other part of the mooring rig that gets worn. One year, the designated person had gone to change over the strop, and found that the new one was too small to fit over the capstan/centre post. Rather than go back and get a bigger strop, the stupid twat hung it around a winch on the foremast.

Later that year in 1999, there was a huge storm in which a dozen or so boats were destroyed. The strop, on which Rich Harvest relied on, ripped the winch clean off the mast, setting the boat adrift. She washed up against the huge breakwater, and because of her long keel, and fantastically strong construction, she survived with only water damage below decks. The yacht club's insurance company had to fork out a huge sum, for a refit.

The boatyard at the marina were given the job. Over a year she was refitted and modified until the £165k insurance payout was spent. The owner, who'd just made a nice few quid on some property, forked out another £100k on new sails, rigging and an engine/gearbox.

Fitted out with absolutely everything needed for gentleman cruising, including crystal wine glasses and a bridge table, she was ready for her maiden voyage to the Caribbean. She was crewed with paying customers, hoping to complete an ocean passage as part of their 'RYA Ocean masters' qualification. 'Clever Trevor with the weather' (as they referred to him) set off to cross the Atlantic as Captain and owner of a truly beautiful, luxury, seventy two feet schooner, Rich Harvest.

Sadly the Rich Harvest refit had many teething problems. She only got as far as the Scilly isles before the owner, while attempting to go astern, lost all power with a bang. The prop shaft detached and destroyed a very expensive Volvo drive system. She was going nowhere soon.

Furious, the owner demanded the boatyard take responsibility. The vessel was towed back to Holyhead and tied to a mooring. Fate played its part here, as the owner Trevor, immediately took ill, and was rushed to hospital for emergency surgery; he'd developed pancreatic problems, and quite frankly would've died, if he'd been still at sea.

While he was in hospital, a strange thing happened. Trevor's boatman, who'd been left on-board to make sure nobody came and 'tinkered' with the evidence, decided to jump ship for the night to see his girlfriend. On his return the next day, he found the boat sinking; another hour, and she would've gone down (not his girlfriend, the schooner).

Luckily, the lifeboat got pumps on in time, and she was hauled out on the trailer the boatyard had made specifically for her. The story was that a raw water pump was left disassembled while a new impellor was sourced allowing water to siphon in, but this sounded very spurious to me as the water would come in as soon as the cover was off, reminding the engineer to turn off the seacock valve at the inlet. No way would he leave while water was pouring into an engine room; I suspected the boat had been scuttled! I remind you that my assumptions are based on information gleaned, which could or could not be true.

By the time the owner came out of hospital, the vessel had received 'first aid', meaning various parts had been flushed out with fresh water, but the destroyed drive system had also been removed, making any blame or claim for damages difficult, to say the least. Subsequently, the owner had been fighting with the boatyard for a few years, while she remained there, incurring horrendous storage charges.

Somebody had agreed to buy her and stripped out quite a bit of the machinery, including the main engine cylinder head. These parts were missing after he pulled out of the sale after a disagreement. In short, the owner had been well and truly shafted, one way or another.

Probably, she'd end up as a 'distressed' boat, sold for a fraction of its worth. This accounted for the negative comments we'd been getting about her around the boatyard. Clearly someone had planned to buy her for a song, and have a birthday. Ever the one to piss on somebody's bonfire, I did some detective work, and traced the owner to Stafford.

Trevor Lyons was a university lecturer at Liverpool. We are worlds apart. First impressions were that he was a Toff, who couldn't hold a conversation without over demonstrating his very adequate command of the English language. He was tall and fit for his age, quite cool, very active, and quite knowledgeable in many subjects. He also had a private pilot's license, a light plane and good business acumen. When he told me he was a lecturer in maritime law, I explained my plans to sell goods in international waters. He was fascinated, and promised to check it out.

He explained the full story of Rich Harvest to me in every detail, but very significantly, said the vessel after refitting, was 'coded' (made legal for use on ocean charter) in 2000, and the vessel build was supervised by Lloyds. Seeing a short cut to us earning a living in the Caribbean with such a vessel, I proceeded to do a deal.

He was so traumatised by the situation in Holyhead, he refused to even go there. I explained my position, and my opinion of his chances of ever getting his yacht back, or winning anything in court. I proposed a complicated plan to buy her, which involved amongst other things, a varying price. It depended on what missing equipment turned up when we started to put her back together, and also what I negotiated the prohibitive marina fees down to.

He agreed to keep our deal secret in order not to upset the yard, or the people expecting to end up with her. Their mutual hatred would clearly have been a problem. Although the deal wouldn't be done until my funds arrived, I was keen to get on with the job. We decided to tell the marina I'd already bought her outright, so as to get unfettered access. We also stood a better chance of the missing components coming back, as they had with the Cornish Maiden.

The next day, he called me, and said he wanted to keep a share in the boat, and also wanted to partner in the offshore adventure. I thought about it for a while before I agreed. A new deal was struck. Trevor would fund the bulk of the parts I needed to rebuild the boat, and I would do, or fund the labour. When my funds arrived, I'd buy two thirds of the Rich Harvest. Some of those funds would go towards his share of stock.

I was well surprised, this seemingly 'stuffed shirt' had taken everything on-board I'd said, taken my word and agreed a partnership without a contract in sight. He was a posh gentleman with 'Bottle', something I hadn't come across before. I'd even detected a sense of humour behind his carefully poised, self-presentation.

When I shake someone's hand, it's my word and my bond. We shook hands back in 2004 and this guy Trevor went the distance.

The Rich Harvest was now to be used for the fag job, with the Cornish Maiden standing by as a backup. Then later, she'd be used in a second operation at a different location when we'd ironed out the creases in the plan. Finished, the Rich Harvest would hold its place amongst any sailing boat around the million quid mark, I couldn't wait! Significantly, the project had now turned into more than just a month or two at sea to bolster the coffers for our Caribbean adventure.

I badly wanted to piss off from the UK, and the shit that'd stuck to me from the cannabis trial. More so, I wanted revenge on the Customs and police, who'd never left me alone since then. If I was going, I was going with a bang.

My old mate John Nelson was out of the project by this time; he'd diversified into the auto diagnostic business which was picking up. He could see a future without getting his hands dirty all the time. In any case, I needed an engineer as my back was too bad for the small engine room. An engineer in his fifties called Ian drank in the Five Alls pub in Stockton. He'd been out of work for some time, but had travelled about on shut down work earning good money. For some reason, which would become apparent later, he couldn't get another job. I quickly recruited him. He was single, having gone through a bitter divorce. He agreed to a full-time deal, staying in Holyhead most of the time until the boat was finished.

I also got a bunch of painters through a mate of mine, Kev Smith. The plan was to blitz the boat in time for the summer. The accommodation on the Rich Harvest could still be classed as luxurious, so it was no problem getting help. I didn't want to get involved with local labour as I didn't yet know, who I'd upset.

Back in Teesside, Phil, my darling son, had become involved with a bad element at his school in Billingham. He'd lived with me for a few years after his mum relocated to the midlands. There were a few incidents, let's leave it at that, and I finally made the decision to take Philip out of school eighteen months early. If I hadn't, he wouldn't be the man he is today; he would've turned out an arsehole. I'd like to think this wouldn't have happened if he'd always lived with me. I had a duty to put it right. My having been on remand in such high profile circumstances clearly hadn't helped.

At fourteen he could do more than most, a competent seaman

with hundreds of hours experience at the helm. I offered to leave him in Holyhead during the week and he jumped at the chance. He was in charge of the guys I had there and reported to me. He mixed with some nice lads, had his own RHIB (rigid hull inflatable boat) and earned a wage. I hoped he'd see a different side of life in a place like that. He rose to the challenge, and revelled in the responsibility.

Everybody liked him. The lifeboat men would take him out for lobsters and crabs; he was in his element, and grew up fast. Every weekend I saw progress, it was a success. He was crew on a racing yacht, which did very well. His friend Greg lived on his father's yacht while he attended university; he was a few years older than Junior, but he had no more about him. In fact, I think he learned from Phil half the time.

Phil learned and understood all of the systems on Rich Harvest, no mean feat considering it has a 230 horsepower engine, AC 220 volt shore power, AC 220 generator, DC 12 and 24 volt alternators and charging systems, hydraulics, diving compressor, pressurised water/gas heating systems, navigational instruments, and radar. She was packed with state of the art equipment.

Better still, when my daughter and his mother sent the school's inspector down to interview him, he showed him round, demonstrating his engineering knowledge, and passed all tests with flying colours, much to their surprise. Phil Junior earned his place on-board Rich Harvest, make no mistake. I bought him a couple of black jet skis to mess about on with his friends; I thought they might be useful later, as covert 'tenders'.

All this time, I researched as much as I could on the subject of cheap tobacco. I had some big players interested, but they wanted to see the project work first. I envisaged much bigger boats in the future, and mooted buying an accommodation platform or 'Rig'. There were many such structures, soon to be decommissioned for not too much money, and mooring one off the Thames estuary looked like a possibility for the future.

Despite trawling through legislation again and again, I could still find nothing wrong with my game plan. The Rich Harvest was coming along nicely as the summer of 2004 approached. We would make a nice few quid, before 'doing one' to the Caribbean in the winter.

CHAPTER TWENTY THREE

TYRONIO

As the plan now involved two boats, I was a skipper short, and needed someone else with the 'arse' to do the job on board the Cornish Maiden. Someone who had the same mindset came to mind, someone who had an axe to grind with Customs. Where on earth would I find such a person as crazy as myself, and with nothing better to do?

I first heard about Tyronio when I arrived at Bristol Prison or HMP Horefield in 1994. Up on the top landing of our wing where all of the category A prisoners were, we'd met a couple of smugglers called Graham Bozormani 'Boris' and Nick Hammer, the 'Captain'. Both were awaiting trial for an importation of cannabis, allegedly on-board a vessel known as 'Abundance'. Customs insisted they'd thrown a large quantity overboard in a storm, under their noses.

While they waited on remand, Customs had tried everything to recover just one bale, but found nothing. Despite employing experts in storm tide prediction, and subsea search and recovery teams, a vicious storm surge had created unmapped currents around the Isle of Wight, which had distributed every bale of precious evidence, far and wide. Or so they said.

I'd introduced myself to Tyronio shortly after I arrived in Belmarsh Prison, and told him I knew his co-accused in Bristol, and all about his case. It was at least two days before he believed who I was. Completely paranoid, he thought I was an undercover plant until I repeated details of the conversations I'd had, that only a friend would know.

Over a couple of months, through Christmas and New Year, we

spent our time not getting captured smoking weed while I helped him a lot with his case. He was ghosted to Bristol for trial, and as I expected, they all got off, despite the 'High-Risk Circus' orchestrated by Customs. I considered Tyronio a friend, and promised to meet up with him when the nightmare ended. He was acquitted eight months before me.

At the launch of a pub I opened in 96, I introduced him to Smiley, a dealer, and between them they arranged a deal to buy two hundred kilo of hashish purportedly owned by his father in Amsterdam. The deal went badly wrong, with Smiley's scouse friends a quarter of a million light. Only then did I learn anything about it, and organised his rescue by contacting his father. Big Ron got his son out of deep shit, using a very big hitter known by every scouse villain. Tyronio had smuggled drugs for him in the past. He kept his distance from Smiley after that.

We kept in touch over the years, I figured he owed me, and called him regarding the vacant position, Captain of the Cornish Maiden, while I was to Captain the Rich Harvest.

For sure he had the bottle, and I was sure he wanted the money as the Polish had moved in over the years, and took the cream from the business he was in. He agreed and travelled to see us in Holyhead. He had two young kids, and I thought I could trust him. He didn't have to worry about Smiley, the heat was off, Smiley was doing a ten stretch for manslaughter.

He'd fallen for the crack pipe and given a crack head whose flat they were in, £170 for some rocks. They beat him to death after he returned wrecked some hours later without any crack. He was half-dead beforehand, and the injuries wouldn't have killed a healthy man. Smiley didn't beat him, it was his co-accused. But Smiley, worse for wear after a three day bender, helped to inject the dead guy with heroin, not knowing it'd be obvious to a pathologist.

All the same, Tyronio was lucky his father was Big Ron. Another reason I thought I could trust him was that I saved his life by giving Boris enough information to perpetrate a rescue in time.

He turned up with a dogsbody called Colin. Colin was alright, but a bit of a ding. It was clear Tyronio was mugging him into all sorts of stuff, and Colin thought the sun shone out of his arse. Tye was a tall, smooth-talking, cool sort of guy, who could hold an audience, and make them believe anything... just like his father. I'd been misled to think he was still a family man who loved his wife and kids, but they went out on the pull on their first night there. Of course that didn't affect his ability to captain the boat. I knew he'd owned a small cruiser for some time, but still overestimated his ability. Game men are hard to find. Tye had the qualities needed for the job to come. He also hated the Customs, they were his sworn enemy.

While I saw Customs as a necessary evil with good and bad, he hated them all, and I knew I could count on that. He'd come back when both boats were ready for sea. Meanwhile, I gave him all the necessary material to study for a skipper's course. What he didn't know, he could learn.

The Cornish Maiden was ready for the water, having been re-caulked from stem to stern. I learned how to caulk from an expert who'd spent years in the historic shipyard restoration facility in Hartlepool. It's a process where planks are chamfered slightly, and fixed almost together onto the frames. Oakum is a sort of horse hair wadding that is swirled and beaten into the gaps with caulking irons resembling blunt builder's chisels. This has the effect of spreading the load along every edge, resulting in a very strong hull, if it's done properly. The seams are then sealed with mastic and painted.

I'd trained a guy from Darlington to do it on the Kandy in Teesside, and left him down there to get on with it. I returned three weeks later and had to pull it all out again. I didn't pay him, and he made his own way back from Holyhead. Junior and I did it together, and what a job we made of it. John's paintwork was brilliant; she was a far cry from the derelict boat we first saw.

The locals were all warning us to get spare bilge pumps on standby. "All wooden boats leak for a few days till the timbers swell," they kept repeating. I refused the offer of pumps and organised the lift in.

Most wooden boats do leak for a while, but only when they've been botched and patched by fishermen or cheap labour, for owners who are quite happy with a bit of ingress. The pumps are on most of the time anyway. Not me, I like to sleep at night, knowing there's no water filling up my boat. A bit of water slopping about in the bilges is good for the wood, but there's a limit.

She was dropped into the water and the beautiful Gardner engine purred into life. We could barely hear it run on tick over. We were directed to a mooring belonging to the marina behind where Rich Harvest was still out on the hard, meaning we could keep an eye on her.

I'd had a disagreement with the Boss, Ed, and his number two, Dick Ed, over charges amongst other things. I also knew by now, I'd stolen the Rich Harvest from under their noses. Their wheeze had failed, now they wanted money, and as much as they could get.

We tied to the mooring with a light line, the boat swung as expected with the current, and I nosed her forward to connect the chain. Clunk clunk, I dropped her into neutral in a split second, but we were still in the shit, the propeller had picked up something nasty; we had no drive. The stern, now snagged, caused the boat to swing round snapping the light line tied to the bow.

Luckily, Junior and I don't go anywhere without an anchor on deck, tied and ready for deployment at a moment's notice, just for such circumstances. In it went and we let out enough slack so that she swung on the snagged prop, but would be safe when she came off.

I borrowed a dry suit from John Walsh who'd been sitting on his work boat watching the spectacle. He told me that mooring was not supposed to be there, and had moved in a storm. If he'd known they were sending me there, he would've stopped me. I asked why they'd directed me there, and he just said, "You'll find out soon enough, I put a price in to clear around there months ago."

I went down only a few metres to the bottom. There were wire strops sticking out of the seabed, one of which was wrapped around our prop. I cut it off, but it took a couple of hours. I checked the seabed for a route out into deeper water and a clear mooring. Later, shackled on safely, we went below to find she'd taken zero water; we locked up and took the RHIB ashore, and on to the pub.

It was a pretty proud day launching the first of our fleet; we had high expectations of the months to come. Of course, we'd fallen for the oldest trick in the book. In some ports, harbours and marinas all over the world, they have areas known to the local boatmen as 'no go' zones as far as navigation, mooring or anchoring is concerned.

Usually this means uncharted obstructions, or quite often foul ground, where anchoring is risky. It's not just for the private sector of small yachts, as in this case. This practice also generates huge spontaneous income for the ports and associated businesses when big ships get stuck too. Some marinas will quite often direct you into tight spots in high winds, hoping for a little damage to occur.

If the ship snags her anchor, the cost of recovery can exceed £100k; the cost to replace it, up to £1mill. If the anchor slips in high winds, and picks up another ship's chain, the cost of local tugs to resolve the problem is unlimited. Worse still, there's nothing better than a shipwreck to boost the local economy of a port. From salvage to pollution control, the cheques keep coming.

In our case, the mooring was only a one ton rating that'd moved in bad weather while tied to a boat too big for it. It rested in an area totally unsuitable for anything more than two feet of draft. There were a number of old steel wire strops sticking up, left over from a salvage operation. There we guessed, it was left for unsuspecting yachtsmen who arrive out of office hours.

The chart shows plenty of water where there's a mooring buoy. Rather than enter the marina and tie up on a random berth, only to be moved again when the office opens, a skipper might tie to it. Snagging such a heavy wire would've caused major damage to a yacht's propeller gear, resulting in a diver, a lift out and a nice few quid for the boatyard.

Not so, with the Cornish Maiden, I'd been going very slow and knocked her into neutral as soon as I heard the clunk. Her prop was massive for the type of boat, and well over engineered. There was no permanent damage.

If I hadn't deployed a light line first and engaged forward to nudge up to the buoy to attach the chain, we'd have remained on only a one ton mooring. Had the weather picked up, she'd have blown aground onto the rocks. I wasn't a happy chappy; we'd had a lucky escape, the devious bastards, whoever they were.

By now, we'd found a seacock (valve) hiding below the main generator support plate, deep in the engine room bilges of Rich Harvest, which was still open. There was nothing connected, it was just spare. We concluded this had been the cause of the partial sinking the last time she was in the water.

We had no proof of this, but the plot thickened. It could have been opened after she was hauled out, but why? As a matter of course, all seacocks are checked, lubricated and rewired to the anode system before re-launch. Anybody who doesn't do that is asking for trouble. Saying that, some don't!

To be safe, I directed that one person be on watch for both boats at all times until we were gone from there, and set up a couple of cameras to watch them, watching us. There were forces at work, I was sure.

CHAPTER TWENTY FOUR

TWO BOATS AND A PLAN

The deal had come through for my land, which was all that was left of my salvage business. I'd sold an option some years before and received a nice cheque every year. I fought to get outline planning permission, despite the surrounding sites already having it. There were some sneaky goings on, but I'd put a master plan into action.

My old pal Jimmy Mason, a relative of some well-known travellers in the area and as hard as a coffin nail, was having a tough time. I consider him one of a handful of true friends. The same age as me, we'd had more than the occasional drink together at various clubs and pubs on the famous Stockton nightlife scene, before it was destroyed by pedestrianisation.

Before my incarceration, he'd spent many a night partying at my house. Quite often, he would pull me aside and say, "What are you doing with these low life pond skaters in your house?"

Granted, the parties were getting out of hand, but business was booming in the scrap and salvage business. "Networking, Jim," I'd reply.

Some of the guests brought their own guests to show how cool they were. It was hard to deny them entry. Just about everybody would try to gain favour, and put 'business' my way. It was the nineties, it was getting out of hand, we had everything from wealthy businessmen to gangsters cling-ons. It was wild!

I got on well with Jimmy's late father, a shrewd auto spares operator from way back. They knew how to 'make a shilling', as they say. Jimmy married a lovely girl Sadie, who not only kept a lovely house, two lads and a full-time job, she kept him on the straight and narrow. Well, as much as she could, considering he was 'cousins' to some of the most famous hell raisers in the North East. Jimmy always went to graft and provided. He could be trusted.

Regulations had strangled his skip hire business. He'd found himself without a premises to operate on, and no chance soon of getting one. My site had been a scrap yard since God was lad, and as such had an automatic permit for such activities. I didn't ask him £250 a week or more; I dealt him at £40 a week. He needed a break, I knew he'd appreciate it, and he wouldn't forget.

I encouraged him to make a mess, which he did. Nobody would be buying any property off plan with Jimmy operating next door. He pulled himself back on his feet by changing the landscape and building mounds of rubble. Every effort was made to shut Jimmy down, resulting in a public enquiry that found against him but by then planning permission had come through.

I got a good deal, and now I had a nice few quid legitimately in the bank. By now Trevor had changed his mind and wanted to retain 50% of Rich Harvest and the venture. He had performed as promised, so I agreed. I was in no position to argue, as the boat was done. A bill of sale and money changed hands. Now I owned 100% of Cornish Maiden and 50% of Rich Harvest. All I had to do was negate a large part of the fees in the marina at Holyhead. This required a cunning plan.

No way were they putting her in the water until a large chunk of cash had changed hands. The ballooning bill had been designed to beat Trevor into submission. Trevor had taken this into consideration when dealing, so any money saved was for both of us.

At this stage, Trevor was in a better position to sue the boatyard for faulty workmanship. During the repairs we discovered the true reason why the drive had failed so spectacularly. The replacement aqua-drive system had arrived new; it was exactly the same model number of the original.

When it was fitted into place with the original mountings, it was found to be way outside the safe operating angles it was designed to compensate for. In short, this device is used to join up the engine and gearbox to the prop shaft and propeller. Where it had been fitted, it was bound to fail.

Furthermore, the unit was a metric version and the prop shaft was an old imperial measurement in diameter. The clamp adjoining the two was designed for two exactly equal diameters. The aqua-drive unit had almost destroyed itself within a few hundred miles, but when she was put astern with a clunk, the clamp failed, causing terminal damage. Without a doubt, this was the fault of the engineers who installed the machinery.

Armed with this information, Junior on standby, I went to the office porta-cabin to meet with the owner and his opo. I was midway through my accusations and threats to enlighten Trevor, when just as planned, Junior rang me, pretending to be somebody wanting a part number. I said I'd go back to the boat and get it, pretending to hang up, and left my phone on the desk. Junior was recording the conversation while I was out of the office.

Armed with the information we gained on tape, I negotiated the fees down from £15k to £4k. The cash was paid up and the schooner Rich Harvest was ready for the water at last. It was a brilliant move, and no more than they deserved.

The big rusty boat transporter rumbled into action. It hadn't moved for four years and took some work to get everything freed off, but eventually she was almost floating when I came very close to being cut in half. They'd failed to disconnect one of the steel strops holding her on the platform.

When she floated, only one strop was holding sixty seven tons of boat. It parted with a bang just after I saw it stressing. Luckily this gave me a split second to jump back almost clear; I caught only a fraction of the impact to the abdomen. It could have been a lot worse. For a boatyard whose forklift's brake was a piece of wood used to chock the wheels, something like this was to be expected.

Both the Cornish Maiden and Rich Harvest were moved to the safety of the pontoons in the marina, although the miserable sods couldn't provide electricity. All systems checked, we went to the pub to celebrate, leaving a watchman on-board at all times from then on.

Trevor declared that he wanted his son Vinnie to be his representative, as he was too busy to participate. Vinnie apparently knew Rich Harvest well, so I could understand his place, also he was there to look after Trevor's interests. But Trevor also wanted Vinnie's mate Ben and his daughter's boyfriend Tim on-board. He exaggerated their abilities, to say the least.

A few days later Vinnie and Ben turned up, but Tim was to join us as soon as possible. They were two pretty good lads it seemed. They also turned up with a big bag of some excellent weed. It transpired a grow room had been set up between a bunch of friends at college, and this had got out of hand, leaving a surplus nobody was interested in selling.

"Welcome aboard," I said. "What's that funny smell, lads?"

"It's weed, Captain. Do we have permission, Captain?"

I liked being called Captain, especially by the other owner's son, who had no preconceived ideas he was any better than the rest. He owed his dad a few quid, and this escapade, was to pay it off.

"I'll have to sample it first," I said. "I don't want any shight on this boat. If it's crap, you're sailing in the Cornish Maiden."

Immediately this broke the ice, and they realised I was cool with it. Tyronio and Colin were next to arrive from Selsey. We sat around the big oak table in the aft saloon of Rich Harvest with a few beers, and smoked a little skunk, while I laid out the plan.

A small, little known pair of islands 29 miles from the German coastline with a population of less than 1,200 was our destination. Helgoland had at one time been owned variously by Denmark and Germany, but was taken by the British in the Napoleonic war in 1807 and ceded to the UK in the treaty of Kiel with Denmark in 1914. It became a hotbed of smuggling and espionage against Napoleon's forces and attracted all sorts of dodge-pots, due to its loose rule.

Eventually it was effectively swopped with Zanzibar, an African island owned by Germany. In 1926, it became a seaside spa and retreat for the German upper class, before it played a role as a naval base. In the Second World War, we bombed the shit out of it, and covered the area in mines.

After the war in 1947, the British set off the largest single non-nuclear explosion in history by detonating six thousand seven hundred tons of TNT in what was then described as the 'big bang'. The intention was to blow the place off the chart so it couldn't be used as a base again against our forces, but that didn't happen. It would take a lot more than that!

The explosion created a third island (the middle land). Next, it was used as a bombing range for a number of years before the Germans were given it back in 1952. It took years to make the place safe again as it was riddled with unexploded ordinance.

To put the place back on its feet, it was awarded a special tax status, which attracted banks and shell companies keen to exploit the system. Ferries arrived daily from other European countries to buy tobacco and alcohol at a fraction of the mainland price.

There was no port big enough for them, so an armada of small boats would ferry the passengers ashore for the afternoon and back again. A ferry runs daily from the mainland for only passengers; cars or bikes are not allowed. A few electric vehicles and a police car are all you'll find there.

A friend of mine had already been a couple of times, until he eventually lost his boat and cargo trying to enter the UK via the Humber River, but our plan was better. I'd already been to have a look, driving through Dover with Tye. The fags were as little as £6 a sleeve and a good bottle of spirit from £3. Although the North Sea can be wicked, this was the ideal destination, much closer than the likes of Gibraltar.

It looked like Ballymory, a children's show on the TV, with brightly painted houses in rows around the port. Not much went on there as far as nightlife or entertainment, it mostly stopped when the ships left, but it was clearly used by some dodgy Germans, up to a bit of fiddling. I quite liked the place, it had potential. We planned to turn up with a big wad of cash, and fill the boat to the gunnels.

CHAPTER TWENTY FIVE

THE JOURNEY BEGINS

The team were as follows: Myself and Junior would travel on-board Rich Harvest with Vinnie and Ben along with Ian as engineer. Greg, Junior's pal whom he raced with, also came along. He had a day skipper certificate, so he had to be good enough to be a watch leader, or so we thought. He'd finished university for that year and needed a few quid for the holidays, so I put him on a wage. Everyone was excited about the upcoming adventure, including me.

We partied hard the night before we set sail. This is always a stupid thing to do, but there you go. Tye and Colin, who were taking the Cornish Maiden, went off to bag the two delightful ladies they'd had before. Meanwhile, we crawled the local watering holes, culminating in a party back on-board, for anyone still standing.

I very nearly ended up in bed with a very nice girl; she was blinded by the booze, our apparent daring, and the size of my 'vessel'. This came to an abrupt halt when she mentioned John Walsh was a relative. Leaving the next day or not, I wasn't about to upset that man! I had visions of angry carrots chanting Welsh, torches burning, sinking boats and burning crucifixion, enough to douse any erection. I'd been faithful up till then, even though my live in girl wasn't while I was absent; it would've been no more than she deserved.

Next day, all fuzzy and hung-over (but also proud of my restraint), we loaded the last of the supplies on-board. I sold my jeep to one of the lifeboat lads, and we were off, both together. We cast off with dozens of friends we'd made taking to their boats to wave us goodbye, horns sounding, flags flying, cameras rolling. Our intended mission was no secret amongst our friends, but I'm sure most didn't take us seriously. Bullshit is abundant in every marina; my own adventures are often doubted, who can blame them really?

To be honest, my heart was in my mouth. This was more than an adventure for me, it was revenge and mischief on a massive scale, for the thirty year persecution I'd suffered because of one bent, vindictive copper's false and malicious intelligence which had spiralled out of control as he attained a higher rank.

The others thought it was a stand against HMRC's absurd tax on goods, an exciting way to earn serious money, and have a jaw-dropping story to tell for the rest of their lives. None of us had any idea of what was to come.

Just outside of the harbour, the main engine warning indicator sounded. I didn't need to check gauges; I pulled up the hatch and saw steam spewing from under the header tank. We had a flotilla with us, we'd built up a reputation of professionalism, and had the admiration of the community for what we'd achieved. I really didn't want to look like an idiot by returning to port!

I called for Ian, who ignored me until I dropped the hatch with a bang. He went into the engine compartment, and found a hose between the water pump and cylinder head that had blown off under pressure.

"We'll have to go back to fix it," he shouted above the noise of machinery.

"Like hell we will!" I yelled. "You, useless bastard, you told me it was done and tested, you're staying down there till it's fixed. We've got sails."

I was furious; I'd asked him three times whether he'd run up the machinery under full load while we were tied up. Clearly he hadn't. We were barely at half throttle when it blew. Like I said, bullshit in abundance!

We set the sails, and instructed the Cornish Maiden to carry on course, as we'd be sailing with the wind. A couple of hours later, it was dark and the engine fired up again; this time with the hose on correctly. It was bigger at one end, but the dozy bastard had forced the little end onto the big pipe and thus, the big end onto the little pipe. It was about this time I realised why Ian wasn't still earning big money. He came out of the engine room, and asked to be stood down.

I'd set the rules on alcohol, but he wanted a drink. I thought he was shaking because of the pressure of working in a confined space with the machinery running; it's not easy at any time, especially at sea under way. I refused, and told him to stand by in his overhauls for an hour to make sure nothing else was wrong. We had a long night ahead, and my confidence was waning.

One mess up is too many at sea, and definitely too many to be qualifying for an early drink! He was the engineer after all. He'd been having an easy few quid living on site for the last four months, getting to the pub early doors every night. He'd had the life of flipping Riley, and now, now it was time to work. My reputation, and quite a few quid, was seriously at stake.

I set him a list of stuff I wanted reports on, a long list. But, he simply couldn't operate; he couldn't think. I mistakenly deduced it was seasickness, and he was too hard to admit it, so I offered him pills. By now it was 2100h, some five hours after he was normally in the pub, religiously!

Why I'd not realised months earlier, I don't know. Ian would sometimes meet up with us during the evening, but it was rare. He'd rather go from pub to pub, and was usually back on-board, in bed by ten. Occasionally, we'd seen him bouncing off the walls of the galley, stuffing any food into his face before staggering off to his cabin, but I thought he'd just had one too many. He'd become a bit too fond of his beer, to say the least.

I'd surprised them all by counting the beers (no matter how many there were) and having them stashed away. For hundreds of years, rum was rationed and mixed with water to make 'grog'. To let sailors drink more than their ration is a recipe for big trouble, not on my ship! The reason an alcoholic goes from pub to pub is so nobody actually knows when he starts and when he stops, or how much he necks in total.

Once I was sure, I had to make a decision; Ian was no good to man or beast in the state he was in. He was rattling like a road drill big time. The only sensible solution was to give him a drink. In five minutes, he necked three large cans of Stella Artois, and was back to normal functioning.

Clearly he'd been operating pissed for months. All we needed to do was make sure he was supervised and we still had a useful crew member (as long as we had enough beer). I missed my old mate Nelson. We both liked a drink, but it was always after graft!

The auto-pilot set, with one person on watch, we sat down for a debriefing. I informed the crew they'd be sailing on their own. I'd watch and only intervene if absolutely necessary. This was a training exercise. I made Phil Junior a watch leader and Greg the same with six hour shifts, or watches as they're called at sea. I wanted checks done, and logs updated on everything from the bilges to the ice in the freezer.

You need some order when you're passage making. It's not the same as cruising when you're in a marina every night, or anchoring in shelter, soaking up the sunshine in tranquillity. When I'm going somewhere, I only stop when I have to.

It's hard at sea, especially the North Sea. It's different when the weather's nice, but it's harsh most of the time. When sailing, there should be no hiding in the wheelhouse. When I'm in charge, if you're on watch, you're outside where you can see. No exceptions. You get a suit on, and get out there!

I'd be asking questions. I wanted charts plotted, bang up to date hourly, with positions derived from other than the GPS on-board, which would be switched off until I wanted to check the accuracy of their plots, positions and calculations.

I wanted everyone on-board to learn the 'ropes' (bar Ian). This wasn't a holiday; the job of Skipper was up for grabs. My back was giving me hell. I needed a rest sometime soon, and I needed to know if my crewmates were up to the task.

The vast majority of sailors never leave sight of land. They dilly-dally around inshore during daylight, and then go back into the yacht club bar for a gin and tonic. Not me. I don't coast hop, I take the shortest route, and deliberately stay away from land. My old pal Jock is pushing ninety and was a very capable sailor who signed on at age twelve as the cook on his father's fishing boat they raced under sail back to Grimsby to get the best price. He once said to me, "Waves don't sink boats, Phil, rocks sink boats!" I learned a lot from Jock.

I know I'm a pretty good sailor, but I'm not as good as him! Another of his favourite sayings as he checked a boat from stem to stern before taking command was, "It's a boat! The idea is to keep the water oot." Priceless, that man, absolutely priceless! Not many men I listen to, but I have all the time in the world for him.

Back at sea, the 'young uns' were looking a bit worse for wear. Phil Junior was too young to go out drinking too much, so he was in his element, and couldn't believe the opportunity of taking charge. He took charge, showing up our badly hung-over wimps as the weather worsened during the night. I was proud of him. He was nearly fifteen, and as much of a man as any of the others.

We never heard any more from the Cornish Maiden, but assumed she'd made good time, as she was out of range of the VHF radio.

Our schooner Rich Harvest performed beautifully; she was gracefully stable in all kinds of shitty seas. Before long, we were on our approach to Plymouth, where we'd pick up another of Trevor's nominated representative's, Tim. Or as we named him later, 'Nice but Dim, Tim'.

As a Navy base, there're all kinds of navigational rules and routes we were not familiar with, which always means a look at the pilot book, a source of information purchased in advance by prudent yachtsmen, which gives precise details about harbours and ports along your route. All the information you need is in it.

In the vast majority of situations, 'Motor gives way to sail'. Not in Plymouth, especially if you have a warship coming or going. Then it's a nightmare. Armed security RHIBs were bombing about, variously shouting orders at us.

Anyone would think we were packed with explosives, trying to intercept a heavily armed ship while doing only seven knots! We had heated words on the radio, until we ignored them when we realised they were taking the piss, and using us an example or a training exercise. Finally we contacted the marina as we entered port, asking for a berth for the night.

The wind was blowing about a six as we approached the entrance to the marina. A boatman came out in a small RHIB to show us the way in (and get a tip). As we sailed past the marina wall before the entrance, I saw the berth they'd given us. I intervened, spinning the wheel round, just in time.

The boatman on the radio asked what the problem was.

I said back, "Looks like a bloody expensive day out, that mate!"

Typical marina bullshit. The chances of getting in there, in that weather, without causing damage, was about 50-50. We went back into the harbour, and tied to a mooring buoy. We had the RHIB in the water in no time. Tim was picked up and came aboard. Still, we had no sign of Tyronio, Colin, or the Cornish Maiden.

After a couple of hard days at sea, the crew asked for shore leave. I was in no position to deny it, due to the fact they'd plied me with skunk cannabis as soon as we'd tied to the buoy and finished checks. Ian made for his beer and bunk, while Phil Junior and I stayed on-board.

Junior would have to remain compos in order to collect them by RHIB. Typical student mentality meant they'd get pissed, but hey, so what? We were on a mission; they knew time ashore would be a rarity in the near future.

True to form, the next morning I had a boat full of useless twats. Greg was lost ashore and efforts were made to trace him. Eventually we got him back to the boat, along with bits and pieces we needed. Tim had been sold to me by Trevor as "training to be an outward bound instructor, who consequently, will have all the skills necessary for the job". Oh really!

The reality was Trevor knew he was an arsehole, and wanted him away from his daughter Victoria, who had no idea he was a knob who tried to shag anything in sight. He placed him on-board to punish him, I'm sure. He knew he'd fail, and ultimately would have to grovel, and remain in Trevor's shadow. Only my opinion.

There he was, bragging about some tart, in the presence of his girlfriend's brother Vinnie, who didn't seem best pleased. They'd also got into a fight, because he'd been bumping his gums at some Navy guys.

I had plans for Tim; his face didn't fit. I immediately saw him as a haversack, who you don't want to be relying on at all, never mind in the North Sea. These were educated lads, from good families, not arseholes without a future. I was about to put him in the picture, when the Cornish Maiden sounded her horn.

She tied up next to us, coming aboard to a full English breakfast before recounting their tale. It transpired we'd nearly killed them. I'd fitted a GPS plotter (the same as a sat-nav) to her. Before they set off, I directed Greg, to input the 'waypoints' or positions to aim for, onto the machine to give them the course to steer, each in sections or 'legs'. Almost catastrophically, Greg had seriously messed up. He had them heading for a very, very bad wrecking on the rocks.

They'd been happily motoring along in the dark on the course directed by the GPS, until the lighthouse became too close for comfort. Luckily they realised the GPS waypoint was behind the rocks they were heading for. In the nick of time they changed course with half a metre of water under them to spare. I didn't believe it at first, and sent Junior with Greg to check it.

We've had GPS on boats since 1990; it's easy to see the data stored in the memory. Sure enough, they seemed to be telling the truth. Greg was devastated, white as a ghost. Everyone could see he was mortified.

Tye wouldn't let go. "You nearly killed us, you twat. I've got kids at home, you twat!"

If only to placate Tye, Greg was demoted while Vinnie was appointed watch leader. When you're planning a passage or plotting a course, you do it at least twice, and check it on a chart, so if it all goes tits up with the GPS, you can go back to getting compass bearings to navigate.

They also lost all electrical power shortly after the near miss, and made for port where they stayed overnight. Next day, a handy sort of 'sea gypsy' discovered the alternator had not been wired correctly. I'd bought new batteries and had the alternator reconditioned before it was refitted by our resident piss pot, Ian. He blamed his eyes. I couldn't demote him, that'd mean me in the engine room.

While we headed to Helgoland, Tye was to take her to Chichester near his home. The plan was to do beer and tobacco runs to Dieppe in France, taking groups of 'shoppers' over for a jolly, legally filling the hold with pallets of beer and wine. Upon notification, they would steam north to Hartlepool, as a backup plan.

She could also carry twelve passengers to and from the Rich Harvest, and provide support for crew changes and supplies. We parted company. Next stop, Helgoland.

Out in the English Channel, I could see the wind was blowing hard, the sea was rough, and this was a good opportunity to put both boat and crew through their paces. By rights, you should reef (reduce the area) the sails when the wind's up, but the sails and rigging should also be able to stand it. I noticed nobody was calling for reefing, and let them carry on until it was too late.

We were howling along, crashing through angry stacks of water pushed up by the gale. The bow was diving under the weight of the huge foresail, then bursting up, sending waves crashing over the cockpit. Greg described it to his father later as, "An ocean of water in the cockpit." Much to their horror, I brought her about time and time again, to the point of broaching. After four hours of total madness, I was confident of the sails and rigging, so I spilt some wind to make life more comfortable.

My crew were gobsmacked, shaking their heads at me.

"What the hell was that all about, Captain?" Vinnie asked.

I told them it was better to have something go bang here, where we can get rescued and get repairs, than to find out later, when we can't. "We also find out which shitty arsed rats scurry for cover," I said, "leaving their shipmates to struggle, DON'T WE TIM?"

Donna had also jumped aboard for her first and last trip. She was petrified, and wanted to get off. Not a chance! I'd known for weeks she'd been misbehaving while I'd been away in Holyhead, and she was on her way out, but she had no idea I knew. I convinced her it would be nice and easy. I thought a bit of 'justice' would do her good! I also had a warm bed and a galley slave for the duration of the voyage. Sound selfish? It was the least I could do!

Being hung-over and seasick is a hell of a combination; one aggravates the other. I learned this many years ago, but it doesn't matter how many times you tell them, it's just the way it is. When you're seasick, you want to die. I've seen grown men offer a month's wages to cut short a day's deep sea angling (I was that skipper who refused it). My crew looked like shit, so I sent them all to bed while I did the graveyard shift myself, knowing Junior could take over, and I could rely on him while I slept in the morning.

I checked the charts, routes and calculations, and discovered Greg was taking us miles off the shortest course. I pulled him out of his cot to explain himself.

"We've got to stay clear of these rigs, this gas field," he said. "It's dangerous," pointing to a section of the chart where a dozen or so rigs were located.

I pointed out to him that these 'rigs' were permanently stationed some five miles apart, and were lit up like Blackpool. They all had a safety boat, a hospital, doctors, some even had a helicopter. "What the hell is dangerous?" I said. "A blind man in a snow storm could navigate through them without a compass. If shit happens, you're in the right place, matey. Set a course through them, and piss off back to bed."

These 'yachtsmen' who do a short 'zero to hero' RYA course to get a qualification are not worth a damn without common sense and experience.

Our ETA came forward by fifteen hours as we sailed through the 'dangerous' gas rigs and on to our dream land of cheap fags and booze. A couple of days of hard sailing in the bleak North Sea later, we entered an area teaming with wildlife, and then the harbour of the crazy little place that is Helgoland.

There was no marina as such, so we tied up on a dock wall as directed by the harbour master, not the nicest place to be, but okay. An hour or two later, a storm from hell came in. We stayed up and battled all night, bursting a few inflatable fenders while trying to keep her off the wall as the swell pitched us up and down, like a sixty seven ton cork.

The bastards in the port office knew the score. They know which way the swell enters the port depending on the conditions, but they were pretty surprised when they discovered we'd no damage. I'd deployed the RHIB to take some heavy lines and anchors across the dock to hold us off the wall, and winched up on them to reduce movement.

After twenty four hours non-stop howl, our only damage was four fenders. They moaned about the lines, the anchors, and our generator exhaust polluting the water. Nice friendly bunch these Germans, I thought. At least the boatyard wasn't getting a cent from us, nice try though. You need your wits about you in these places!

CHAPTER TWENTY SIX

HELGOLAND / HELIGOLAND

The sun came up on a completely different island the next day. The storm had passed, and judging by the locals' reaction, it was a common occurrence. We later saw pictures of the whole place covered in horizontal ice, where the seawater had frozen in the wind. This was not the place to be in the winter that much was for sure.

That day however, large ferries were arriving from all over, dropping anchor in the shelter of the islands, before deploying dozens of small motor boats to ferry the passengers ashore. A flotilla of local rowing boats swarmed around to ease the congestion, and line the pockets of the boatmen. The place was buzzing with bargain hunters, racing around like ants in a rubbish bin. Clearly, every day was like the 'Boxing Day' sales in Helgoland. I sent the crew ashore to get the best prices for what was on offer.

We had a large amount of cash on-board; I wondered if this would change their attitude towards us. Before they went scouting, I gave them all a serious talking to trying to explain that we were there on business, with a British flagged boat, in a place we tried to blow to smithereens after we'd hammered the Nazis into submission. "Some of the surviving Nazis are likely to be living here now!" I said. "For Pete's sake, behave yourselves please. The next nearest place is two thousand miles away!"

Each had a set amount of cash with instructions to split up, trawl the place, get as much information as possible, and see who could get the best deal by the end of the day. The prize was shore-leave, and light duties for the duration of the stay. Phil Junior won hands down. I took him everywhere and taught him well. He knows how to do a deal. From age eleven I'd take him to the trade market, and stock him with all sorts of stuff to sell at school during breaks. His only competition was the kids whose parents worked at the local crisp factory. Business got that good the school decided to open a tuck shop, and asked him to run it.

Out there on the island, he also found out some very interesting information, which paled the others' efforts into insignificance.

It transpired that Helgoland had a large stock of old cigarettes, soon to become relatively worthless, due to the fact that the warnings on the packets were not up to spec for European countries. In a matter of days, they would have to export these fags outside of Europe. They were already significantly cheaper than new stock, but the potential for a deal increased greatly, with my little man's detective work.

Furthermore, although there were many shops, they had limited stocks. Only a few big fish imported, and held the island's stock. As usual, they'd have all the power in such a small place. I'd need to speak with these men soon. The shopkeepers were variously acting out a standard strategy, ringing the prices.

Some would pull us aside, acting all secret and clandestine; as if the whole place didn't already know what we were up to. A large German Customs cutter entered and docked across from us. Our camera trained on them, theirs on us.

Rather than play silly games, I went to the Customs office and spoke to the director, who listened very carefully as I explained our intentions. To say he was surprised would be an understatement. I could see him calculating the ramifications for Helgoland, if what I said was true. Technically, boat owners could buy as much as they wanted, and do the same off mainland Europe.

These guys were used to tracking down smugglers. I told him he didn't need to tie up his patrol boat, crew or cameras. He/they were quite welcome aboard at any time. I left the office and him, flummoxed. I'm sure the telephone lines of the German Customs headquarters were busy that day. Some high rankers arrived by helicopter with half a dozen suits. We were followed everywhere from then on.

All of the local shopkeepers started to put up and 'ring' their prices. My next stop was an old local, we shall call him Hanzfag, who ran a very successful import business. I introduced myself, and sat down to talk. He was fascinated with the plan, which opened up all sorts of possibilities for his operation.

I told him we would need a partner, someone we could trust. We didn't want to be coming here every time we sent a boat to restock. We wanted co-operation for mutual benefit. This place had less people on it than Holyhead. I'd found Helgoland's 'John Walsh'.

He took the bait, the prices came down, and every shopkeeper was allowed to sell us old stock. I decided to draft, translate and print a flyer which introduced us, telling we had informed Customs, and were openly buying old and new stock for our venture. It worked; I gave a deadline and allowed them to think we were close to our quota. Some of the shopkeepers defected from the new lower fixed prices, and offered even better deals, but only in the dark!

Clearly Hanzfag was playing his cards close to his chest, but that was to be expected, we'd only just met. Time and good business bring prices down; we were still paying over the odds, but needed to earn trust. I also had some other ideas about re-stocking, but knew I could get stuff here with a clear profit margin without delays. In a completely new business, you're learning all the time.

Tim was trying desperately to get out of the trip back. Donna had suffered enough, and frankly so had I (of her), so we arranged a flight home for her and then Tim, who by now had managed to find a strong enough reason to flee, a relative was ill. He'd been very unhappy, finding it tough going. Clearly sailing was not going to be his chosen speciality; however the experience counted towards his intended qualification.

The Rich Harvest was almost full and we still had deals pending. Various repairs and further work was completed, including re-lining three huge water tanks running above the keel totalling five thousand litres. Vinnie, always as game as a badger, had been inside them with buckets of watery plaster. When he came out, the only solution was to throw him in the dock to save blocking up the shower drains. He wasn't like his dad; he made a big effort to be 'one of the lads'.

In all, we were there ten days. We had money to change, but again, the money shops were 'ringing' the rate, so I tried a different tack, paying by debit card. That didn't please the shopkeepers, who were trying to get rid of their old stock. By rights, they could write it off, and here they had people buying it for cash. The last thing they wanted was to put it through the books. Very soon, I could pay in Great British pounds, and let them haggle about the exchange rate themselves.

I also got a large amount of Euros from the bank, direct through my account from Trevor. He'd been a bit cautious, waiting for us to test the water. Then after consulting Vinnie, he transferred his end. Who could blame him? The plan was unique!

Vinnie and Ben also invested some money of their own. Just how two students had cash to spare would seem a mystery to most, but these two were pretty astute, despite their propensity to smoke copious amounts of high quality weed. They were both good 'crack' (interesting to talk to), Vinnie was clearly missing his girl, but never once complained, he just got on with it all and was a credit to his pop.

Ben, on the other hand, couldn't give a damn; he was a surfer sort of guy, who made great effort to appear as laid back as possible. Just having the sheer arse to be on the boat commanded respect from me, and I remember being just as daft when I was a student. A single lad, he was busting for a woman, but Helgoland was definitely not a land of milk and pussy. He tried his best and came close, but his lack of German, and his stoner attitude beat him numerous times.

Phil Junior was having a ball; he got his good looks from his dad. He was followed around constantly by a few local girls his age. When I quizzed him, he said they ran away when he tried to talk to them. I deduced they weren't interested in his looks or the big roll of Euros in his sky rocket, they were simply spies for the cigarette traders, but I didn't tell him. He'd soon learn by himself.

Greg was learning another side to life. He thought he was a bit of a tearaway in Holyhead, and liked to hold court with a few stories of his antics. After listening to many an after dinner drawl in the Rich Harvest saloon, he'd learned his place, but was clearly looking forward to the fame this trip would bring him for many years to come. He couldn't handle his beer, and quite often made a prat of himself, but accepted the ritual ribbing the next morning. Again, he had the sheer arse to be on board, no mean feat by any standard. For that, he has to be respected.

The Customs patrol boat never moved, watching us constantly, and I don't mean covertly. We were getting close to departure. Everyone was itching to get on with it, but the weather forecast was shitty. The North Sea can be an evil place. Even on a biggish yacht like ours, it was going to be an uncomfortable trip back to Hartlepool.

The last night approached. The crew went out for a final crack at the very limited nightlife while we took a large delivery of 'Blonde Fanny' (Golden Virginia rolling tobacco), and stashed it in the aft water tank for a rainy day.

The vessel was full of fags and booze of all makes and brands. We wanted it to be like an offshore shop, instead of an obvious staging post, with only the usual smuggled brands, such as Lambert and Butler and Benson and Hedges. I sent Junior to pay the harbour master, and collect the final stores, and I notified people in the UK of our imminent departure next day.

At 0400h I heard a distant commotion, I went topside to see my trusty crew trotting up in a right state. They'd been to the only club on the island, high up on the 'upper land', another level above the shopping streets. In time-honoured fashion, they'd got ratted, and started singing 'Rule Britannia' and other such inflammatory songs to wind up the locals, who responded quite understandably, by hurling rocks at them on the steps down to the town.

My crew retaliated and threw some back, resulting in an angry gang, swelling at each turn into a lynch mob, chanting anti-British insults, and scavenging makeshift weapons on route to our boat. I could see it was going to get pretty shitty, I wasn't about to let them pelt our boat, even if the crew got below safe. Phil Junior gawped in disbelief as I snapped out orders to make ready certain equipment to repel boarders and marauders. We already had a loose plan to ignite a pool of petrol with the flare gun, when the Customs boat lit up like a Christmas tree. Her horn sounded general quarters, while blinding searchlights lit up the motley gang on the dockside. They stopped in their tracks, and scuttled into the darkness.

I'd contemplated staying another day, but somehow; I thought we'd better do one, bright and early!

There was no point ragging them in that state, I couldn't get a straight answer. As usual, it was blamed on the other parties as the aggressors, and my innocent crew were vastly outnumbered, etc, etc. I sent them to bed awaiting the wake up call. Next morning, bright and early, we fired up the motor, slipped the lines, and headed into the cruel North Sea to escape the impending official investigation into the first British and German conflict on the German Byte since world war two, for Pete's sake!

The wind, on our nose was staying there for at least thirty six hours. I set a dog-leg course for two reasons: first, to use the wind, second, to give the Customs boat following us, as hard a time as possible.

Their sleek aluminium patrol boat was designed to go fast, and would've been quite happy banging head on at speed. On our course, they were rolling from gunwale to gunwale almost horizontally to hold station at the speed we were going. We had a seventeen ton keel and four working sails to stabilise us.

Poor bastards, they must have suffered as much as my crew, who were again, sick as dogs! Without a hint of mercy, I had them trimming sails relentlessly all day and night, until I thought they'd suffered enough for their riotous, near disastrous behaviour.

It's the Captain's responsibility to teach his crew the lessons every young buck needs to know. Sometime in the future, I hoped they'd be taking it easy the night before a voyage, but if we did go back to Helgoland, I'd need a different crew.

Finally after two days and nights, the 'Zoll' left us. They'd taken to zig-zagging around in an effort to stay upright, and were probably short on fuel. In any case, we were on our own and headed to the North East. Funny thing, we thanked them for the escort on the VHF, but got no reply. The weather was a little kinder, we had Ian's drinking under control, and we began to get excited as we neared the UK after three days hard bash.

There were some rumours bandied about, that we'd bought a stock of children's rubber dinghies in Holyhead, loaded them with pre-ordered stock wrapped in black plastic, letting them go from the stern at pre-determined points, so that other boats could collect them without coming close to the 'Mother Ship' and alerting Customs.

This would've been a good plan (if it were true) because the radar target would be absolutely minimal in anything more than half a metre swell. A good sailor would know which way the dinghies would drift, taking into account the tide and wind.

If it were me, I'd throw in a plastic drum first so that the following boat had a visual before anything valuable went over the side. Then each dingy would go in at regular preset times.

If it were me, I wouldn't use dinghies anyway. That method, I'm led to believe, is used more when the cargo is somewhat denser. Cigarettes and tobacco float, especially wrapped up watertight, with a little extra buoyancy.

The cargo would be vac packed, then sealed inside black bags with polystyrene. This creates an almost zero radar target. If the operation is done in the dark, the chances of detection are very slim. Bags would be tied together or loose, depending on the sea state and visibility. A simple tracking device designed for animals, even boats and cars, costs less than £100. This could be attached to a buoy, enabling pick up in any weather.

If it was me, and decoys were needed, a plastic drum or refuse sacks filled with tin foil scrunched up, make an excellent radar target.

The radar operator, after numerous false signals, 'tunes' them out, in the same way as they tune out the wave crests.

A floating battery lamp can be used to distract unwanted attention, whereas a black bump on a dark night is almost impossible to spot, unless you're expecting it.

Thermal cameras can be fooled with hot water bottles floating on polystyrene blocks. As they cool, the heat signature fades; this gives the impression of a motor cooling down or moving away when there's no other data to rely on.

Tricks like this can tie up resources very easily. Of course there'd be no radio contact, virgin 'pay as you go' phones for coded text messages only, would be needed to avoid detection. If it were me, I would send 'disinformation' via VHF, and my own phone.

All of those silly rumours aside, we approached our target spot thirteen miles off Hartlepool and began organising ourselves. We'd sent messages out, and there were public on route. It'd been a long time since we were home. Land in sight didn't help the yearning for a hot bath, a warm bed, a hot woman, and a room that didn't move.

A yacht like Rich Harvest should have been anchored in a blue, tranquil bay, crewed by topless females, glistening with suntan lotion and sweat from washing the decks, not crewed by unshaven blokes, anchored thirteen miles from the nearest bar!

CHAPTER TWENTY SEVEN

DISASTER

Later it was Saturday evening. We'd moved to avoid a contour on the seabed that was causing us to roll as the water moved up the ridge with the tide.

We dropped anchor in about ninety metres of water. It was the second time we'd used the anchor and winch. We'd tested the equipment in Holyhead, but both the hydraulic winch and stainless chain were virtually unused, and cost a small fortune. The last thing we anticipated was that it would fail.

A roller system housed in the bowsprit fitted by the boatyard wasn't up to the job of carrying ninety metres of vertical chain, and the spacers collapsed, jamming the chain. The winch was just not strong enough to move it.

We kicked up the main engine to change the angle the chain was to the boat in order to un-jam it while we pulled it onto the main roller using a winch attached to the mast. Twice the plan very nearly worked. On the third attempt, the ratchet failed in the mast winch while I still had hold of the handle.

Sixty seven tons whizzed the handle around and mangled my fingers on both hands before I could pull them free. The chain was staying down, and I was about as much use as a chocolate fireguard.

Two fingers were completely dislocated. Acting tough, I pulled and banged them into place within about ten seconds, spraying the deck with claret. I looked round at the gob-struck faces on the crew and said, "You might want to get me a towel, you've only got to clean this up later."

Phil Junior rolled a five skinner, and poured me a half pint of

Jack Daniels, while Greg practiced his first aid certificate. Shame he couldn't stop baulking!

The young-un came to the rescue and finished the job whilst Greg took command of the VHF radio, and while dreaming of recounting the story as an after dinner speech, hit the mayday button! It's the captain's decision to shout 'Mayday', but it was too late to preserve our secret position.

All modern VHF radios have a 'missile' button, which can only be activated by removing a cover. It sends out an automatic distress call giving the ship's name and GPS derived position. Other stations, especially the coast guard, receive it, and alarm bells are ringing in seconds. This is in case the sailors in peril can't get the message out for any reason. Before I could intervene, they were scrambling a helicopter!

"Cancel that helicopter, Greg," I whispered gently, "or it'll be you they're fishing out of the freezing water, you daft twat!" I knew I had to go to hospital, but also knew the only way a helicopter picks a casualty from a sailing boat means the casualty jumps into the water, and drifts clear of the rigging before the copter crewman, dressed in a full emersion suit, is lowered in to attach the harness.

Number one, I didn't want the drama or publicity; number two, the cost of a helicopter would be far better spent on someone in dire peril; and three, I didn't fancy paddling about in the freezing North Sea with broken, heavily bandaged, bleeding and mangled fingers. We convinced them to only send out the lifeboat. Despite cracking jokes, I was in first stage shock and very clammy. My hands needed professional attention, tomorrow wouldn't do.

I could see Hartlepool where the lifeboat was stationed and figured forty minutes out, forty minutes back, Hartlepool General for two hours maximum, and in the local before last orders.

The five skinner had been replaced by another, along with more Jack by the time the lifeboat approached. I was getting dizzy. Greg was firing orange smoke flares off the foredeck in dramatic style, posing for the cameras. We were the only boat for miles, so there was no need really. It was just the lifeboat checking that we knew the drill.

The coxswain approached the port side a bit fast, and crumpled the safety stanchions as I jumped aboard. A bit of damage is expected in such circumstances. Nobody complains, not if you have the slightest idea of what those guys do.

I appointed Junior as skipper, which made him beam with pride as I waved to his crew. All but him had pleaded separately their cases for coming with me. I told them to hold station until further notice.

On-board the lifeboat, there were twelve crew. All of them very interested as to why we were anchored so far off. Our mission was no secret. For sure the Germans had passed on intelligence, we had a radar target shadowing us, but it was too far away to get a visual. UK Customs were on the case for sure, so I told them. After all, they could go out on a training trip, and collect their just deserts for giving up their Saturday night to rescue me.

I was met by an ambulance and ferried to hospital where, after a couple of hours stitching and dressing, I discharged myself, went home, ate a delicious Teesside Parmo, and retired to a warm still bed to sleep off the litre and a half of Jack Daniels. Painkillers would've been better, but I was trying to be hard. Damn, my hands did hurt!

My head hurt as much as my hands in the morning, so I took painkillers, and went back to sleep till one. The phone had been going non-stop for a while till she woke me to show me the paper. There I was on the front page, in full colour, jumping onto the lifeboat.

Little did I know there was a reporter for the Northern Echo on-board called Neil Hunter (crime correspondent). He lived on the marina in Hartlepool, and often jumped aboard (brave man) in search of a good story. I couldn't blame him; he was a nice enough bloke.

He laid bare our business in the article. The other calls were from other news agencies, TV, radio, you name it, and they all wanted to speak to me. My plan for publicity was originally word of mouth from a few ads, placed on the notice boards of various boat or fishing clubs along the coast.

That and my network of contacts would surely empty the boat in no time at all. Now, I had BBC, ITV, SKY and even Reuters doing the story. Hell, what had I done?

The operation was discussed on radio and TV by experts. It was already big news; my mate working in Kuala Lumpur called me to say he'd just seen me on the news. I agreed to do interviews as HMRC issued statements, condemning the operation as illegal.

I knew the crew on-board Rich Harvest needed a break. Tyrone, Colin and the Cornish Maiden were days overdue, and I couldn't contact them. Trevor, quite amazingly, agreed to take command while I was recovering. I'd doubted his bottle, and for that, I'm sorry.

True to his word, he didn't back down, and nor did I. We were sure we were right; I'd checked the legalities a dozen times before Trevor even knew of the plan. An academic like him being involved only made the story more interesting.

Apart from the fact he kept purporting to own Rich Harvest and failing to mention my shares, I couldn't fault him. We did interview after interview defying HMRC, challenging them to list the regulations they were relying on in their statements to the media, and to sit down with us around a table. We knew we were correct, we didn't need solicitors, and there simply was no regulation in place to stop our business.

The brand new forty two metre Customs cutter, the HMCC Valiant, steamed north from the English Channel where it was more justified to have a £5mill vessel patrolling our coast. Customs men occupied the coastguard stations, and were deployed to watch every inlet and landing point from as far south as Whitby, and as far north as Newcastle.

Every possible place was covered 24/7. They openly advertised their threat to seize any craft going near our vessel. The press were fuelling the situation. I was called a pirate; it was fast getting out of hand, and becoming political.

The scale of publicity took all of us by surprise; the chances of us emptying the boat in a week had evaporated. Tyrone finally turned up with some lame story, but one I couldn't disprove. The weather forecast was atrocious for the time of year. The Customs cutter repeatedly warned of a storm. They wanted to get back to land as much as our by now, very bored crew.

After a very rough twenty four hours, Trevor made the decision to head for port. During a telephone call on 9th July 2004, the Customs agreed to sit down with us around a table. We were told we could declare our stock, hold it on-board, and be free to leave unhindered, that was their promise.

Let's face it, we had more chance of catching whales than selling any fags. Nobody, bar a few brave men, ventured anywhere near the 'Baccy Boat' as it became known in the news. There were reports of jet-ski activity at night. This was true; there were a number of visits made by beach-launched craft in the dead of night. The riders were more in it for the adventure, rather than any profit. Steve (The Greek) Odysseas and his brother Mike were extremely daring and even got lost one night, landing quite a few miles away from where they'd launched.

I'd negotiated a discount for our boats at Hartlepool Marina by promising publicity. I certainly kept my part of the bargain. The place was buzzing, TV crews were filming a steady stream of customers who'd heard about charter boats to take them out, arriving by the bus load.

Everywhere I went people were cheering and clapping. We were in the news constantly. The TV crews were on hand as Rich Harvest entered the marina and tied up at 2100h. Customs were stationed inside the lock office. Rather than play to the cameras, we left them to it and went for Chinese food close by. All of the crew needed a good feed.

Trevor then made the declaration as captain of the vessel entering port, that by rights we had twenty four hours as we were not tied to a wall, but rather a floating pontoon which is classed as a buoy. If we tied to a wall, we would have had to declare within two hours.

The next day, Customs were astounded to discover how much

stock we had. They acted quite decently, but then we were given orders to leave within twenty four hours, or our stock and vessel would be seized. The guy on the ground was only relaying what he was told, so there was no point in arguing with him.

We asked to transfer the cargo to the Cornish Maiden as we had repairs to do. They refused without any good reason. We didn't want to risk Rich Harvest being seized, so we agreed to make ready, and sail with the next suitable tide, which was more like thirty six hours.

This treachery was only the start of things to come. There was no more mention of the arranged sit down meeting. We had some bits needed doing or getting. Amongst other things, we needed an anchor rope as Trevor had left our anchor chain at sea.

Later in court, the reason given for the refusal to transfer cargo (cooper) was, "It might have been seen to be landing the goods." How this could be possible, while both boats were tied together is beyond me.

We worked like hell, and spent a couple of grand on everything we needed. I should have been resting my bandaged hands, but had to grin and bear it. By 0300h in the middle of the night on 11th July 2004, the vessel Rich Harvest was ready for sea again with just six hours of the illegal deadline still to go. The crew were shattered.

Everyone had pulled their puddings out despite them being well overdue a rest ashore. The storm had passed, the game was on again. We weren't about to stop, we had a point to make. Customs had broken their word about talking to us. We took that as a victory.

Clearly they didn't want to hear what we were saying, and had nothing new to tell us. They just wanted to continue blagging the press, and bullying the boat owners. The significant thing to remember here was that none of us were arrested, or detained for any offence at any time!

Customs were acting illegally by ordering us to leave unprepared, and declining our request to cooper, or transfer the stock. Clearly they thought we'd give up. They had no right to order any vessel, even a British vessel to sea, regardless of its cargo. Our intention was to call their bluff, and do just as they said! But sue later!

As they had no intentions of honouring their word, we'd sail around the UK, dragging the 'circus' with us. The running costs of the cutter with its combined horsepower of 5,400 and hundreds of extra officers on overtime along the coastlines were already attracting ridicule from the press. I went home for a well-earned rest, promising to be back before they sailed.

Later that morning, I was on my way back, when Phil Junior called me to say the Customs had stormed the boat team handed. They were acting on instructions from above. More than a dozen civilian workers attempted to board Rich Harvest along with a dozen Customs.

Trevor quite rightly objected, and refused access to the civilians, forcing only Customs to unload the boat. Their outrageous behaviour demonstrated they'd clearly been told to provoke an incident, whereby police would be needed. It transpired later that two minibuses full of cops expecting trouble were on full alert, waiting just out of sight.

They trashed our beautiful schooner, throwing personal items about while laughing in our faces, and squaring up to the crew like a bunch of thugs. They threw valuable stock about like bags of rubbish, ripping open boxes and throwing loose sleeves into open plastic containers.

When I got there, the boat reeked of booze as numerous bottles of spirits had been smashed. With broken glass and booze puddles everywhere, it was a disgustingly sick attempt to provoke us, and have us arrested for 'obstruction'.

They mistook our band of educated and restrained young gentlemen for mugs and thugs. We behaved impeccably, and just laughed at them, much to their annoyance. Thompson, the senior officer on the ground, was heard to say on his mobile, "Stand down, stand down, there's no chance of a section sixteen (obstruction)." They wheeled the stock from the boat in the pouring rain, and left it out, waiting hours for the truck, despite firm and lawful protests.

Some of their own officers were clearly shocked and embarrassed by the others behaviour, and sheepishly offered apologies on their behalf. Not all uniforms are power-crazed dickheads, but there's always some who relish the chance to bully, and abuse their position. These bastards would work for nothing on days like that.

We weren't smuggling heroin or crack cocaine, but they treated us like we were. Unfortunately for them, they failed and had none of us in custody, which was obviously their plan! The worst we did in return was clap!

A very valuable cargo was left out in the rain at the directions of their superiors. This total abuse of position was clear for all to see, the perpetrators laughing gleefully as they sheltered under a nearby canopy, while watching the labels slipping off expensive bottles of spirits, and boxes of cigarettes soaking up the puddles.

Sad, sad types, not one of them could hold a candle to our crew. A hundred years ago, the same type of sicko would have been hanging some peasant farmer, for keeping a few chickens back to feed his family. I re-iterate... not all of them!

The public hated them for what they did; they embarrassed their own authority by acting like criminals at the behest of some stupid arse above them. How proud they must have been, relaying the story to friends and family. I bet a pound to a penny, none of them told the truth! 'The Queen's men'? She wouldn't let them walk her corgis!

We sat down and discussed options. Clearly the law had been broken, which left us in a position to sue the arse off them. Granted, it was going to take time, but the evidence was clear. They'd agreed to us coming in from the storm, which in maritime law relates to 'force majeure' (any vessel is entitled to seek shelter without fear of interference).

They ordered us out unprepared, and then broke their agreement to allow the goods to be sealed on-board. We were in a win-win situation. The Cornish Maiden headed back to the south coast, and everyone else, went home.

The media and public cried foul as we were left in the dark. Trevor consulted his solicitor friend, who frankly had less idea than us. It seemed too good to be true. Customs had made a monumental mistake under pressure. Clearly their legal team had got it wrong, or they had been ignored.

Customs are well known for thinking that the law doesn't apply to them. At some point a few days later, their mistake must have been laid bare. After consultation at a very high legal level, they had no choice but to admit their mistake. In writing, they asked me to take our stock back onto Rich Harvest. In an astonishing climb down, that must have hurt deeply those officers who perpetrated this disgraceful abuse of power. We'd won another point.

After consultation with Trevor, we refused point-blank, citing our distrust of Customs. We feared they wanted to seize our beautiful schooner, as well as the stock. Why would we trust them? Where was the meeting they promised? Their idea of a meeting, it had transpired was us getting arrested; and them interviewing us under caution. Dirty bastards!

CHAPTER TWENTY EIGHT

ROUND TWO

We were in no hurry to conform to Customs' demands; they'd messed up, why should we dance to their tune? They had something planned, and constantly plagued us to arrange the return of stock. As far as the public were concerned, the climb down was a victory for us, and proof our operation was legal. We liked that, and wanted to perpetuate it for a few more weeks. We were celebrities around the marina, and famous everywhere else.

Tye was becoming difficult to reach and owed me around £12k. I got high readings on my bullshit meter every time I managed to catch him or his wife on the phone. He'd spent time grooming Ben and Vinnie who'd both put a few quid into the venture. Ben was due a windfall from the sale of a house, and Tye, ever the opportunist, had his eyes on it.

My money was long overdue when again Tye's long-suffering wife lied about his whereabouts. I jumped in the car with Junior and drove through the night to be at his door in Selsey at 0700h the next day. He nearly shit a brick!

Tyronio was living on his dad's fame; he'd fallen out with him over the situation in Amsterdam. He'd nearly got himself killed after losing a gang's money while purporting to be acting for his father. I was aware of this, or I wouldn't have turned up at his door. I'd smelt a rat since he hadn't arrived as planned in Hartlepool. Another vessel would've given us a number of options; that'd been the plan. He'd failed us badly.

I made it quite clear that I wanted the Cornish Maiden back in Hartlepool, and my money paid back pronto. He said he had another trip booked, and would head North when it was finished. He was a smooth talking, likable fellow who's easy to believe. I didn't want to fall out with him, but I'd noticed a change in him when his dry lining business failed. He'd become quite the family man with two lovely daughters, but now his priorities were shagging about, blag, blag, blagging about his brief encounter with gangsterism, and his dad's awesome reputation.

A week later, I got a call. Apparently they'd pulled into Grimsby for fuel, and a purported wiring fault, and they were staying overnight. Phil Junior and I headed down in the car next morning to surprise them and see for ourselves. We were only fifteen minutes away when we called to ask for specific directions to the boat. By the time we got there, they'd vanished, leaving the boat unsecure, and a Peugeot belonging to Tye parked nearby.

She was indeed short of fuel, which begged the question, where had they been? I'd topped her up in Hartlepool, and by my reckoning and past performance, she should have been at least half full. I knew Ben had been on-board, as it was him I talked to.

I never got to find out exactly where they'd been or why his car was left there. Finally I got through to Ben again. He passed a message from Tye, while pretending to have a bad signal.

"Look under the fuel pump," he repeated a number of times then he texted the same message.

I assumed they must have lost their bottle and dumped the boat, leaving my money hidden, so I wouldn't be turning up at his door again. We went down into the hold and removed a cover from the pump housing, and found three vacuum packed bags of skunk cannabis.

My young son's arse twittered as we realised what it was. My heart pounding, I expected Customs and police waiting outside to catch us red-handed. It had all the hallmarks of a classic set-up.

How was I going to get out of this? We replaced the cover and wiped everything down before going topside. We put the kettle on, trying very hard not to look suspicious. There didn't seem to be anyone watching us, but even that made things worse. All their phones were switched off.

Of course the Harbour master would be on the lookout for this boat, for sure everyone knew it was there. Had they been caught up to no good, and agreed to set us up? My brain was racing out of control, the dirty stinking bastards!

We finished our tea while I texted the following to all concerned: "Found Cornish Maiden tied up, abandoned and insecure at Grimsby port, crew assumed safe as I got a message to look at fuel pump, nothing wrong, maybe held by Customs. Securing vessel, and awaiting contact. If anybody has any information, please reply."

I knew Customs were monitoring my phone, but this text would help in court, if we got arrested leaving the boat. We shook hands and hugged before we went ashore, expecting the worst. If we were getting knocked, it'd most likely happen before we left the port.

We left the vessel, and his car sitting there, the skunk still in its hole. We drove around every corner expecting a roadblock until we cleared the port, and onto the public roads. We got back to Teesside, still expecting a pull.

Quite often with a set-up, the knock comes when you enter a particular county where the slimy bastards are based; this ensures the credit for the bust is given to the right office.

After ninety long minutes, we arrived home very puzzled to say the least. Next day, Customs were onto us again about returning the stock. It appeared (or they pretended) they didn't know where the boat was, so I told them. Honesty is the best policy if you've nothing to hide. In any case, it was likely they already knew and had photographed us at the boat; they could easily check where my mobile had been. To deny it would be stupid, and lead us to look guilty. I still had the problem of the skunk on-board, and needed to know what'd happened.

Whatever it was, it'd put us in real danger of getting nicked. It was awkward as I didn't know if Trevor's son Vinnie was involved with Ben, or even if Ben was a willing partner. Both had been thrust at me by Trevor, who was as straight as an arrow.

I tried to contact them for days before I finally got to speak to

Tye, who all of a sudden was doing an impersonation of his father. He just laughed it off, and said we were 'square'.

He purported that I should be grateful he paid me back at all. He valued the skunk at four grand a kilo, and would throw in the Peugeot to sweeten the deal. I deduced they'd been using the boat, and her legal operation as cover for bringing back ever increasing volumes of skunk. They'd used my money, my boat, my fuel, and then my crew to double up from the day they'd left Plymouth. No wonder they didn't turn up. Then I doubted the near wrecking and repair story, as they'd had time for a run, then must have realised they hadn't called or texted. After all, we were sailing along the coast where there is ample mobile phone signal. Like a tumbler lock, it all fell into place. When will I stop trusting people?

Instead of giving me £12k, he left me the skunk that would've cost him £5k, and a banger worth less than a grand. As far as he was concerned, he was a on a higher level like his dad, and could do anything he wanted; a bit like the movie The Layer Cake. I told him to stick his cake, his skunk and his car up his arse, and to wipe my number from his phone. At the time of writing some ten years later, I've not spoken to Tyrone, Colin, or Ben since.

I later discovered from Trevor that Ben had bought a boat for £20k which Tye eventually stole and sold. He also forwarded an article translated from Dutch. Tye had been caught at the Dutch-Belgium border with a boot full of skunk while driving a car hired by his wife.

He escaped custody by telling the judge that he was under pressure from serious criminals, after becoming involved with some big gangsters in the cigarette business, which was well publicised in the UK. Of course he meant Trevor and I were the gangsters. He supported his mitigation with paperwork and newspaper cuttings to prove his involvement in the business.

The Dutch judge believed it, and only fined him. It transpired later that his wife had been intercepting texts from his supplier, a woman in a coffee shop in Amsterdam. She'd grassed them up in anger! He was living in a caravan facing divorce, all good news! The snake, living up his dad's arse.

I started to put two and two together, and deduced maybe Tye had intended to rip off the Scouse firm in Amsterdam, but was ripped off himself, but I'll never know the truth. It was ten years since my trial, and I was sick of dealing with dodgy arseholes who couldn't be trusted regardless. These experiences cause me to see things more clearly, like having epiphanies. The more I get, the wiser I become. When you mix with life's characters, don't expect an easy ride!

In any case, I now had to get the Cornish Maiden to Hartlepool. My hands were still not capable of handling ropes, so I was as much use on a boat as a snooker table. We enlisted the security guard from the marina in Hartlepool. Dave, an ex-trawler skipper, was getting on a bit, but still went to sea for a month at a time on Guard boats (ex-trawlers guarding cables, rigs and pipelines).

He was a big strong bloke you wouldn't want to tangle with and looked like you could sand wood on his face. As hard as a coffin nail, he'd sailed out of Grimsby hundreds of times in similar boats. He liked to tell a story, and jumped at the chance to get involved. He was the man for the job.

We got dropped off at the Cornish Maiden, and made ready for when the forecast suited us. We cleared the wheelhouse of two bin bags of rubbish, which I put in Tye's car. The skunk went into the dock on video. Even if I was tempted myself, my son witnessed the affair. What use would all the time I'd spent with him be, if I sold drugs? Imagine us sailing into Hartlepool and getting searched... game over!

I'd rather blow the money than teach him wrong. I'm not saying we didn't open a bag and take out some personal, it would've been rude not to, but I'm not saying we did either.

By dumping the skunk on camera, I negated any observations, or any risk of a set-up. Obviously, the bastard couldn't lie straight in bed. I still didn't know if I was getting a knock on the door sometime in the future.

Sometimes it can be months after the fact, before you get a tug, and then they make it look like we're involved in a much bigger conspiracy. He'd lied convincingly to everyone from the start of the venture. I'd have been stupid to trust him now we'd fallen out.

To anybody watching, I was simply throwing it out. The thought of Customs searching and finding said skunk had haunted me since I found it. The text messages were enough evidence against me. Whenever I smoked it, I only bought personal, and I'd leave it in a waterproof box away from the house, retrieving only what I needed, on route to the shop.

In all the years, I only came close once (apart from three point seven tons in my boat). Boris was staying at my house while looking for diggers, and other plant to export to Morocco. It was shortly after my acquittal, and the police were watching my every move. I'd been developing a new, high-tech hydroponic system, and even advertised them openly as a flat pack.

There was nothing illegal about it, but after getting a sun-bed in a bedroom next to the heating boiler outlet, the police spotter plane sent a squad of twelve burly coppers to kick down my front door, early one morning.

Within seconds they had me cuffed, sitting at a dining table while the search team went straight to the 'sun room' and a cupboard used for propagating seeds under lights. They returned looking pretty daft. They'd found a sun-bed, and some tomato plants in the cupboard. We'd been on the razzle the night before, and my head was bouncing, but still, I couldn't stop laughing at the two Reebok heading the raid.

Just then, as Boris came through the door, cuffed in his pyjamas with a plod, one Reebok found an ounce of hashish in the next room on the coffee table, in an ashtray, with a half-smoked joint.

The grin vanished from my face. How could he be so stupid? Of course the Reebok boys now had my grin; at least they wouldn't have to pay for the door. Even though an ounce would only justify a caution, it would still be the only official mark on my character.

"I've just seen you take that out of your pocket!" Boris shouted. "I watched you plant it!" he went on, doing an excellent impression of a shocked, innocent victim, absolutely appalled by what he'd seen. He even had some of the uniformed coppers convinced, with his best boarding school accent.

I got my grin back from Reebok as they bundled Boris into a police car, threatening a twenty four hour lock up unless he changed his mind. Boris was laughing at them. "Do you think twenty four hours is going to reduce me to a quivering wreck? I've spent eighteen months as a category A, and done a year in a Moroccan hell hole, you silly boys!" Of course, he had a point.

We both ended up at Stockton nick giving statements lasting forty minutes. If the cops are wasting your time, waste theirs! Babbling for forty minutes on tape means they'll spend many hours typing up your statement.

They were as sick as hell by the time I'd finished explaining how and where we'd been out, with whom and why, how drunk I was, and that I couldn't remember if the person smoking a joint in my living room was a girl, or a ponytailed man as I'd spent most of the time calling for Hughy down my toilet... I didn't know for certain if the spliff belonged to the ponytail or, as my friend said, you planted it.

One young tech held up the half-smoked joint in a sealed plastic bag, and said, "Do you think your DNA will be on this joint?"

I replied, "Do you think your boss is going to authorise a DNA test for an ounce of spliff? You dickhead!"

His mate cringed, and laughed at him before they bailed us for a month. On the way out, I couldn't help winding them up. "Your mates couldn't get me for three thousand seven hundred kilograms; now it's thirty seven grams? You're in the big league now, boys!"

On the due date, we faxed our co-ordinates from the sub-Sahara desert, surrendering ourselves, and asking for a helicopter to take us to the nearest airport where they should have tickets waiting. They replied saying the enquiry was dropped! What a joke!

Back to the skunks' skunk; I was relieved when it was done. I wiped the keys and left them on the back wheel of the Peugeot where I found them. We untied and cleared the dock, leaving behind the pungent aroma of Dutch grown 'White Widow' floating in the dock. I almost had a tear in my eye as we sailed out for a wonderful trip to Hartlepool on still waters, lit up by bright sunshine, just how it should be. Whenever I bought a tiny £20 bag of cannabis afterwards, I remembered that day well.

We sailed into Hartlepool, tied up and went home. Trevor was lecturing at Liverpool, so he couldn't travel straightaway. Customs were irate; they had HMCC Valiant on standby again, twelve miles off the North East coast. Our intelligence suggested there were already a number of people engaging in similar activity, with supply boats from as far away as Russia, peddling fags and vodka on the high seas around Scotland, before returning with fish. Customs needed to send a clear message; something was brewing.

I was approached by dozens of illicit fag dealers, offering to buy any and all of the stock, but only if we got it ashore. We knew we had little hope of making a profit, but my motives included revenge. Trevor's motive was, he was simply correct, and intended to prove it. We had by now offered to call a truce, and cease operations with certain conditions, but to no avail.

The day came, the Customs arrived with a load of rain damaged goods into a police controlled, cordoned off compound next to Cornish Maiden. It was a stupid circus played out for the TV cameras to put off anybody who had similar ideas. Trevor brought one of his yachty friends called Nigel, and few good bottles of red wine. He was very unimpressed during his stint on-board Rich Harvest, because we only had beer and spirits.

Officer Thompson was barking orders, and threatening to seize the vessel and goods unless she set sail immediately the goods were loaded. He cited security risks, because of the hundred plus people watching the spectacle. We pushed our luck, and left Phil Junior in charge of loading while we left to "procure vital spares", as Trevor put it.

On our return, Thompson was steaming mad. He complained bitterly that our security arrangements consisted of only a young boy.

I rounded on him and said, "Who going to steal anything, you daft twat? The place is crawling with cameras, police, Customs and daft bastards who unload cigarettes into puddles. My son's got more about him than you have, matey. Now piss off, I'm busy!"

I had to show Trevor where everything was. He quite rightly refused to leave until he'd become 'familiarised' with the operation of everything on-board. Clearly, Thompson was performing to a script from above, and would, no doubt be recounting his version of events to a judge later. No amount of threats swayed Trevor from his duty as Captain, he was completely calm.

There was less than a hundred thousand pounds worth of stock being transferred in broad daylight inside a gated marina. The security farce laid on for the cameras, and later for the judge was extraordinary; anyone would think we were moving the bloody crown jewels!

In contrast, the 'bonded' warehouse where our stock, and millions of pounds of other goods are stored, is guarded all night by one unarmed security guard... on minimum wage! At the dockside however, there were literally dozens of Customs, police, and warehouse staff involved, on high alert!

Trevor Lyons and Nigel Copping took the Cornish Maiden, laden with fags and spirits, and set sail for the twelve mile limit, along with four bottles of very good Italian red wine, and a pack of cards to play bridge. After dropping anchor, they settled down to a quiet night under the watchful gaze, and protection of the five million pound HM Customs Cutter Valiant with her huge crew, already sick as penguins in a desert, bobbing around hundreds of miles from their home port, waiting for... damn all to happen! The ports, harbours, inlets and beaches all along the North East coast were guarded by roving Customs rummage patrols, twenty four hours a day. God only knows how many real smugglers took advantage of this ridiculous circus.

CHAPTER TWENTY NINE

GAMES, SET AND MATCH

Now please remember, the Customs had played some pretty dirty tricks to date. The latest attempt to infer our security arrangements were inadequate, were outrageous, and completely irrelevant, but clearly a case building exercise. The press were keen to get hold of any information, however small.

The Northern Echo newspaper planned a trip for Neil Hunter on a charter vessel to test the Customs response. We had plans of our own. One of them included a tiny black speedboat bought on eBay. I bought it for Phil Junior to restore. We called it 'Little Flea'.

We had a perfectly good RHIB hanging from the davits of Rich Harvest, which we'd already used for crew exchanges, but it was too red, and too big. We also had a brand new Tohatsu eighteen horsepower two stroke outboard motor, which was a spare for the RHIB (Trevor thought of everything, bless him).

Half a day's work for us, and it was married to Little Flea. We fitted LED lights, compass, anchor and warp, life jackets, flares, first aid kit, knife, torch, brandy, a hand held VHF radio, and she was ready for sea. We looked ridiculous; it was barely ten feet long. I set the throttle stop to two-thirds, and added extra oil to the fuel as the engine needed running in. We launched her inside the marina at midnight on 16th August 2004.

We were perfectly entitled to go through the loch, and out to sea, so we radioed the control room to open the gates. The guy in the watchtower couldn't see us, so we flashed him with a big torch. The gates opened and our tiny little craft motored into the loch. The four Customs officers sitting in an MPV, couldn't believe their eyes, or hide their surprise.

They saw the outer gate open, but were looking out to sea for a boat coming in when we tootled past them, ignoring their calls to stop. Of course we couldn't hear them above the motor only two feet away. I just waved as though they were seeing us off. We got into safe water, and mischievously turned the navigation lights off (they were getting hot).

A metre high swell was well enough to make radar useless. To all intents and purposes, we were invisible in the dark night. We even had black coats over our life jackets and 'balaclavas' to keep us warm. Search lights began sweeping the area frantically, a bit of mist vastly reducing the visibility range, so we remained undetected throughout.

Later, we had some adjustments to do to the throttle linkage, so we headed into the commercial dock and hid by a visiting yacht, which was tied to a pontoon. The owner, a Dane, was just coming back from the bar, and spent half an hour talking to us while we were jammed under his transom, adjusting the linkage.

Obviously, we had to motor through the entrance, so we'd been seen and reported on. Cars were screaming around the dock roads using headlights as searchlights. Customs men were running around, checking every metre of waterside with high powered torches. One shouted to the Dane, and asked him if he'd seen a little black boat. "Not around here, I've been here all night," he shouted back.

An hour later, the search was still on. Our scanner picked up radio traffic confirming they were still on full alert. They thought we'd managed to slip out to sea. Valiant weighed anchor and conducted a search pattern while we were having a smoke and a brandy. There'd be nobody sleeping that night. After a couple of hours more, we got bored and thought a bit more 'winding up' would brighten the night.

We fired up the motor and headed out between the piers, turning south for the marina, staying in close to shore, picking our way round in the dark to see how far we could go, before they spotted us. Trevor wanted a couple of things dropping off, so we were going back to the marina to attract attention, before setting off into international waters.

Little Flea was performing very well, but we hadn't had a chance to open her up yet. We were tickling along at five knots to keep the noise down, when all at once, she slewed sideways, and then back again. We looked at each other in horror! Rocks! Mini currents are only caused by tide over rocks. Hell!

We killed the motor so as not to damage the propeller, quickly deploying paddles to poke about in the murky water. We were both frantic, what a pair of twats we'd look if we needed help, we'd never live it down.

After a minute of hearts thudding and splashing about, we sat silent. I took my bearings; I'd been sailing off there for thirty years. Even at low tide there was enough water for a much bigger boat. We deduced there must be a sunken boat around, so paddled further out in order to clear it, before restarting the motor.

It was during this paddling when we started to discuss what level of madness we were at to be out in the North Sea at 0300h in a ten foot plastic boat. Granted, it was calm, but 'rocks sink boats, waves don't'.

I squeezed out of my seat, swivelled onto my knees and leaned over to pull on the starter cord, just as the boat slewed violently to port. "Sit still, you loony, you nearly had me in then!" I shouted behind me to Junior.

"Dad, Dad, Daaaaad!" he screamed back as Little Flea squirmed violently, almost doing a three sixty.

As she spun, I saw what he was screaming at. A big black fin was coming straight at us. The still water instantly became violent.

With pure reflex reaction and no planning, I swung my paddle down hard in front of a creature easily bigger than Little Flea. It dived so close under us, I could have touched the fin, and its tail scraped the hull as we swivelled again.

My arse was twitching as I nearly pulled the motor off its bracket with the starting cord. It fired first time, I rammed it into gear before the revs could fall, Little Flea lunged forward, nearly landing me in the drink. I squeezed back into the cockpit as she picked up speed at the same rate as our hearts.

We didn't know which way to go. Do we run onto the beach, make for the marina or go flat out to sea. It's not something you have a plan for really. I slowed down, not knowing where it was, or if it was coming up under us. The last thing I wanted was a collision at speed. I hoped the motor might scare it off. We slowed and levelled out at about seven knots, then set a course for the marina entrance, our heads spinning around like the girl in The Exorcist, hoping and praying it'd gone away.

A couple of speechless minutes passed, by which time I'd realised there should be no sharks that would attack us anywhere in the UK, never mind off Hartlepool. I thought, nobody's going to believe this, just as the big fin broke the surface, right next to us, going the same way at the same speed. We squealed like little girls, until it opened its blow hole, spraying us with water before kicking forward, flicking its tail and sending a torrent into the boat, soaking us.

"It's a dolphin," Junior gargled, now he could control his jaw.

"Yeah, but still big enough to sink us, so let's go, sharpish!" I said as I hit the throttle and brought her up to twenty knots. I didn't care about being detected. Even if Flipper was playing, he should be playing with someone his own size.

Junior doesn't like brandy, and only has it on his Christmas pudding, but we made a serious dent in a litre bottle during the following five minutes. We'd had enough fun for one night, and I was sure from the smell, that Junior needed the bathroom! Trevor could wait till tomorrow.

We entered the marina trying very hard to look cool in front of the bemused Customs, who had no idea where we'd been, or why we were dripping wet. We tied up behind Rich Harvest and splodged on-board, leaving puddles everywhere!

Next day we recounted our adventure, expecting nobody to believe us. It transpired this lost dolphin was actually one of two that had made the news in recent weeks, hanging about the Tees estuary, playing in the bow waves of boats. Well, nobody 'flipping' told us. What a pair of prats; we wouldn't be doing that again in a 'flipping' hurry.

That afternoon, a charter boat had been arranged to take out some reporters who were going to buy some fags and booze from the Cornish Maiden, to see what the Customs did about it. We had a plan! We loaded what Trevor wanted into Little Flea, and set off an hour after the charter boat Geronimo, which had a top speed of less than ten knots. We had ample time to get there, at about the same time.

The sun was out, the forecast was good, getting a bit fresher later in the afternoon, but nothing to worry about. We whizzed there in about forty minutes, and tied to the stern. Geronimo was rafted alongside; her passengers gawped at our little boat before realising who we were.

The Valiant weighed anchor and circled us closely with all of her five thousand, four hundred horsepower roaring.

The wash created by this stupid manoeuvre bashed hell out of the boats, bursting fenders and causing significant cosmetic damage. People were hanging on for dear life, as both rolled violently, throwing gear about. It was simple bullying, abuse of power, dangerous and irresponsible, but typical of HMRC!

Some interviews and posing sessions later, Geronimo set off for Hartlepool. Our information, gained from the scanner, was that the cameras were waiting on shore to record the Customs forcing the reporters to declare their goods and pay duty on them. Customs were playing along by arrangement, and intended to send a clear message. It was going to be a well-choreographed, stage-managed affair.

Valiant dropped anchor again and deployed her RHIB and four crewmen to follow Geronimo, close enough for good photographs. Clearly they intended to escort her in for the circus ashore. I was pissed off with them for damaging the paint on my boats.

John Nelson had insisted on spraying the hull with expensive paint, despite my assertion she was a work boat. The preparation and finish he achieved was the envy of Holyhead marina, now I would have to roller it.

We put some fags and vodka on Little Flea and watched the radar. I wanted to time it right and arrive at the same time to confront them on camera, something they'd avoided so far.

We set off just about right into a more choppy sea, the tide had changed and the swell was building. A safe speed was about fifteen knots, still uncomfortable in the chop, but safe enough.

Little Phil was driving again, my right hand still in bandages. We'd been going fifteen minutes when I looked behind and saw Valiant had weighed anchor and was following us. We assumed they too were going to play for the cameras. It seemed our adventure during the night was only the start. I nudged up the throttle as Junior gave me a dirty look.

"Dad, we're going fast enough, she's just running in," he shouted responsibly above the noise of the engine.

I don't know how long it was before I looked again, but Valiant had made a lot of ground. She was crashing through the waves at near maximum speed, about twenty five knots. Obviously, they were steaming on the same course as us; we were going to the same place. The collision regulations state that she should pass on our starboard side in a safe and responsible manner. I started to feel like this could turn messy.

I'd seen what the wash from these engines had just done to two heavy boats. It didn't bear thinking about what would happen to us if they came too close. The forty-two metre, one hundred and fifty ton, five thousand four hundred horsepower HMCC Valiant, was bearing down on our tiny three metre, two hundred kilogram, eighteen horsepower Little Flea. If we stopped, they couldn't; they were far too close, the wash would continue and capsize us for sure.

What looked like getting messy had now turned into real and present danger. Phil Junior, bless him was blissfully unaware of the situation, totally in the zone, white knuckled, jumping the swell.

I reached over and pushed the throttle up to the maximum. The little Tohatsu liked that, it was in its power band now! At twenty two knots we were banging and crashing across the swell.

"What the hell are you doing, fatherbean?" he screamed, spitting seawater at the same time. He reached for the throttle as I put my bandaged hand on his, and held it in place. He glanced at me, pulling his 'Have you lost the plot?' face.

I smiled and gestured for him to look behind.

If his little face looked shocked at the sight of Freddy the dolphin's fin at 0300h that morning, now he looked like he'd been swimming with great white sharks with a nose bleed; he was petrified! The Valiant was almost on us, now at full speed judging by the smoke from her stacks. We could see the welds in the hull plating and the evil bastards' faces on the bridge, and she was still gaining ground.

I grabbed the wheel and changed course carefully about twenty degrees to port. I needed to get clear before we slowed down. The Valiant was going to win the race back, end of story! I released my grip on the throttle before turning to give them a 'victory' salute.

To our horror, she was heeled over and coming at us again, still at full speed. They were trying to run us down or capsize us with the wash.

As a boatman from being a lad, I know real danger. The problem was, we just couldn't believe what was happening. As far as we were concerned, they definitely had intentions to do us harm, if not drown us! Getting my head round it and deciding my next move with only seconds to spare, was a bit stressful I can tell you, from the bottom of my heart.

We accelerated again and changed course, this time towards a favourite spot of mine, which I knew very well indeed. The Longscar buoy marks a small, but treacherous crop of rocks, which are submerged most of the time, but still lurk high enough to rip the arse clean off a vessel at high speed.

I'd fished off that buoy so many times with my dear old dad Joe, we'd scattered his ashes there from the Pisces a few years before. There was a way through and I knew it. He'd be dancing with Davey Jones if my plan worked, but I'd need to outrun the Valiant for that to happen. We had to dispense with the throttle stop… and go wide open!

I had no chance of doing it in a proper mechanical fashion. We were on course for getting run down again. We had no time to stop long enough to adjust the Morse cable. I grabbed the cable, ripped it off the bracket and rove it out, as far as I could.

Blood was pouring out of my bandages as the little two stroke revved its nuts off! The engine screamed for mercy as Little Flea shot up to over thirty knots, banging and crashing across the chop. It doesn't sound fast, but try it at sea level in a boat no bigger than a decent bathtub on a two metre choppy sea, and then, "you'll be a man, my son".

'IF' by Rudyard Kipling is my favourite poem of all time. It fitted my situation perfectly, and gave me great strength in jail!

Phil Junior, bless him, had a face like he was falling down the stairs.

"Drive the boat, son. I'm not letting go, SO DRIVE IT!" I bawled.

And he did drive it, admirably; he was just turning fifteen, in charge of the scariest roller coaster in the world. One mistake and we were history. Lose your bottle, you're gone! We brayed the living daylights out of poor Little Flea that day. It was to be her last.

The Valiant fell behind. We tried waving, but this proved difficult as our white knuckles were welded into position. Each time she came down on a big one, we got the wind knocked out of us. They must have realised my plan, and changed course. It was a great pity the bastards gave up before I could lead them to 'Joe Berriman's locker'. He would've been damn proud.

We slowed right down in shallow water, just above the rocks, safe from any more attempts to capsize us. I thought about my dad, took a big guzzle of vodka and lit a spliff. After a few minutes, we heard them on the VHF diverting the RHIB from the Geronimo, just before the big publicity stunt was about to happen. This was a massive victory for us, talk about David and Goliath. There'd be no Customs boats in camera shot when Geronimo landed her passengers. The timing, as it happened, was perfect.

We headed towards the marina at Hartlepool until the RHIB approached with blue lights flashing. We stopped, just as you should. We couldn't outrun it, and my hands were wrecked. They came almost alongside, shouting that they were coming aboard. We both burst out laughing.

"Where the hell are you going to sit then?" I said.

They tried to look serious and menacing in their paramilitary style uniforms, but an inflatable boat was not going to intimidate us. I glared at them. I hadn't quite got over the 'attempted murder' by then. It clearly wasn't their doing, but screw it; any uniform would do today!

"Errr we have information you've just come from the Baccy Boat in international waters, and we're going to search your vessel," one of them said.

"Piss off," I said.

"Sir, we are going to…"

"Piss off," and so on and so forth until he got sick.

"We need your name."

"What for?"

"We need your name."

"Piss off, we're doing nothing wrong."

"Listen, mate…"

"Don't you mate me! You bastards, you just tried to kill us!" I took another swig from the blood spattered bottle of Vodka, opened my fags and lit one, grinning at them like a demented gargoyle.

Truth was, despite the spliff, I was still blood spattered and raging mad, and my hands were killing me. I had claret running down my arm where I'd ripped open the stitches for the third time. The cockpit of Little Flea looked like a butchers sink. I knew they weren't coming on. Repel boarders? There wasn't room for one, let alone four of them.

After what went on minutes before, I was in a zone where I don't like to be. My fuse was lit. I eyed up the big sharp knife in the sheath we'd fastened on the dashboard, and mooted 'gutting' the nearest hypalon flotation tubes of their RHIB, but, in couple of seconds, I concluded that Customs would turn a bit of harmless criminal damage, into an attempted murder charge.

The four guys in the RHIB clearly thought I was a nut case, and decided against boarding the boat. Apart from the fact, there was no room for us, never mind any fags, I also think he was scared.

"Give us your names and you can go," he conceded.

I saw the opportunity to extinguish a dangerous fuse and took it. "Okay, Phil Berriman and Phil Berriman Junior."

Their heads swivelled about in disbelief as the penny dropped. They'd had no idea who we were before then.

I don't believe the Valiant was trying to run down a random bloke, and a young lad with a litre of vodka and two hundred fags, in a ten foot boat! And they certainly wouldn't have called the RHIB away from the publicity stunt waiting in the harbour, not when they had land-based officers who could easily intercept us on shore. We had two theories, did they want to stop us spoiling their staged press circus, by delaying us, or capsize us to make us look foolish, and demonstrate to the media how dangerous flirting with HMRC can be?

Clearly things were getting out of hand!

It is possible the Valiant told the RHIB to pretend they didn't know who we were, to negate any accusations later. In any case, we headed for Hartlepool. No one from HMRC came near us that day; it's a good job too.

Next day, despite numerous hot Radox baths, I ached like I'd spent the night in a dungeon with a dominatrix. I was black and blue from the chest down. My arse felt like I'd been dragged down the road by my feet to test speed bumps. Junior was no better. We surfaced and found our Little Flea was no more.

We'd taken all the valuables off, and left the bilge pump on automatic, thinking most of the water in her was taken over the bow, but she'd been leaking all the time. The battery had gone flat because someone unplugged the charger on the pontoon. We couldn't prove who it was, but had a bloody good idea.

In any case, we hauled her up on the davits to remove and flush the motor out. Two stroke motors easily survive a dunking. We let her drain out for inspection. She'd taken such a battering, the glass fibre had stressed and become porous at the strengtheners, sadly she was a write off, a casualty of war. Before we left her at the skip, we concluded it was by far the best value craft we'd ever had in terms of excitement. Her story will last forever!

There was talk of this episode having been a well-organised diversion, in order to float off large quantities of cigarettes, which were picked up by two black jet skis, launched from Saltburn beach. I can say, quite categorically, that this libellous story is complete and utter nonsense. The Customs were watching Saltburn!

The media circus continued as the public turned their anger on HMRC. The scale and cost of the operation was becoming a public joke, but the Crown had billions at stake. As an island with thousands of miles of coastline, they couldn't hope to police it all. The prospect of hundreds of fishermen turning offshore shop keepers was very real.

Amazingly, the weather forecast indicated another storm coming. Customs wrote to me to say that if the Cornish Maiden came in for shelter, the goods would not be considered secure enough on-board, and would have to be removed, stored and returned by a Customs approved operator at our cost, and their convenience.

I replied stating that Trevor was the Captain. If he chose to come in, he was entitled to the same rights and protection of the law as any other vessel claiming 'force majeure', sheltering from a storm.

The law is in place to stop authorities all over the world taking advantage of a vessel needing shelter, or repair. It would be an excellent boost to a local economy, if the Customs could simply impose their will on any vessel they choose.

"Okay, Captain, we think there are rebels in the area. We're going to unload all the containers off your ship, store them at my cousin's warehouse, and bring it all back for you when it's safe, but you'll have to pay the bill beforehand." Lives would be at risk – rather than seek shelter and risk the cargo, a Captain might take chances. Customs were setting a dangerous precedent.

In any case, they indicated a bill of about £1k. I had no intentions of letting them break the law, and take control of our stock. I made enquiries about hiring a high security container with built-in satellite alarm, and got permission from the marina to locate it in the secure area.

This newly invented concern about security was ridiculous; the marina is gated with twenty four hour guard and CCTV. Even if the Cornish Maiden could be smashed open, it would be in full view, with nowhere to run. It'd be easier ram raiding Asda.

Trevor brought her in demanding the same treatment as any other ship. Customs said they were unloading her in twenty four hours. I procured some steel grate, a welder, and fabricated a security cage for the hold hatches, complete with the biggest hasp, staple and padlock, money could buy.

They said it was still not secure enough, and refused to allow the use of the container. Clearly, they were taking our stock whatever we did. I said we would leave within twenty four hours. They said that's not an option. Thompson said he would call the fire service to gain access to the hold if I was not there to open it. Not secure? My arse!

As far as the law and we were concerned, Customs were well outside the box. That was game, set and match. We protested first but Trevor wanted to let them do it, but only with a condition. We agreed with Officer Thompson and his boss to assist the unloading by moving the boat to a suitable location. In return, they agreed to let us declare some goods and have them seized by Customs officially. This would enable us to proceed and test the matter in court, where we knew we'd win.

Trevor lost his bottle at this time, and agreed to have his half of the stock moved to an approved warehouse at his own expense. He was quoted a reasonable estimate by Customs. I knew he was making a mistake. I knew it was an illegal seizure. We would see who was right, and who was wrong.

The time came for Customs and a crew of haulage employees to empty the hold. Again, they over-dramatised the situation, getting police to secure an area, and cordon if off as though gold bullion was being moved.

Despite us having agreed the lawful way forward, they waited until it started to rain, then unloaded the goods onto the dock side, taking cover while the crates and open cardboard boxes filled with water for the second time. It was simply disgraceful, Nazi-like behaviour.

Of course we recorded all this as I went out and shouted at them, pointing out a tarpaulin which could easily have been used. The damage was already done, but I had them. No court in the land would allow that to go on in the Queen's name, or so we thought.

When the wagon finally turned up, it transpired it had been waiting for instructions, out of sight. Now the stock was truly soaked again, it was time for them to go home. I asked Officer Thompson for the 'symbolic' goods that it was agreed they would seize. True to his word, he instructed a female officer to put them aside.

His boss, a skinny slinky bloke, spray tan, resembling Jerry Springer, overdressed in a fake shiny suit, intervened and stopped the agreed transaction. Basically, we were getting screwed again! Jerry was strutting around for the TV cameras, and he looked for support from the rest of the crew as we protested. The truth is they were sickened by what they'd been ordered to do again, especially as an agreement had been reached.

These were the same people who'd unloaded Rich Harvest into the rain in a totally illegal swoop, and then had to take it back. The details were public knowledge, and the cameras were watching again as they criminally destroyed our stock. Only Jerry was proud of himself. There were no smiles or laughter that day, only embarrassment and shame.

Junior recorded the events, including my scathing verbal attack on Jerry for his treacherous behaviour. If I'd thrown him in the water, I don't think there'd have been a stampede to pull him out. He was clearly about as popular as a pig farmer in a mosque.

Officer Thompson apologised for having no choice but to break his word. To be honest, he was alright. None of the abuses were his decisions, and he was simply acting on instructions, shovelling someone else's shit downhill!

Half a truckload of our money left the marina, never to return.

Customs had made so many errors; to sue them in court was a done deal. Later they sent a bill for a ridiculous three thousand pounds after we'd been relayed an estimate by Thompson of one thousand pounds. This is exactly the criminal behaviour the law of 'force majeure' was designed to prevent. British Customs had acted like a tin pot banana republic's militia. Even I was shocked how brazen they were.

It was now up to us to appeal the seizure as illegal in the town's Magistrates' court. Any decision by the magistrates had an automatic right of appeal to a higher court, so it was really irrelevant. Ultimately, the Customs had discriminated against us because of our activity, and this would likely need to go to the European Court of Human Rights before justice may be done.

Both vessels remained in Hartlepool while we awaited British Justice to run its course. A few weeks later, Customs wrote and offered us the stock back – if we paid the bill. We refused, the stock was ruined, and we wouldn't even get our money back. That'd been their plan; each time they deliberately soaked it.

They were worried. By now their legal people had examined every detail and concluded that we were on a winner. The media eagerly awaited every bit of news. We knew they were in no hurry; they'd stopped it for now. Their plan for the future was to direct as many resources as it took to know our every move, and then mess it up! To tie me with a criminal enterprise would do them the world of good in court.

The public eagerly awaited the outcome, HMRC were dreading it.

I didn't just sit about, I ran as an independent candidate at the Hartlepool by-election after Peter Mandelson left to become an MEP. After I entered, I couldn't believe the attention we got. I'm not sure if it was meant, but the surveillance was very much over the top, even blatant, like they were trying to scare us. The people of Hartlepool loved me. I think they saw me as a threat.

I put together an election communication document under the protection of parliamentary privilege which was scathing to say the least. It was so inflammatory that the postmaster refused to send it out without legal advice, a sneaky move, as we were close to the deadline. I came third last. Out of forty seven thousand letters, only a few hundred were delivered. I was furious, and disrupted the results presentation along with members of the Fathers for Justice party. The police surrounded me and bustled us out as I tried to speak to the press and state my case, but it went unreported.

In the few weeks after the election, I had friends and colleagues reporting back that they'd been followed after seeing me. I knew we always had company, but the manpower used on this farce must've been a fortune. I don't know which agencies were involved, but everybody I mixed with was looked at, some even had official visits at home and business premises, such as vehicle checks, stop and search, health and safety, VAT, hygiene, employment records and so on. Just sheer bullying, and they made no secret of it, dropping my name at the same time.

By December 2004, I'd had enough. It was ridiculous. I started to realise how much a threat I must have been to the status quo regarding excise duty, and believed I had more serious agencies on me, such as MI5 or MI6.

My relationship was about over, and my back was causing a severe limp, made worse by the cold weather. We'd used each other for selfish reasons, and it was time to break. She was already looking for a house closer to her family, but said nothing. I would much rather she'd been honest, and could have parted friends. My brother Alan (RIP) was going to Thailand over Christmas with a few blokes I knew. I decided we needed to leave. I'm sorry to all those genuine people I seemed to ignore. I was doing you all a favour!

Junior and I flew to Thailand via Holland, but not before we got a really serious pull at Teesside airport. It comes to something when you get searched and questioned on the way out of the UK, but of course it came as no shock. What on earth a person can smuggle from the UK to Thailand and make a profit, I have no idea. My only credible conclusion was they were looking for cash. After we'd taken the piss a little, we continued our journey.

I was looking forward to Thailand; the British establishment have very little influence there. I could relax for the first time since my spell on remand. We still had some spare funds to work with, and would be looking to invest in something profitable while we waited for the legal machine in the UK to crank forward.

CHAPTER THIRTY

THAILAND - LAND OF SMILES

Always looking for a business opportunity, Thailand was no different for me. Mosquitoes were the only problem with Thailand. We had no problem in our suite high up, but at sea level, they were a nightmare at sun down. The vast majority of products available were mostly ineffective or very short lived.

We wanted something to do, and saw an opportunity. We began ordering and experimenting with all sorts of products and compounds. Eventually, we arrived at a product we were very happy with and decided to call it Buzzzofff. By the end of 2004, we had a product on route.

Meanwhile, the Customs appeal had been heard at the Magistrates' courts in Hartlepool, despite my notifying them that I needed an adjournment. I wasn't worried; we had thirty days in which to appeal, then it would go to Crown court where we would get a fair crack of the whip.

We returned via Teesside airport to the usual welcome. Customs forensically examined our luggage, telephones and laptop. They take such items on the pretext of x-raying them, but in fact they download everything from the memory including personal documents and photos. It's a diabolical liberty they get away with more frequently than you could believe.

If I was up to no good, I wouldn't dream of taking sensitive info through an airport or ferry terminal. Quite often, if your name's on the shit list, they search your gear before the baggage belt then copy anything they're 'building a case' with. Some mugs think they've slipped through undetected, but in reality, they haven't.

On ferries, teams use dogs and often burgle vehicles before docking. That's why they won't let you near your car. Search warrants? No chance. If they so want, they'll give you a tug, pretending it's a random act, knowing full well what they're going to find. In any case, after an hour of blatant abuse of power, we continued to our vessel in Hartlepool marina.

As a matter of course, and purely out of habit, I set tell tale 'indicators' on doors, draws and cupboards, a hair glued between a door and frame to tell if some nosey bastards have been through our stuff. Every nook and cranny had been searched. The marina had an excellent CCTV system, but the agencies have free access to it as usual. Who's going to question them? I'd long since learned to live with the fact that nothing I had or did, was private.

I applied to appeal on the last day possible.

We attended and got the matter moved to Middlesbrough Crown Court without much drama, apart from my first meeting with the Customs appointed QC James Puzey who seemed to think he had some sort of authority over us. It wasn't long before he was put in his place. We stayed in the UK under very heavy surveillance. Whenever I met with friends or associates, I became the 'kiss of death' to anyone who had the slightest fiddle going on. I couldn't wait to get away again.

Later the same week, I bumped into some people I knew from back home and had a drink with them. One, a guy called Craig, stayed a couple of nights with us. He was good pals with Benny the Bell, mentioned previously. One of his gang we met up with was an ex-copper who'd been the landlord of his local pub. I don't know anything for sure, but our life in Thailand took a bad turn, a week after his visit.

We quickly realised our house was under heavy surveillance, and the attitudes of the Thai's we had contact with changed dramatically. It was like they'd been told we were buying babies. The pool cleaner and housekeeper couldn't look at us. They disappeared. We got new staff from the estate agency we got the house from. The agency also changed their attitude, demanding further deposits, and outrageous charges. It was all becoming too familiar. We'd been here before.

We went to get paid, and replace stock in the pharmacies and other venues, only to be given the remaining stock back, along with the money owed. We were losing customers hand over fist. No explanation was given, only 'Boss man'.

I knew something was badly wrong when my daughter rang to say her house had been raided by Customs and police after I'd sent a parcel there by carrier. Included in a bunch of other gifts were a couple of rechargeable security torches bought for less than five pounds in Baht. I had no idea they could also be used as stun guns with a little modification.

There was no indication on the box whatsoever. I'd been sold them by the new pool cleaning guy, and packed them to make up the twenty kilos parcel weight. She went crazy. I couldn't apologise enough. Worse still, there were another four on route, packed with some other stuff we'd bought for the boat.

Later, I had to properly examine a torch before I could work out exactly what it was, and how to use it. They'd not been discovered with a random x-ray. A person would need to unpack it from its box and take it to bits. Clearly HMRC thought we were up to something sinister, and were forensically examining our parcels.

Luckily, the next lot got through as we'd changed the parcel carrier because we were trying out different services before we started shipping our product about. Nikki called panicking, so I e-mailed her a letter to take to the police station, along with the four torches/stun guns, thereby negating any criminal charges relating to the first parcel. Of course, I told her to get a receipt.

We went further afield with our product, only to find the businesses who said yes at first, would cancel before delivery was due. It was like someone was following us about and putting the boot in. Then one night, as I was looking around my bedroom for bugs as the patio doors had been left open, I noticed something on top of a door frame that didn't move.

Thinking it must be a flying roach or even a baby gecko, I armed myself with a fly zapping bat (much like a stun gun for insects) and used a stool to stand on. On closer inspection, it was a radio transmitter, a bug, but not one that got there on its own. This particular bug was powered from the telephone line running around the doorframe. Crude, but effective.

Downstairs there were two more: one in the office, housed in an electric clock, taking power from it, and the last one was in the sofa I sat on, powered by a battery, scarily meaning the buggers had to have regular access to change it. I had to box clever. I told no one. I was used to being watched, but the others would give the game away if they knew.

I went to an electronic market and bought a mini camera, digital recorder and a passive infrared switch. I hid them in the alarm box. Two days later, I watched our new pool cleaner transform into a secret agent, changing the battery and copying the previous day's work from our computer, while we were all still in bed.

I had no idea what the UK agencies had told their Thai counterparts in order to get them involved, but it can't have been good. There were clearly forces working against us. I could see little point in hanging around, and although I had limited faith in UK justice, I had zero confidence there, and really didn't fancy putting it to the test. It was time to go before we had something planted by the pool man, and I don't mean a bush.

I arranged for a carrier to collect two and a half tons of our products, seven pallets in all and store it securely pending a delivery address. We flew back almost immediately. I felt a great sense of danger in those last few days there, and I'm usually spot on. The usual hassle at the airport was nothing more than expected. I left Darren and his girl to vacate the house, and sell or post the things that we'd bought.

For the first time in many years, I'd enjoyed being left alone in Thailand. For almost six months, I'd been free to think and relax. I had no intentions of staying in the UK for it all to continue again. I decided we would quit the UK, and set off on Rich Harvest, getting agents for our product on route to the Caribbean, where the mosquitoes are a real pain.

We'd spent nearly £70k on the project. Dosh was running low, but we were confident of success away from HMRC. We sold the Cornish Maiden for a song and cashed a few motors we had which were lying about. We set about preparing our vessel for a long voyage. We would need to up the fresh water capacity, so the Golden Virginia we found still stored in two of the three water tanks would need to go ashore. I still can't believe we'd forgotten about that!

Our stock was coming by sea, and would take six weeks. As it transpired, these six weeks would be very significant indeed.

CHAPTER THIRTY ONE

A MURDEROUS VOYAGE!

We stayed on our schooner at Hartlepool and rather than bring the agencies' attention to our friends and acquaintances again. We kept a fairly low profile and saved them the hassle. We had a month to kill until our stock reached Europe. I didn't want to bring it to the UK, just to take it south again, and I just knew Customs would mess me up if I gave them the chance. The company was based in Thailand, and had nothing to do with the UK.

I had no intentions of getting involved with licences in the UK or anywhere else; that would be the job of the importer or agent in the various jurisdictions we intended to visit. I contracted the carriers to send them to Portugal where they'd be held as 'goods in transit' by Customs until I collected them with Rich Harvest. Portugal was on route, about ten days sailing. November/December was the soonest we would cross the Atlantic due to the hurricane season.

The plan was to sail to, and around the Caribbean to find agents/ importers for the product on route, using our yacht as a promotion tool.

Finally we had a hearing on 9th June 2005 with Judge Taylor. I was representing myself. Trevor had as much to gain, as by now the Customs had 'disposed' of his share of the cargo, which he stupidly agreed to have stored through them. His solicitor had failed to respond to or pass on a notice from Customs. I say this was a deliberate act, no accident. Trevor had complied fully with Customs, now he had nothing but the hope of me winning my case. He'd boxed clever, and left the risk of failure and costs to me. If I won, he'd win.

At court, I did really well, surprising everyone there. I was winning hands down until I had Jerry Springer on the ropes. The judge seemed to panic when some points were made; then he advised me to abort and get a barrister. I wanted to continue as I knew I'd taken them by surprise. I don't know if he was saving the witness or the result. He was adamant I should abort. He even adjourned to check I could get legal aid, and all but promised it, telling me he'd grant a 'Representation Order' citing the complexities of law which would guarantee support for legal counsel, and that I risked failure if I did not. With that, I agreed to abort the case on his advice.

Amazingly, much later, almost a year, and just before the next hearing, the Judge retracted and apologised for misleading me. Clearly he'd been overruled. There would be no legal aid; the 'complexity of law' had evaporated! Does this stink or what? I personally think I took them by surprise. I was winning all by myself, but that couldn't happen, could it? Rather than have me, an uncouth layman embarrass the legal profession by annihilating their arguments, they lied to me to have the case aborted. British Justice? I'd been in this place before. The saga would have to continue on.

This is when I met Nicola. She lived close by, and spent some time with Junior after we'd seen her in the marina paddling a big kayak along with five young people, all with various disabilities. We were doing a barbeque and invited her later. At twenty two she was a bit old for Junior, but they seemed to get on really well. He was more man than boy now, and could make his own mind up.

She had a degree in disabled sport development, and had played hockey at international level. She had a nice gaff close by, a nice car and a good job for the council. Junior spent some nights at her apartment while I was entertaining. I encouraged it, and made her very welcome. She was an absolute star, and a real good catch. Pity we were leaving soon.

After a couple of weeks, she passed our boat, and asked if it was okay to come on later. The Tall Ships were at Hartlepool at the time, and we'd been out most of the day. Later, she arrived just as Phil called to say he wouldn't be back till much later. She might say different but the fact is this had been planned, and she seduced me!

It transpired Phil wasn't the least bit interested, and was using her flat to entertain some local girls. She'd had the hots for me since Vibes, Junior had been singing her praises, and was part of the plot. He saw Nic as a cool stepmother.

She didn't do make-up, high heels, handbags, drink or smoke, and had only one previous owner, the opposite to my usual choices. I put it down to a one off and played it cool. We were leaving soon, and I didn't want to make it difficult. Women and boats don't usually mix. I know a few lucky sailors whose partners are just as keen, but the vast majority sail under duress, if at all.

With no commitments or promises, we spent a bit more time together, with Junior still putting the pressure on. I knew I wouldn't see her again after we set sail, so despite the age difference, I let it happen. By the time we were ready to leave, I was trying hard not to get too close. She was on contract to the council, it couldn't be.

I had other options on the table also, but knew for certain we were heading south. I couldn't put up with the constant invasion of our lives anymore. Phil Junior was growing roots again, and my mission was always to show him a different way of life. He was doing well; it needed to continue at least another year. No woman was going to follow me wherever I went, and it would be silly to think they would.

The outlook on my back injury indicated I could soon be in a wheelchair; the advice was to keep moving, despite the pain. The anti-inflammatory drugs were playing havoc with my guts. I wanted to sail our boat for as long as I could. I was limping a lot then, and the cold in the UK made it worse, especially after forty degrees in Thailand.

I paid up the marina and waited for the right weather. I didn't want all the goodbyes and drama. We would be back for the court case when we got a date a year later. We slipped our lines at 0300h on 3rd August 2005, went through the loch gate, and sailed into the night with only Nicola there to say goodbye. Both us of had tears streaming down our faces.

At twenty-two metres, four working sails and sixty seven tons, we were extremely short-handed, but easy sailing is for pussies, so a forty something half cripple, and a lad nearly sixteen, set off doing the job of six crew.

The wind was strong, but in the perfect direction. We thrashed the boat full sail, and made the Thames estuary in thirty hours, me without sleep, and Junior taking power naps. Soon we would be in the English Channel heading west. To change course, we'd need to reef some sails as the wind was blowing a six, but we'd wait until then.

We were almost in the busiest shipping channel in the world, when we headed upwind to reef the huge Yankee cut foresail with an electric roller reefing system operated by remote control. The timing of the operation is critical, or the boat loses speed, and manoeuvrability. At just the right time, the sails start to flap; that's when it's time to change it all.

I pressed the button. The aluminium 'foil' around the huge forestay (big wire that holds the top of the mast to the front of the boat) began to furl the sail throughout the height of the mast. It only turned about five times before we heard a huge crack! Then the forestay parted. The twenty metre foremast whipped backwards, sending a thick, scary shudder throughout the hull, before bowing and flexing dangerously close to snapping.

I thought the mast was coming down, and after we paused momentarily to shit ourselves, I bawled, "Life jackets and grab bag NOW!"

Junior didn't need telling twice; he was back in about seven seconds, life jacket on in fifteen. The 'grab bag' is a waterproof floating container which contains all the stuff you need for the life raft, such as handheld VHF, flares, chocolate, brandy, and emergency cannabis smoking kit. If you have time, wallet and phone goes in there too.

The halyard (rope that pulls the sail up the foil) miraculously held, stretching further than I would ever have believed. The sail caught the wind and pulled the bow round. The foil, now the top of the sail, was at forty five degrees. The boat picked up a couple knots as it found its own centre, pulling us round further until we were 'running' before the wind.

The rest of the sails and rigging were banging and flapping. It was hard to think, but I knew one thing – while we were running, the weight would be on the foremast, the 'stays' beside and behind it, and not where the forestay should have been. We had a slim chance to avert disaster, if we worked fast.

The stainless steel bracket holding the furling gear had ripped its bolts off from one side and twisted. We had no idea when it would part completely. To make matters worse, we were heading into the path of a huge tanker ploughing towards us. At the speed we were doing, we would pass in front, but it would be very close. Then I had to consider that we'd slow down as the sail area came in. In short, we were on collision course!

I had to make a decision. If I turned with a full foresail, the mast would come down. The safest way was forward, and hope for the best. If it got too close, we could jump ship, and likely we'd be picked up in no time. Forward had to be the plan. I fired up the main engine for the first time since we cleared Hartlepool, so we could maintain speed and steerage to avert the impending disaster.

I got on the radio to warn the ship of our situation. He had no chance of stopping, and changing course would take too long. We had less than five minutes to work with. Junior went forward, and let the halyard down a metre while I slackened the sheet (rope that pulls the sail tight). As the sail flapped, I wound it in a metre with the roller reefing that was amazingly still working.

This operation was repeated a dozen times, until it was half in before the engine stopped dead. Now, we were in trouble (as if we weren't already). I couldn't waste time on the engine. The plan was working. I could see a way to minimise loss, or more or less save everything. All we needed was the rest of the sail in before it was too late. The dickhead on the bridge of the ship didn't help by blowing his horn, and blabbing on the radio every thirty seconds. I had no time to answer.

I kicked in the auto pilot to hold course, and went on deck with my brave little fellow, who by now was wondering if he'd see his sixteenth birthday, which as it happened, was the next day. He never flinched, did exactly as he was told without a wasted breath. The vast majority would be screaming and panicking, but not him, he wanted to hear every word I said; I was his best chance of seeing sixteen, and he knew it!

As the sail furled in metre by metre, and was almost at deck level on the port side, she started to veer off course. The autopilot couldn't handle the imbalance with a full mainsail and staysail still up and connected to the aft mast. The little fore staysail couldn't help the rudder. In short, we had too much sail area aft to hold a course, and were seriously in danger!

We needed literally just another minute to lash the fallen stay, sail, and furling assembly to the hand rails to be safe. With no other option, I took out my knife and slashed the halyard of the staysail. It came crashing down flapping furiously. A big sail has a heavy steel eye that'll break your bones if you get in the way. My first job was to catch hold and lash it. A short struggle and it was done. We frantically lashed the gear alongside before I dashed back, disengaged the autopilot, and swung the wheel hard to port, heart pumping like a blood worm with a hook up its arse.

She swung round quickly due to the full main, which on a staysail schooner is the one at the stern/back. I did a one eighty degrees with about fifty metres to spare. The ship was so close, her bow wave lifted us violently, but thankfully helped push us away to safety. Half a dozen crew on deck gawped in disbelief as she stole our wind. We were beam on and stationary as her huge wake rolled us gunwale to gunwale.

There were more ships coming, we had to get her moving again without putting any weight on the foremast. We frantically messed about with what sails were still up for an extremely stressful fifteen minutes; finally doing a steady course at about three knots (walking pace). Any other direction, and she wandered off course.

Unfortunately, we were heading across the busy shipping lane diagonally. Every ship in the lane must travel the same course. If you cross the lane, it has to be at ninety degrees. Phil Junior protested, citing navigation and collision rules, danger, drowning and other negative remarks. I explained the ships pilots didn't have a crystal ball; we had to maintain a steady course, so other ships radar could calculate our speed and course to avoid us. Our only steady course would take us to Calais. Pissing about, with a mortally wounded rig would create serious confusion in the busiest section of the busiest marine motorway in the world; so, even at speed of three knots, Calais it was. We'd been in the news enough!

He was white as a ghost. I could see he was scared, regardless of expression, and he had every right to be. I told him to get the fishing rods out.

"Are you joking, fatherbean?"

"No son, I want mackerel for breakfast, and it'll take your mind off the shit in your shreddies (underpants)".

With the autopilot on, we caught six nice fish as the nearby ships altered course, and passed within throwing distance.

Within an hour, the barbeque was on and Junior's nerves returned as he saw the funny side of a story many wouldn't believe in the future. We had brunch amid blowing horns. We didn't reply to the VHF only for pan-pan messages at intervals.

Pan-Pan is an urgency signal, not the same as a mayday. It went, "Pan-pan, pan-pan, pan-pan; this is schooner Rich Harvest, schooner Rich Harvest, on your port bow heading one ninety degrees, be aware we have rigging and engine failure, we cannot manoeuvre, please alter your course as necessary, and keep a sharp look out, pan-pan."

When all was squared away, we found the problem with the engine. The fuel filters were blocked with grey sludge. I switched over to the reserve filter, and started the motor. It ran for ten minutes before they also blocked. I replaced both sets of filters, but left the engine off. We would get as far as possible into Calais, and only use the engine for docking.

I began to investigate the rigging failure. We'd been all over the North Sea braving horrible weather. The rigging and sails were nearly new at a cost of £60k. We unravelled the sail and found the forestay hadn't parted, but unscrewed from the top of the mast as we reefed.

Further examination under a cover at the base where the roller reefing system was mounted revealed the cause. A thick stainless steel pin designed to stop the stay turning had been removed. It couldn't have just fallen out or broken, as the bits would still be under the cover. This was sabotage, plain and simple.

We limped along at a snail's pace, contemplating the ramifications of this. Later as we approached Calais, we saw we were being shadowed by a boat a mile or so astern of us. We ignored it and continued into the dock as darkness fell. We easily found the entrance to a smaller dock, where our pilot book showed mooring buoys we could tie up to for the night.

Out of the darkness came a French Customs patrol boat. They were only thirty metres off our stern when a huge spotlight burned into our cockpit, blinding us. Our own handheld device hardly made a difference as we lit up their bridge, furiously gesturing for them to turn it off.

I got on the VHF to protest. It was reflecting off our screen and bright work, we couldn't see anything ahead. The spotlight turned off just in time. We fired up the motor as our vision returned to normal, furled the two remaining sails, and motored to our mooring as the patrol boat passed us, tying up on a wall close by.

I thought that was it, silly stupid bastards! We dropped the RHIB and were about ready to go ashore, when ten armed men in black paramilitary assault garb roared up in a big RHIB, storming the boat with guns drawn. What a shower of shit! It's much better to keep both hands free in such circumstances. Two of them nearly went in the drink during the scramble, and one had to jump back on to tie it on!

They were wide eyed and scared, some were taking cover, some were kneeling, all were pointing guns at us, shouting and bawling. We were drenched in spotlights from three or four places. Regardless of what they order, the safest thing to do is stand still, with our hands on our heads; there was no telling what these dimwits were thinking, apart from we were extremely dangerous. Shouting various orders to confuse us is standard drill. I'd seen it before in the Helford pass in 94. I assumed the position, and gestured at Junior to do the same, saying to him, "Don't move!"

I smiled cockily as two approached, guns levelled with both hands. One of the bastards was shaking, he couldn't hold his gun still. He was stood down as soon as the leader noticed, and replaced by an older guy who seemed to have more sense. We were cuffed, searched for weapons, and ordered to kneel on the deck. I refused, shaking my head. They knew we were no danger by now. I walked two metres and sat on the aft lockers. Phil followed. We were sweating like rapists, still in our weather suits, which didn't help, because we looked guilty as hell. Two guarded us, the rest did a commando style sweep of our boat, no doubt looking for machine gun toting desperados, complete with suicide vests. Drama queens, watching too many cheap movies!

Laughing really took the jam from their donuts. They just couldn't fathom it. These guys had obviously been told all sorts of bullshit by our own agencies, and responded accordingly. They looked genuinely scared, while we were genuinely confused.

When it became clear there was no one else on-board, we were taken down to the stern saloon as the SWAT team began to tear our boat apart without mercy.

What on earth can be smuggled from the UK to France to turn a profit is beyond my wildest imagination. Even after half an hour, we were still cuffed, so I began to make a fuss, demanding to be released so we could take off our sailing suits. We were sweating like smack heads in a chemist. Eventually we were allowed to get comfortable. I poured a mega brandy, lit a fag, and settled down to wind them up. I also recorded them.

When they relaxed a little, I poured another brandy, got another fag and pulled a nine millimetre Berretta from under the cushion next to me. Before the three clowns in the saloon could get a breath, I lit my fag with it, and nearly choked laughing. They didn't see the funny side, but we did!

After an hour of showing the boss the court papers, newspaper cuttings and news videos, he started to realise they'd been duped.

Little Phil had been helping some of them to gain access to spaces they wanted to look in to prevent further damage.

One picked up a pair of red ladies knickers from under his bed, waved them about, then asked him if he was homosexual.

He'd had a hard day bless him.

"Piss off, Dickhead," he spat at the guy, and squared right up to his face.

I remember thinking I'd have to keep my eye on him.

We did have something they were interested in, something very dear to us, a plant we called Harriet. It was a baby female 'White Widow' variety, so named after the slang for skunk which is 'Harry Monk'.

After finding nothing else apart from the knickers, one of them clocked it, and asked if it was cannabis.

"No, no," I said. "It's Sativa, very similar, but for rope and textile production."

He leaned over, and scrunched a few leaves to smell it.

I grabbed his arm, shouting at him, "And it's very expensive."

He backed off. We were very fond of Harriet.

They'd made right twats of themselves. We took the piss, big style, clapping and jeering at them as they got back in their RHIB. We videoed them as we shouted insults. They'd wrecked our boat inside. The mess was catastrophic. As is the same everywhere, not the slightest apology was offered. Bastards, all of them! If you make a mistake, own up, make up and apologise.

We decided to chill for while, putting the kettle on before going ashore. Tea on the table, my son sat down, and burst into tears, something I hadn't seen for years. It was a shock, believe me. We'd been at sea some forty four hours and barely snatched a kip between us. After nearly losing the mast, almost getting run down, discovering sabotage, making it to safety, only to be stormed by armed thugs who trashed our boat, it was just too much for a young lad. He broke down. It was a rare 'father and son' moment, I'll never forget.

I've got to give him credit where credit's due. I have more bottle than any man I know, but it was wrong to expect him to cope at his age. He didn't buckle under pressure when I needed him; he was more of a man than any father could possibly dream of. I was so, so proud of him. I have tears myself while writing this. I know plenty of hard sailors, who'd have crumbled, long before him. Me? I had brandy!

I cuddled and comforted him as a terrible rage built up inside me. I could have lit a cigarette with it.

"Come on," I said, "get a Red Bull into you, it's your birthday in half an hour. Let's go celebrate being alive, son. We can deal with this shit in the morning."

He forced a smile on his tired face, and set about finding some clean clothes, mumbling, "Frog bastards, dirty frog bastards!"

We shipped ashore, and headed for the town where there was a funfair on all night. As our anger turned to adrenaline, we painted the town red, ending up in a bar full of British wide boys, based there for smuggling. I scored some nice cannabis I'd need to smoke, and drink myself to sleep, my head was farting. Did that really happen?

Tomorrow was another day. Phil was no worse for his experience, and he'd kept his cool throughout, I could see a man on his sixteenth birthday. Happy days!

Next day, hung-over, we surveyed the damage. The main problem was the engine room, where they'd climbed over machinery, damaging pipes, wiring, and fittings; they'd used junction boxes as steps, ripping them from the bulkheads. Both alternators were damaged, engine sensors were broken off. There was chaos in every cabin; it took us all day to tidy up.

I set about the engine and drained over 50 gallon of fuel, only to find the same grey sludge. I checked the deck filler fitting, and found the pipe blocked with newspaper, scrunched up into balls. It would've taken a few hours to get so much in the tank. Luckily the starboard tank had been isolated as it was lower than the port tank, and could only be opened when the levels were equal.

As we had a clean tank with clean fuel on the starboard side, I replaced the filters, and we had power again. I decided there was too much work to do in Calais. We would limp to the UK, and do it there. The engine would be okay in bursts without the wiring and sensors we needed. I botched the pipe work, and wired up one alternator as best we could, with what we had.

If any of you reading this think that no government agency would do such a thing as what we believed, but have no proof of, remember in 1985 the Greenpeace ship Rainbow Warrior was bombed and sunk by the French secret service in operation Satanique to stop them demonstrating against a nuclear test. People died. The trail of murder eventually went all the way up to the president. The agents only served two years.

CHAPTER THIRTY TWO

EASTBOURNE AND AWAY

After a couple of days of repairing what we could, and waiting for good weather to limp over, we decided on Eastbourne as our next stop. The bits we needed for the rigging were impossible to find in Calais. At 0500h just before first light, we slipped our mooring, and motored past the sleeping Customs patrol boat on the 8th August.

Amazingly, they'd left their big fancy RHIB tied to the stern, instead of hauling it back on-board. It appeared someone had slashed the inflatable tubes, and removed the hull drain bungs during the night. It was all but sunk, except for the lines attached. I decided to take the shortest route to the twelve mile limit, out of French Jurisdiction, just in case they decided to blame us. A nice bit of Karma that. Little Phil was convinced it'd been me, as he'd found puddles of water on board when he got up, as if!

After a pleasant uneventful trip, we tied up in Eastbourne. Our plan was to repair the rigging, and check everything from stem to stern. It was only a year or so since it was all done. The boat hadn't moved, prior to our departure, but clearly some dirty bastards had tried to mess us up. The next leg would be the Bay of Biscay, where you really don't want any surprises.

Dave, the ex-trawler skipper called to ask if he could jump on, and meet his girlfriend and her daughter in Portugal. I agreed to them all staying on board for the week; a good hand would be useful, especially after the mess in the channel. As a trawler man, he'd have seen his fair share of bad weather, but had never been out of the North Sea. As he now lived on a sailing boat, he needed the sailing experience to increase his credibility in the marina.

Nicola also called, explaining she'd swung three weeks holiday if she first took a group of guys with special needs to the lakes, camping for two days. I didn't think it was a good idea, but couldn't say no. She'd never been to sea before. Biscay takes no prisoners. It took me by surprise that she seemed very keen. What could I do? We got on with the repairs, awaiting their arrival.

We had a couple of crab fishermen on-board a few times for drinks. Realising who we were, they told us a Navy boat was hanging around offshore, which was unusual in that area. I must say, we had no bother at all at that marina; everyone was great, although we made absolutely certain she was never left unattended.

The repairs were almost complete. Nicola was on the train four days after we'd arrived. She called to tell me she'd been badly bitten by mosquitoes, as apparently the council hadn't provided her with a tent. She'd slept outside in a sleeping bag; she seemed quite upset and worried.

When she arrived, it was quite a shock. She'd been to accident and emergency. Her body had gone into toxic shock, the doctors wanted to keep her in, and certainly wouldn't let her travel, and I could see why. She'd been eaten alive, and had a face like a plate of scarlet porridge. She had a bag full of medication, and had ignored the doctor's advice.

What a state! She was petrified of me seeing her, and thought I wouldn't let her on. That's why she didn't say anything, till she was on the train. Women, eh? I started to see something special in this one.

I grabbed her bag and said, "For Pete's sake, woman, get down below before anyone sees you."

Talk about keen! I gave her a cuddle, and a bunch of our anti-mosquito towels, which were also excellent for soothing bites. She insisted on helping out, so I gave her light duties.

I have to say, I was well impressed. 99% of women, and most blokes for that matter, wouldn't have ventured anywhere but the hospital. She was in a right state. I made light of it, and told her I'd only shag her doggy style till she was better. Apparently, she was already a lot better. It was hard to imagine her being any worse.

A couple of days later, it was clearing up. Dave arrived and we set sail the next day, after being there a week. Next stop Portugal. We split up the crew. Nic would be on watch with me, and Junior with Dave, who wasn't too impressed at being under him. Phil knew the boat, and had earned his place. Dave had been a skipper a long time, but a trawler is a completely different animal, and I wasn't about to demote my little hero.

I always do the graveyard shift from dusk till dawn, which nobody else wants. It's much harder, especially as we never use the wheelhouse steering position, only the open cockpit, exposed to the elements. It's safer and keeps you awake. Too many yachtsmen have come to grief in a warm cosy wheelhouse with the autopilot on. Condensation inside and rain outside is, without doubt, a recipe for disaster. Good visibility is what keeps you safe at sea!

After two days plain sailing, we were at the western end of the channel, not far away from turning south. Nicola was shaping up very well. She could keep watch while I went about various tasks, and she soon knew her way around the navigation electronics. We were thirty miles from land with nothing about as we'd kept out of the shipping lanes. It would be light in an hour. I was below, knocking up some breakfast, when she shouted for me.

When I emerged, she said the alarm on the depth sounder had gone off. Frankly, I thought she'd made a mistake. We were in sixty metres of water, and would be for miles. It wasn't long since I'd checked the chart as I was teaching her to navigate. I checked the alarm display, which was still set to fifteen metres, and assumed she'd been fiddling with it.

After a few minutes I went below again, leaving her feeling a bit put out. She could tell I wasn't taking her seriously. I told her not to touch anything, and just keep watch. Ten minutes later, she shouted it was happening again. We were tired, and I was a bit stroppy as I came up. Sure enough, the alarm was buzzing. The screen showed we were in ten metres of water then it was eight. I disengaged the autopilot and swung the wheel to starboard, causing the sails to flap violently.

The sounder went back to sixty metres as the other two came

up to check what'd happened. I got them to trim the sails while I double-checked our position on the chart, plotter, and the radar. We were bang on. Dave started chuntering about women on boats and other chauvinistic shight, typical of a fisherman. He was glaring at Nic.

I jumped to her defence. "Ow, steady on big fella, ye grumpy old twat, go and get a cuppa, you're on in half an hour."

Being a skipper for so long, and as big as he was, he wasn't used to being talked to like that, but there's only room for one Captain, and it wasn't him. He scowled at me, and I laughed in his face. He quickly realised he was on a loser, and was almost in the door when the alarm went off again, showing twelve metres. We were five hundred metres from the last alarm. He went white, mainly because he didn't know I'd already double-checked where we were.

"There's sixty metres of water here, Dave. It's not rocks. Calm down, it must be a whale, messing with us," I said, which didn't put anybody at ease. The sounder alarm went silent, showing twenty metres, then twenty five, then thirty, and then back to sixty metres.

"Nicola, Phil, I apologise," he said, which was big of him. A man like him was not used to saying sorry.

We went back to our original course as the kettle boiled. Nicola, chuffed she'd been exonerated, and keen to show her mettle, stayed on watch for another thirty minutes while we supped our brew.

"Phil," she shouted, "I've got a target on the radar right behind us."

I shouted back, "Check the range, it should be on twelve miles. There was nothing close when I looked."

As I went topside, she confirmed it was still on twelve miles. Sure enough there was a target; I flicked the set to two miles range. The screen lit up with a target just less than two miles away on our stern, no lights, nothing to see. We were flummoxed as to why we hadn't seen it before. Only minutes later, as the sun was just lighting up the horizon, we saw it was no whale, it was a submarine. We could make out a bow wave and coning tower with the binoculars. By the time we'd all had a look, it disappeared, and didn't bother us again.

Later about 0800h, the only other incident on route which could possibly be linked to surveillance, was a light twin engine plane just before we turned south. It approached from the UK side, came down low, circled and flew back on the same route. It could hardly be described as covert. Maybe, it was just a pilot on a jolly who wanted a closer look at our beautiful boat; we'll never know for sure.

Perhaps the submarine needed a visual to confirm who they'd been following. Back in 1994 a nimrod airborne radar search plane had been deployed to find us in the Atlantic. On smuggling operations, the Navy are used to track and storm vessels at sea, often using elite groups like the SBS (Special Boat Service). In any case, it didn't need to surface. I deduced it was a show of force, a warning.

I played the whole incident down, but didn't sleep well that day, despite being shattered. I didn't want to scare my crew, but personally, I was worried. It wouldn't be first time a submarine had sunk a yacht or a fishing trawler for that matter. Just because I'm paranoid, doesn't mean they're not out to get me...

CHAPTER THIRTY THREE

BISCAY, A YACHTSMAN'S NIGHTMARE

We headed into the Bay of Biscay later that day. Most yachts going south will 'coast hop' around the bay, staying overnight in shelter. You're a long way from help if you take the shortest route. I've done it a few times, always going straight across, about three hundred and twenty miles. If you catch the weather wrong in a small boat, you're in Shit Street for sure.

We needed to make up time. We were late now. The five day forecast had been reasonable. I'd studied satellite weather predictions before we left and I was confident it wouldn't be too rough for Nicola, although there would still be plenty of wind to make good time. Of course, there're plenty of horror stories about 'The Bay'. As I wound them up a little, the three 'Biscay Virgins' were apprehensive, to say the least.

One absolute bonus to taking this route is the wildlife, which is just as interested in us, as we are in them, especially a sailing boat without the engines running. Dolphins, whales, sword fish, marlin, tuna are always worth watching. For my Virgins, this leg was fascinating, as every sighting was a first. When the dolphins first surrounded us, as they do, their faces were an absolute picture. Nicola and Phil were in marine Disneyland. If I have one video of dolphins, I've got twenty.

Only two things went wrong across the bay, both at night, while I was on the helm. The staysail top eye parted, sending it crashing down to the deck. A little bit of drama and a bit of stitching rectified it the next day, then the main sail boom runner came off its track with a bang, after pulling the track up from the boom. Both failures were clearly the weakest points, but had held before, in much stronger winds.

I blamed Dave for tightening everything down too hard. I'd told him a couple of times not to do it, but he was an old guy, set in his trawler ways. He'd waited until we'd gone to bed then 'Hardened' everything down, as he put it. I was taught to leave a little 'give' in the halyards and sheets (ropes) to absorb any shock. We weren't racing a few miles offshore, we were passage making.

He was a big strong bloke, and always wanted to bend the winch handles before he stopped. Yachts use expensive braided rope, trawlers use steel wire and cheap polypropylene. Now he'd seen the downside of his stupidity, he stopped doing it. I was in a foul mood, and let him know. He was told to follow my instructions to the letter, or leave the boat at the next landfall. I stitched the eye back into the staysail, modified a spare runner, and re-fixed it to the mainsail track, and made everybody watch as I set the strain how I wanted it. We had no more failures.

With Spain in sight, there's always a feeling of pride for any sailor, after the notorious Bay of Biscay. Nicola's first trip was one that would piss on the bonfire of many a bar bragger in the future. Phil Junior had completed the leg as coxswain at just sixteen, no mean feat on a big boat like ours.

Dave could now add this one to his short list of interesting sea yarns, and get some extra respect in Hartlepool where, like most marinas, the vast majority of sailors never leave sight of land. The infamous crossing of the Bay of Biscay is, for sure, a gold star on any sailor's log book.

A lot of sailors put into La Caruna in Northern Spain, but we continued nonstop to Portugal. As we cleared the bay, we passed Cape Finisterre, which again, is notoriously rough, and this time was no exception. Nic looked a bit dodgy. She was well overdue a sleep, so I sent her below to 'batten' the hatches and bed down. She soon discovered there are two positions to close the hatches, one is proper shut, and the other lets air circulate the cabin leaving a thirty millimetre gap. Not what you want in rough seas.

We took a wave over the bow that came over the cockpit, and all the way to the stern. We heard a scream, and laughed. Thirty seconds later she came up like a drowned rat. At least she wasn't tired now. Nobody, even your girlfriend, gets any mercy in this situation. We ribbed her for days, but couldn't fault her resolve. She dragged out the soaked bedding, and cleaned, dried and remade it before she stopped to sleep. What a woman!

She'd had passed a very arduous interview with flying colours; she had the potential to be the soul mate I'd always wanted. I knew this would complicate our plans, but even if I only had her for holidays, it would be enough for me after a string of worthless gold diggers. Junior thought she was great; he spent time passing on what I'd taught him. Nic was an extremely keen student. She wanted desperately to earn her place as a sailor, and not be judged for sleeping with the boss.

As we cleared the North of Spain, the weather was great, the sea alive, everybody relaxed as we sailed sweetly to our destination. Those good days are what sailing is all about; when everything is perfect, there's no better peace and tranquillity, and it's priceless. There are few days in the UK like these, and they don't usually land on a weekend. Being self-employed all my life, I would drop everything to go fishing or sailing on days like those.

We arrived at a place just north of the historic city of Porto, where the best port comes from. Lexious had a commercial port, as opposed to the River that Porto is built on. We were refused entry to the marina because there had lately been a catastrophic fire at a chemical plant close by. The fallout had covered the place with horrible toxic ash that'd damaged shit loads of stuff.

There were still boats in there, but it was closed for visitors. No doubt because they'd be getting paid for 'loss of business' from the chemical plant's insurance. I couldn't understand why they were dredging it, but was soon to find out.

They directed us to an anchorage area by radio. I checked the pilot book. It indicated the ground below us was 'good' for anchoring. The book also shows what the ground is made up of, which helps to select the right type of anchor to use.

A minimum four times the depth in chain is required. We set down five times the depth and a 'Bruce' anchor which 'ploughs' into the ground. The forecast was 'freshening', so we waited a while till it peaked to make sure our anchor was set. As the wind gusted, we slipped a little, so laid out double the chain. We still slipped. I put on a mask and fins, and went down for a look.

I've never seen anything like it. The water was clean, but the ground was covered with two feet of grey slippery silt. It soon transpired the cleanup after the fire had washed thousands of tons of chemical ash into the water. What else could they do? Vacuum it! Still, you'd think the dozy bastards would warn everybody. It's the harbour master's duty to keep all vessels safe.

We rigged two anchors, and added weights to the chain. She was held fast, time to relax. We could clear immigration tomorrow, when we were sure it was okay to leave the boat. Dave was up early, and gone to catch a train to meet his girlfriend and bring them back to stay on-board. The silly sod had taken a ride ashore from a boat close by, taking his passport, making a proper correct crew declaration impossible.

It was a Saturday, the Customs and our agents were not open till Monday. We had to wait to get our stock from Thailand. The dock was filled with dozens of kids in little dinghies sailing about. A fair few cruisers arrived and anchored. Junior took it upon himself to greet them in his RHIB to warn them about the anchorage problem, and often took them ashore, earning a few euros each time.

We quickly realised we were being watched by a couple of rank amateurs, but we had nothing to hide. I was fairly sure by now HMRC in the UK had sent some sort of bulletin around about our vessel, but had yet to discover just how far they'd gone.

CHAPTER THIRTY FOUR

ROBBERY, PLAIN AND SIMPLE

We contacted the agents, Gefco, who were responsible for our consignment, which we had been told, was hauled across Spain after the ship had docked on the east side. A couple of hours later, we received a demand for VAT and tax on our goods, and also an import license.

I put them right straight away. The goods were not coming into Portugal, and were clearly shipped as 'Goods in Transit'. I knew the law; they were to be held in the Customs compound until we put them on-board, and exported them in our vessel. There was absolutely no requirement to pay anything.

We were told to meet a Customs 'Agent' who basically asked how much cash we would pay for our stock. I refused to pay anything under the table. I was determined to keep everything 'squeaky clean'. I'd paid good money for transport, including all agents' fees. It seemed like a simple ransom, but there was more to it. I knew that much. The rules are the same throughout Europe. I was doing nothing wrong. Using an agent to ask for the bribe provides a buffer.

We went back and forwards to the Customs office, made dozens of calls and wrote countless e-mails to Victor Caravello at Gefco. We got nowhere. The Customs there refused point blank to put anything in writing, a clear breach of regulations. We were scowled at by everyone in the offices around the port. It was bloody obvious they were convinced we were serious criminals.

The surveillance became farcical; it was like the Keystone Kops, Charlie Chaplin and Inspector Clouseau were all on us. They set up mobile wireless cameras on the dock side as we kept waving at the clowns pretending to be fishing. We took the RHIB up close to the cameras to take photographs. Days turned into weeks. We were getting nowhere.

By now, we had a solicitor. Trevor had acquired him after a chance encounter on the steps of the university with an ex-student of his, or so the story went. This ex-student worked in London with a top man who would represent us on a no win, no fee basis. I'd resisted his appointment because I had every confidence, and wanted to present the case myself.

I called, and wrote to him and got no help whatsoever. He refused to respond or take calls. I was furious. I wrote to the solicitor dealing with our case at HMRC. He denied knowledge of anything. I finally got an appointment to see the boss in the Customs office, going equipped to record him, armed with documents and press reports. I was going to set the matter straight.

I wasn't expecting what came next. He told us our stock had simply 'disappeared' from the Customs compound. We had a row lasting an hour, all recorded. He said that HMRC had circulated information that we and our vessel was "the top of the list of international smugglers". They'd been told heroin was being transported from Thailand.

This confirmed what I'd already suspected, but to hear it, and record it direct from the boss, seemed at the time to be a bonus. At least I would have some ammunition to threaten them with. I gave him a crew list demanding he put our names and passports through a complete search. He was very surprised; our boat and none of us had any record whatsoever.

I believe heroin is the worst scourge on earth. To have those horrible, vindictive bastards at HMRC link my name with it, and then transmit it around Europe, made my blood boil! The director could clearly see I was furious, and he started to listen and look at the evidence I presented. I called the Customs solicitor Fred Phillips, and blasted him while on speakerphone. I ridiculed the surveillance methods the Portuguese used on us from the start, and demanded he tell his staff the truth.

He promised to find out about our stock, but again would not provide anything in writing. During eight weeks at Leixoes and dozens of visits to the Customs office, WE NEVER GOT ONE PIECE OF PAPER OR E-MAIL FROM THEM. They simply refused! I went to solicitors, but it was very hard to convince any of them without a single document. We did get one firm who agreed to call their office. When we returned, he asked us to leave.

From that day with the director, everybody there treated us much better. Clearly, we wouldn't still be coming back to the office if we had anything to hide, but we still didn't get our stock. I presumed it was being unpacked, and forensically tested until they were absolutely satisfied there was nothing in it. I believed we'd get it back shortly, albeit with some missing or damaged.

Nicola's three weeks was up. She went back to England, getting tortured at both airports by Customs, who questioned her about everything she'd done.

She hadn't been gone a few days when disaster struck. Junior was taking a dump, and I was in the stern saloon, when a huge crunch shook the boat, followed by the unmistakable sound of splintering wood as a sixty foot catamaran crashed along our starboard side.

The Big Green Lemon, or Grand Citroen Verde as it was known to its French owners, had only just arrived at the anchorage, and despite Phil's polite warning, hadn't dropped enough anchor chain, or even bothered to wait. The French family had gone ashore as the wind freshened.

Their boat was now bouncing down the side of ours. That wasn't the main problem. When she slipped further, her anchor would catch our chain, and uproot our own anchors, setting us both adrift in a tangled mess. Phil Junior jumped aboard as I threw him a line. He made it fast to the capstan in less than a minute; she'd slipped past us, and was hanging on our stern with the anchor chain jammed between the top of our rudder and our hull.

Phil jumped onto the RHIB in the water, and moved it clear before getting back to me. We fired up our main engine to take the extra weight off our anchors and leave them well buried, as they had been for three weeks.

As is usual in a dodgy situation, the wind picked up quite quickly. We tried with the engine to un-jam the chain from our rudder, then with the RHIB, pushing each variously sideways to no avail as darkness fell. I fired up the generator with the intention of cutting his chain, and just in time, the owner and his family came back in a dingy. With more hands and both his engines running, in an hour we managed to disentangle his vessel, and reset his anchor.

I knew we had damage above and below the waterline, so invited him aboard, and recorded his admission that he was 100% to blame, before he contacted his insurance, who in most cases, would tell him to deny liability. Next morning, they did just that, but the Frenchman had no choice but to admit it when I played the recording to him.

He wouldn't accept all the damage until he snorkelled down to see it, then it was case closed. His insurance would be paying for any, and all damage, or I would be claiming his boat for salvage. Technically we'd saved an unmanned vessel from destruction; better still, I had it all on video.

The Frenchman reported the accident to the Port Captain, as you should. Amazingly, our boat was arrested while he was allowed to continue. Because we had rudder damage, we would need a survey and sea trial to determine if we were fit for sea, by a surveyor, appointed by the port, but paid for by us. As there was no English-speaking engineer, so we had to wait until one became available. Our ship's papers were taken from us until it was done. We were now under their control, not an ideal situation.

We discovered much later from the insurance surveyor, that the Frenchman had set off south, and promptly ran a small fishing boat down in broad daylight. They were all below with the autopilot on having tea. When they came up, there was a Portuguese fisherman hanging on each bow, and the remnants of their boat floating astern. Oh dear! He too had now been arrested. If a foreigner hits another foreigner, they're not too bothered, but a local is another matter.

After a couple of weeks, Nicola came back out via Stansted to Porto. She was again subject to a forensic search, and interrogation at each airport. She brought with her all sorts of stuff we couldn't get. One geezer picked up a Weetabix box and asked, "What's in the box?" to which she replied, "Weetabix silly." They pulled out all of the biscuits and checked them while they downloaded data from her phone.

Finally, the ports engineer arrived to survey our boat after a ludicrous payment that was tantamount to robbery. All was well apart from a weakened support for the hydraulic steering ram, which we already knew about, but needed the report for insurance purposes. We could easily botch it, until we got to a boatyard.

We were led to believe some progress with our missing consignment was close, so we waited patiently, still under surveillance. We were into late September now; there was no point thinking about the Caribbean without our stock. Money was getting short after all of these unexpected costs.

I'd been directed to a yard in the marina at Villamoura in the south which had a travel lift big enough to get us out. I thought a week was easily long enough for repairs. I tried everything to get our stock back, but it was starting to look like we were getting proper screwed. I was seething mad.

The brief in the UK still refused to get involved. I really couldn't understand it; of course this matter was relevant to the case in hand. This was abuse of power on an international scale. I don't blame any officer for carrying out his duties given instructions, information or intelligence. This circulation of false and malicious intelligence came from the top. My goods had 'disappeared'. The only proof of which was a secret recording.

It later transpired he had worked alongside the same solicitor I was fighting with in HMRC. Now, how's that for a coincidence? Was it a chance meeting, on the steps of the university? My arse it was! Trevor had been mugged by his 'ex-student' who'd been sent there, specifically for the job.

I'd copied everything to Trevor, who strangely didn't want to get involved. This is when I discovered he was not in fact a 'marine lawyer' as purported to me, and reported by the media, but a lecturer. He found it very difficult to believe what I was telling him. All he could say was, "You have the bill of lading; they have to give you your goods, bills of lading are my bread and butter." It all sounded a bit farfetched, and way beyond his knowledge, but oddly, he as much as refused to help.

Let's face facts here; we're in a foreign country, albeit a European country. The Customs will not, or cannot produce our goods, and refuse to provide written reason or any other document. What can we do? Part with £5k upfront to a lawyer who's going to be told we're drug smugglers? What's the point? We're going to get messed about from pillar to post in Portugal. Again, I don't blame anybody for treating us like criminals when the horrible bastards at HMRC were peddling false and malicious intelligence.

I contacted our solicitor/director in Thailand, and also the shippers. The cargo was insured at cost, but any payment wouldn't have come close to what that stock meant to us in our present position. New stock would take at least three months to manufacture and ship. We had to face it, we'd been screwed!

Finally we got our boat documents, we were free to leave. Nicola had already gone back to the UK, and was due back in a week. She couldn't stay away, she was perfect in every way, more than a consolation for the shit we were taking. As she had a flexi-time contract, she'd worked her little socks off to get back as soon as she could.

I'd found my Girl Friday long after I'd given up looking. To her, this was a huge adventure. She'd tried to join the army, but because of an operation on her feet she'd been refused. She took extremely well to life at sea, and wanted to learn everything.

Due to the damage to our steering, we decided to coast hop to Gibraltar, where I thought we could get repairs done. After a favourable weather forecast, we notified the port of our intentions. They protested we'd only been given permission to limp to Villamoura. I'd researched the limits of their power; I knew they were bullshitting. We set off after nearly eight frustrating weeks of trying to collect our goods.

We called in at Peniche to refuel as we'd had to motor most of the way, due to picking calm weather. We continued on the same day, as there was a weather front coming in we wanted to miss, and Nicola was due in Gibraltar to meet us. As we sailed down the coast, I kept a close eye on the weather forecasts after noticing conflicting reports.

As we got to the south of Portugal, I became worried. Call it a sailor's nose, but weather conditions were changing rapidly, and not nearly as predicted. I sailed closer to land to get a mobile signal. Nic was at the airport when she rang to say she was going to the gate at 0600h. I told her to go directly to an internet desk, and get an accurate update. It didn't matter if she missed the plane, it was very important.

She called me back to tell me a freak tropical storm was forming, and headed our way. I knew Villamoura wasn't far away, so pushed the throttle up, and let out full sail. The last place you want to be in a tropical storm with a steering problem is the Straits of Gibraltar where there're strong winds guaranteed, most of the time. That's why they host world wind surfing competitions there.

With full sail we began to run (in front of the wind) with the engine, bollocks to the steering gear. We could use an emergency tiller apparatus, if it failed. The storm would seriously whip up the sea in the bay of Cadiz. I wanted to be in as quickly as possible. I'd nearly come to grief in 1988 in the same place, on the one hundred and twenty foot yacht Aubriender I'd bought in Gibraltar.

If the hydraulic steering had been okay, I'd have headed for deep water and rode out the storm, rather than run for it. It was a good decision; we rigged the emergency steering in advance, which also allowed us to physically help take the weight of the rudder as things got pretty violent.

We were surfing down huge rollers at speeds of fifteen and sixteen knots in winds gusting to 70mph as we surged along into Villamoura and safety. We were tied up at the well-sheltered reporting berth when the worst arrived and battered the yachts tied in the marina. Sailors get a huge adrenaline buzz which can last all day after a leg or race like that, that day was no exception!

When you're in it and responsible, you wonder what the hell you're doing there, but the buzz afterwards is priceless and indescribable, but granted, not for the faint hearted. Phil Junior had again performed so well under pressure. I was a proud father, make no mistake.

After two hours of torrential rain, the sun shone, and it was beautiful again. Pity we were still in Portugal.

Nic had called from Gibraltar and was on route, no drama or whining; she'd had hassle at Customs who wanted to tax a mountain bike she'd bought for my birthday coming up. She knew the law and refused, telling them it was for collection by yacht and therefore not subject to importation tax.

They had to allow it. She left it at the chandlers on the marina and dragged her bags and supplies through into Spain then Portugal, eventually arriving at 1800h with a huge smile and not the slightest complaint, what a star! The marina agreed to lift us out into the boatyard when the national holiday was over. They were very nice to us; we were allowed to stay on the long reporting/fuel berth which had room for another five like us.

We spent four days relaxing in sunshine then prepared for the lift out. On the day, everybody came back to work, their attitudes changed completely. Clearly, we were scum drug smugglers again. They directed us from the safe berth to a pontoon far too small for us in high winds. I refused, saying it was too dangerous to manoeuvre until the weather improved. Later at their perpetual insistence, I made the move perfectly, much to their annoyance.

They then informed us we were too big to lift out there. Their excuse: the machine was not operating to full capacity and the engineer had decided against it. They said the authorities wouldn't let us leave until the vessel was repaired. We'd need to be towed by an authorised tug to the shipyard in the next port. This was going to be expensive!

Luckily, we found it hard to understand his poor English and would be able to claim ignorance if we were caught slipping out during the night. Dodgy bastards them Portuguese! Once they knew an insurance company was responsible, they wanted it all. We were gone and soon in Spanish waters. I'd had enough of Portugal.

CHAPTER THIRTY FIVE

SNORTOGRANDE

The boatyard in Gibraltar had been sold for development and the nearest place big enough in Spain was a yard in Sotogrande, a very posh, expensive marina twenty miles into the Mediterranean. The insurance company would be paying, I'd visited it when it first opened and knew it to be very nice, a good day's sailing through the straits and we were there.

On route, we'd chopped up poor Harriet, who by now had "flowered" many succulent buds which would need to be dried before smoking. We again tied up on the reporting/fuel berth and arranged the lift out in a few days with the pleasant and accommodating staff there.

Sotogrande is a huge sprawling development where many respectable affluent people live. It is, however, also known as 'Snortogrande' by some, due to the vast amounts of people snorting cocaine on a regular basis. Just like many new developments on the Costa Del Sol, it has a fair amount of villains based there. Property (before the financial crisis) was the order of the day to clean ill gotten gains. As a relatively new development, prices were rising all the time, so it attracted a lot of 'new money'.

After a couple of days, they asked us to move to a spot near to the entrance which they marked on the berth plan. The main engine starter motor was removed for servicing, so it was easier to pull our boat with the help of the marineros and our RHIB. We were all tied up safe again within an hour, then left in a taxi to Gibraltar for the day.

In Gibraltar, I showed Nic and Phil round before collecting the mountain bike Nic had bought me. When we tried to cross the frontier into Spain, the Customs wanted VAT and import tax on it. She produced a receipt to prove its purchase in UK, complete with VAT number. I reeled off the relevant regulations to the letter (much to their surprise) and refused to budge. They'd no choice but to allow us through after thirty minutes of standing firm. VAT and import tax cannot be charged twice in Europe.

We took a taxi back to our vessel, arriving in the dark. Before the kettle had boiled, a dull thud echoed from the stern. We thought a boat had come adrift and collided with us, but there was nothing to see. It happened again. We ran around like demented chickens before we realised we were aground on something. I knew from the marina plan we had a minimum of four metres there, so I assumed there was something else under us as we needed only three.

I had the good sense to instruct Phil to video the whole scenario from start to finish. I used the VHF to call the tower and ask for help. A boat arrived with one of the guys who'd moved us. The camera was rolling when I told him there was an obstruction under us, possibly a car. He replied it was a rock. I said, "Impossible," and pointed to the sign on the wall which clearly said four metres to which he replied, "I am diver, trust me, is rock."

"Why did you move me here?" I asked furiously.

He gestured towards the office and shrugged his shoulders.

They wanted to pull me clear, but why would I trust them? I was going nowhere until I'd put a mask on for a look down myself, just to make sure there were no more rocks 'growing' up. On inspection, I found a big clump of rocks in the corner. Our keel was scraping on them, close to the rudder.

A fin keel yacht wouldn't have been a problem, but we had a full-length keel. They knew this because I'd provided drawings and photos to the office, normal practice in advance of a lift out. It was either a really stupid mistake or a deliberate action, we weren't sure. How a marina such as this could claim and advertise a minimum four metres, when they had only two and a half metres in places, is beyond me. Furious, we moved our boat into plenty of water.

The huge 157 foot super yacht Va Bene came in that night

and tied close by. She was one of the most successful charter yachts in the world, bought by Eric Clapton after he'd been a customer. On route to the Caribbean for the winter, she'd stopped to collect a huge amount of luxury goods, which took days to load on-board.

Some of the crew spent time on-board our boat, in particular, a Rastafarian called Coy who was very impressed with Harriet's flowers. He introduced himself as 'De Painter', but was clearly more than that, and proved very interesting company. We did a bit of barter and ended up with a few bits and bobs, you know, for eBay.

Finally we were to be lifted out, it was too windy in my opinion, but we negotiated our way to the narrow dock through a narrow corridor of expensive boats. As we waited, doing our best to hold position, the yard manager, who became known to us later as 'Hitler', changed his mind and wanted us in, stern first.

He knew fine well we were committed in the cross winds. He'd set us an almost impossible task, probably resulting in a nice bit of work for the yard. I managed to turn around with our powerful bow thrusters, one of Trevor's better buys. We had just a few metres spare, but hit nothing.

Rather than wait, trying to hold position as he further instructed, because the crane operators hadn't slung the slings correctly, I steamed out clear of the other boats, waited till all was ready before sailing back, doing a one eighty on her axis and backed into the slot perfectly, much to the amazement of the marineros, who clapped and cheered. However, Hitler didn't look happy at all.

The machine put us down in the corner, nearest to a posh mirrored building on the other side of the wall we towered over. We could see ourselves clearly in the reflection, it was quite weird. We photographed the damage from both the catamaran and the grounding.

The insurance engineer called Makowlski arrived to deal with the claim. He was hard work. We fought hard. I threatened to sue for loss of use and even claim salvage for saving the vessel. He soon capitulated and negotiated a good price for us to do the work ourselves. They would also pay the bill for the yard, which, by the way, was eighty euro a night.

At that price you'd think we'd have got a key to get out of the gates or use the toilets/showers, but no, we had to telephone and wait for security to get in or out, outside of business hours. Screw them and their new rules. We dropped the RHIB into the water and used it to move about the marina freely, which they didn't like, but could do nothing about, or they'd have to stop everybody else.

Clearly, our friends at HMRC had traced us there. Whoever they had watching us, wanted to control our movements. The yard was pissed off because they wouldn't be getting any work from us. We needed funds. If there was anyone getting paid good money for repairs, it was going to be us. I wouldn't trust another boatyard to repair her. At least in this place, it seemed to be only the bosses that'd been poisoned. The regular workers and punters were all very nice. I decided to have her properly surveyed to progress the chartering option as I had diminishing confidence in getting our stock back.

I'd taken off the keel strap and a huge Teflon rudder bearing damaged by the grounding and presented it to the office, alongside photographs of the chunks out of the keel, asking about repairs. They'd sent me away to show Hitler, who couldn't speak a word of English. I assumed they would sort it out; it was clearly their fault and they had no way out.

Nicola went home, only to hand her notice in. When she'd worked it, she was moving out for a life at sea with an old sea dog and his son. Most women would desert a sinking ship, this one jumped on, complete with savings and credit cards which funded the repairs until the insurance coughed up. We were still hopeful of getting our goods. Now the boat was safe, we could step up the pressure.

We got a date for the hearing on 17th and 18th November, followed by a demand for funds of £8k by our no win-no fee solicitor. I refused point blank, and set about preparing the papers ourselves. We produced a full and comprehensive case in readiness and sent it to the court and our supposed solicitors, who said they were applying for legal aid.

We'd also completed the repairs relating to the collision, and billed the insurance before we set off back for the hearing. The plane was delayed overnight due to a collision with the mobile steps. We would still make the hearing the day after. We stayed with Nicola in Hartlepool. The solicitors called to say that Judge Taylor, the same guy who promised legal aid then backtracked, had refused to hear the case without representation.

It was months before I discovered this was a lie. Our 'solicitors' had engaged a local representative to ask for an adjournment, stating I'd arrived from the UK and instructed them to abort. He didn't know we hadn't arrived. We'd spent the night in a hotel near Malaga, at the airline's expense. They didn't want me to present the case myself and lied to get their own way; it was becoming quite obvious there was something sinister afoot.

We moved Nicola out of her apartment. I acquired a big old transit van and stuffed it full. We headed back to Spain by road, collecting Junior on route from his mother in the midlands.

We arrived back to our boat on 7th December. The marina still hadn't done anything to repair the damage done by the grounding, so I went to the office to demand an explanation. To my absolute amazement, they denied point blank that any such incident had occurred, even denying the existence of the rocks.

I told them I'd dived on them. They said I could be arrested, as it was forbidden to dive in the marina. I laughed, retrieved a copy of the video from the boat and left it with them. When I returned, there was hell on! I threatened to post it on YouTube and sue them for loss of use of our vessel. We were going to be stuck in a boatyard over Christmas and New Year, when we should have been in the Caribbean.

Of course they had no choice but to organise the repairs. When complete, they wacked the marina bill up more than double. They wanted 16,400 euro, but after a long standoff, we gave them 4,600. The relationship with the yard boss, Hitler, had become very tense. As we had no access to toilets outside of working hours, we used our own on-board, which flush into a tank that needs emptying from time to time.

After many attempts to get the yard to fulfil their duties, but mainly because the tank was bubbling full of liquidised human waste, one night we had no choice but to 'relieve' it, before there was an accident. A couple of big wheelie bins were commandeered to transport said shit to the dock, some fifty metres away.

I was cooking dinner while a hired hand called James was pushing 300 litres as fast as he could, while Nicola, bless her, was pulling. The base of the bin caught a bracket fixed to the ground which ripped out the base and dumped the lot. Both of them were instantly up to the knees in shit before it levelled out to cover a large area. The stench was gagging. They were horrified. I was howling, tears streaming down my face. They quickly subsided as we realised we'd have to clean it up.

Wellingtons, shovels, brushes and hose pipes all spring to mind, but the most important was dust masks, soaked in Olbas oil to stop us gagging. The hose did more damage than anything else; it just sprayed the shit about and transported it further afield. The area had multiplied when security came to the wall. They demanded we stop work, as it was after 1900h. I tried to explain, but they absolutely insisted we stop.

Next morning Hitler arrived with the general manager banging on the hull. I got up to find ten masked yard crew cleaning up the mess; they didn't look happy either. I showed him three written requests to have the tank emptied going back weeks. I turned it back on him. He got the blame. He hated me.

A week of hot weather later, the yard still stunk of shit. Just over the wall, the posh punters were going crazy complaining. I was up on deck one morning having a smoke, while watching Hitler do his round of inspections. He opened a wheelie bin close by to check it'd been emptied. I swear I didn't know it'd been left full of shit, but shit it was. A bubbling, festering turd soup had been cooking for a week in the sun.

He wasn't very tall this man. He was on tiptoes as he lifted the lid with two hands, stuck his head under the lid and dropped the lid as he gasped. The dropping lid sent a waft straight into his gob. He fell to the floor retching, finishing up on all fours, puking till he could feel his arsehole in his mouth. Good enough for him, I can still see it now, what fun we had!

There was an Irish bar/restaurant in the port. Half the bar staff there had a serious coke habit and were well known for striping the customers. The regulars insisted on paying for each drink as they got it, to prevent being lumbered with someone else's bill. After being caught out a couple of times, Nicola noted our drinks one night, until we got the bill. Armed with cast iron proof, I kicked off in the bar big style until I got my money back.

I contacted Mr O'Riley, who came down to see us from Jerez. A proper nice man, he had lunch while I grassed the lot of them up, explaining the methods used in detail. They'd been ripping thousands while damaging his business reputation. He wasn't happy, I can tell you that.

Pretty soon after that we were in the water at a vastly discounted rate. We decided to sail to an anchorage close to Gibraltar and Spain, which was in effect, disputed waters due to the age old dispute between the two. We'd been spending time there. Nicola joined a local team, and also played hockey for the national side. Phil Junior got himself a girlfriend also on the team. We were in danger of growing roots, but paralysed there because of the stolen stock.

At least the anchorage was free; we simply had no intentions of entering any port or marina for as long as we could. All we'd received wherever we went was shit. I'd continually complained to HMRC in e-mails, but the surveillance and interference in our business continued relentlessly.

We had stupid, gormless amateurs sneaking about, taking pictures and following us everywhere. I would sit in a bar and ask them openly if they could hear us alright. Some would pretend to be fishing while watching our boat from land. We knew which ones because they'd still be fishing in an Easterly wind when nobody ever caught anything. When they relieved each other, the fishing gear stayed put, only the blokes changed places, it was farcical.

Every single time we went through the border from Spain to Gib or back again in our van, which was about four times a week, we got searched. If we took our RHIB into the port, we got serious hassle, even though others did it regularly. One night, Nic and Junior had gone in to pick up laundry in the little boat, and were threatened with twenty four hour lock up. I went back with Junior, daring them to lock me up.

Later they would nick our boat and take it to the police dock, if we left it unattended. Each time I challenged them, they referred to new regulations they could not produce, but assured me they were contained in the "New Port Ordinance". I managed to obtain a copy and took it with me the next time we landed. No such new regulation existed, they were furious. We continued to land in Gibraltar, while they continued to take our boat, until they got sick. We knew whoever was watching us from the shore didn't want us shooting into another jurisdiction within minutes in our little RHIB, they'd obviously had a word. It was cat and mouse while we waited for the date of the hearing.

CHAPTER THIRTY SIX

JUDGE FOX AND VICTORY!

On 8th April 2006 we had a new hearing back in the UK. We'd spent months preparing the case ourselves, with no solicitors help whatsoever, no Trevor and no legal aid despite what Judge Taylor had said. The case was not even reserved for him, as he'd ordered. The solicitors demanded funds for them and the barrister, supposedly ready to take the case on. I refused, not least because we didn't have £14k. He'd refused to do anything about our missing stock and I didn't trust him.

I'd always been straight; I wasn't paying them anything up front. Trevor at some point capitulated and contributed £4k. I had promised the same on the condition he submitted no more documents without my prior approval, and then he did just that. He got nothing from me.

I was confident of victory. We were far better prepared this time. I'd abused my position last time and taken advantage of the usual leeway which is granted to persons representing themselves. We'd served everybody with documents on time. I was ready. I flew back with Nicola, who would be my assistant, while Junior took charge of our boat.

Amazingly, the solicitors sent a QC with an assistant, despite not receiving any funds. He was wholly unprepared with eighteen hours to go, and hadn't even been given a transcript of the last hearing. Documents they used in court were all taken from my own. Jeremy White QC was horrified; we were up most of the night preparing stuff he didn't have. The brief had done nothing, despite asking for £14k. I was livid and almost told them to piss off.

I was very suspicious of the fact that Judge Taylor had been replaced by Judge Fox, who had a fierce reputation not to be messed with. However, he was just as pissed off with the actions of HMRC and their abuse of powers, just as Judge Taylor was previously. He conducted a very fair and unbiased hearing, resulting in a well earned, but anticipated victory. My only problem with this was that the 'legal team' would get all of the credit while we had done everything. The media went wild. HMRC were furious.

Judge Peter Fox criticised Customs for their "impermissible conduct" and "unilateral closed mind". He said they were "wholly unreasonable" by refusing to consider options for secure storage of my goods, and that the Cornish Maiden provided "impregnable protection" in the gated marina against theft. He praised Trevor and I as "characters" but there was no disgrace in our business opportunism, nor any grounds to say we acted unlawfully. While quashing the order, he actually said we were both "men of honesty and integrity", something I'm quite proud of.

He concluded by saying that I had not breached any Customs regulations, because officials were acting without proper legal authority. I was totally exonerated.

It was only a matter of time before we got compensated now. We flew to Italy for an international hockey tournament where Nicola scored all her team's goals, before returning to Rich Harvest.

We had by now discovered our Thailand stock had actually been imported from the Customs compound by an as yet unnamed company that had paid all taxes back when they first arrived. Portuguese Customs still, ten months later, refused to reply.

The stock was apparently with a storage company, Warelog, controlled by a Louis Pinto who was now demanding outrageous storage charges. At one point we didn't believe this to be true, so we offered to pay their demands. The price went up another £3k.

We'd appointed a shipping agent in Gibraltar with whom we had deposited the original bill of lading, when the shippers finally agreed to pay all charges to prevent being sued. The document went missing, and he denied we'd left it with him. We had no receipt, only an e-mail to Warelog, in which he confirms it was in his possession.

What could we do? As we were the shippers and the consignee, the document was not absolutely necessary as an original, but all parties refused to go further without it. The shipping agent's family are in politics in Gibraltar, where the abuses of power continued to thwart our lives. It was a mistake to trust him, but I have no proof, which is why he's not named here.

In any case, I wouldn't blame him. If a high ranking police or Customs official asked him for a favour regarding some heroin smugglers, he would surely comply. It now appeared we'd never a chance of getting our stock. I instructed our solicitor/director in Thailand to file a claim to the insurers of the cargo, some ten months after it arrived. He wouldn't reply and wouldn't take calls.

Our information later was that he'd been arrested and interrogated for three days about us. Poor Pong, he was just another victim of the relentless smear campaign conducted against us. Why would he believe us? He didn't know for sure, if or not we'd planted something in our cargo while we had possession of it. To all intents and purposes, he too now thought we were smuggling heroin. It can't have been much fun for him, that's for sure! Clearly, it was a good move to vacate Thailand when we did.

We had to face facts. £70k investment and six months work, plus all the grief we'd endured waiting around, had come to nothing. We'd been proper screwed over! Of course HMRC still denied any knowledge, but I continued to accuse them by e-mail. We consoled ourselves with our victory and would use some of the compensation to order new stock. Every single person who'd got samples had raved about them afterwards.

We'd discovered that Rich Harvest had not in fact been licensed for ocean chartering at all. She'd had gone through the process and survey, but wouldn't pass a stability test due to her always being slightly stern heavy because of changes to the original design when she was built, and the fact more weight had been put further up the masts due to additional furling gear fitted by Trevor. Furthermore there was no Lloyds certificate for her, or any trace of it.

Our deals were based on these claims. It meant we couldn't legally charter her, losing a potential £10k per week in season, and given the attention we and our vessel were getting, there'd be no chance of anything unofficial. Our asset value went down considerably. We weren't happy. We needed something to do, and fast.

One day we met a bunch of guys after a hockey match at our favourite marina bar in Gib. They were mostly Scots and Irish. We got to talking about spring-loaded fishing hooks, fish waste reprocessing, crab pots and the like. They said they were looking at businesses to invest in and recruited me to give a presentation. It transpired they'd bought into some biotechnology they were launching into the UK.

Amongst the markets to be targeted was the fishing industry. Their chemicals preserved fish and shellfish much longer, cleaned diesel fuel in ship's tanks and even cleaned contaminated soil. A big, 'money no object' two-day seminar was held in a posh hotel in Marbella, followed by great dinner parties at Banus port. We got paid and had a great time.

I have to say, my paranoia got the better of me. Lots of things didn't stack up. They didn't know much about their own products. There were also one or two dodge pots present who made no secret of their past. I was so used to undercover bullshit, and this lot seemed too good to be true.

I researched them and checked up on things I heard. Not much made sense. It was like they'd won the lottery and were buying a technology they knew nothing about. I thought it was something dodgy, maybe money laundering, and pulled away from an opportunity, which may have been a mistake.

One of the guests there introduced me to a man in Gibraltar called Manoli, who was an agent for a crane company there. I'd bought some aircraft loading trucks at the MOD sale and wanted them moving. Manoli, it transpired, had been a prolific smuggler during his life. In Gibraltar, there are thousands of ex-smugglers. It was the national vocation when Franco shut the border with Spain.

We got talking about the many ships' anchors and chains abandoned in the bay of Gibraltar. He said his friend had a barge and crane licensed in Gib, capable of raising them if there was a way to locate and connect to them. I did some more research and proposed a joint venture as the sums looked very good. We bought a magnetometer to scan, but discovered there was so much metal, the readings were off the scale.

I found a company who had an old Cherokee work class ROV sitting in Scotland doing nothing. We did a deal to split the proceeds of what looked like a good project. Manoli said he could get the equipment, which filled a forty foot truck, into Gib and onto his friend's barge. All paperwork would be done by the time it got there. I got an Indian/British guy, Paul, to invest for shares of our share in the profit. We decided to go for it, as we were due our money soon anyway.

We returned to the UK to deal with the valuation of our damaged stock and to negotiate a settlement. To our horror, HMRC appealed the judgement of Judge Fox on the last day possible, throwing everything back to where we started. A long protracted appeal process designed to frustrate and pervert the true course of justice was about to start. The issue was about whether or not Judge Fox had the right to take into account the Customs failure to be proportionate, when he made his judgement.

The main reason behind this appeal process was that HMRC had lost an appeal on this very point in a case known as 'Newbury' whereby the appeal court had found in favour of Newbury when Customs had acted disproportionately by seizing his car. HMRC badly wanted this ruling overturned, and with the help of 'accommodating' legal personnel, this was their opportunity to have this done. The hearing would take place in London probably a year later in 2007. Incredibly, HMRC indicated they would pay legal costs to have it argued by Queens's Council. I screamed conspiracy, and was determined to take charge of proceedings, but Trevor was dealing with solicitors despite protests and acrimonious exchanges.

The appeal hearing in London was set. We'd been having heavy exchanges with Trevor and the legal team who were on a nice pay day, whatever happened. We'd acquired a Luton bodied van in

Gibraltar which needed a few jobs doing. In no time we had it all ship shape, and ready for a road trip back to the UK for the hearing. I made it quite clear I wanted to represent myself, or at least be part of the hearing. I strongly suspected a conspiracy and had no intentions of letting it go smoothly for them. I believed I already knew the outcome was going to go against us, but wanted to witness it for myself.

Five days before the hearing, we packed up the van with equipment going back to the UK we didn't need. Our clothes, legal papers and personal items were also on board. We intended picking up some excellent red wine we'd found and had labelled up in Santander, which we'd promised to various friends and family. We knew we could bring as much as we wanted, as long as it was not sold. Of course we were pushing our luck, but were sure we complied with everything, including personalised labels, to win any challenge. Nicola went off to fuel the van, while I secured our boat.

The port police stopped her demanding paperwork for the van. It was still registered on a Gibraltar number plate, and would be until we had it tested in the UK and registered there. We knew of the regulations regarding a non-Gibraltar resident not being allowed to drive a Gibraltar registered truck in Spain, unless driving for a company with a covering letter. Because of this, we had agreed with the company to postpone transfer of ownership until we arrived in the UK. We also had a covering letter, as per the regulations.

Nicola was ordered to drive the van (accompanied) a mile or so to the Spanish Customs compound at the frontier between Spain and Gibraltar. On arrival, the van was forensically searched before being seized. She was instructed to get a solicitor and sent away. We returned to the Customs office we'd passed through hundreds of times in the past two years on route to and from Gibraltar. We'd never had a problem; Guardia civil officers knew us and joked while searching us, sometimes twice a day. That day was different; clearly they'd been told we were enemies of the state!

They messed us around from pillar to post, sending us here, there and everywhere!

We had the people we got the van from turn up with company

documents but they too were abused to the point they refused to do any more stating; they'd been told we were smuggling drugs, and they wanted nothing to do with us. The office shut at 1600h. All our stuff was in the van so we stayed with friends, returning the next morning for round two. Same shit, different day. It was like being in Portugal again. We spent a fortune on taxis. They sent us to one town then another to various offices, demanding we get Spanish NIF number before we could pay the import or VAT on the van. This was impossible as we lived on our boat.

I took advice and got a Customs agent, agreeing to pay a deposit until the van got to the UK. This is a standard procedure and went as planned until the agent came out of the Customs office with a face like a beetroot and told us to return the next day. I demanded my passport back in his office, but he refused saying he'd left it with Customs and put up the shutters when I went outside for a smoke.

I was going to fly back the next day in time for the hearing, and tried to retrieve the paperwork appertaining to the case, from the van. Without my passport or the paperwork, we were done; we both knew we were being deliberately impeded from attending the hearing. In all we were there four days until the day of the hearing on 17th May 2007. I walked into the agents' office, he asked for two hundred and fifty euros which I gave him, along with a signature, and in thirty minutes we had a document stamped, allowing us to travel in Spain. I've taken vehicles all over the world, even across land to Pakistan, and never been messed about so much in all my life.

We drove back to the UK via the ferry from Bilbao and landed with a load of wine from Santander. We had a number of offers to buy this wine but refused, we had no intentions of blotting our copy book. Of course the appeal hearing went against us and the case was referred back to the Crown Court for re-hearing. The judges quashed the ruling on 'Newbury' meaning Judge Fox should not have given weight to the disproportionate acts of custom. It would be another year of torture and abuse before we could move forward. I was sure by then that our brief and the Customs brief were in cahoots. They'd all had a pay day, the Crown had their troublesome ruling quashed, and we were sent back to Crown Court.

We bought some salvage equipment, and a jet ski to cheer us up on route back to Spain.

CHAPTER THIRTY SEVEN

THE DON INDA

Meanwhile as the months ticked by, I prepared a detailed proposal, and had meetings with the bosses at the Spanish Port of Algeciras across the bay. The abandoned anchor problem was very serious. They were just as keen to be seen to be doing something about it. It all looked very good. Gibraltar port was desperate to increase their safe anchorage area. To have both Gibraltar and Spain cooperating over a maritime issue was a massive step. Many ships come into the bay to take on fuel from the twenty or so 'bunker boats' operating from Spain and Gibraltar.

It seemed we would be the first ROV firm to survey the bay. It was all very exciting. The truck arrived at the frontier only to be held up. Apparently, the paperwork regarding a tax deposit was not completed. It was stored in a compound on the Spanish side. As weeks passed, we discovered Manoli was only the Gibraltar agent for the crane company and his friend Pepe was only a representative of the barge company, belonging to his wife's family.

In business since I left the fire service in 1979, my word and handshake were always my bond. I'd taken these men at their word and been blinded by meetings at the highest level. There was however, still serious potential for profit, but the barge had got another job to do first. We had a couple of weeks to wait. On 18th May 2007 something happened that would scupper everything.

The Odyssey Explorer, a Tampa-based treasure hunting ship arrived in Gibraltar carrying seventeen tons of silver and gold coins from an unnamed wreck in the Atlantic Ocean. The cargo worth an estimated $500mill was granted an import license, and an export license, as two cargo liners arrived to fly it to the USA, all on the same day it arrived!

The Spanish government went ballistic. They knew these coins had come from the Spanish vessel Mercedes, which sank off Portugal in 1804. Despite the company having a good claim, they lost judgement after judgement in Florida. Later Wikileaks exposed a secret deal, where a painting in a Madrid museum worth $15mill, stolen by the Nazis, would be returned to a wealthy socialite family in New York, in return for the courts to find against Odyssey.

The last paragraph demonstrates the price of treachery, perpetrated against a US publicly owned company by the US judiciary on the behest of the US Government, on behalf of one 'connected' family. A simple call to the Judge, then justice is only a perception; same all over the world. In any case, our project was pretty done after that day the ship arrived.

All cooperation ceased. There'd be no permissions granted for any subsea work, especially from Gibraltar, who they perceived had assisted the 'robbery'. We had no choice but to wait and see if common sense would prevail.

The guys who owned the ROV were getting pretty pissed off at this stage, even though I was paying all charges incurred. We decided to buy a new type of multi-beam sonar between us and fit it to Rich Harvest in order to survey the areas covertly while we cruised about. Our goal was to acquire targets for further attention later.

The system was a fantastic leap in reasonably affordable technology. At £50k it could do the same job as the Odyssey Explorer, but only in depths of less than 300 metres. A few years before, this capability would have cost millions. The speed, cost and capability of evolving computers enabled this breakthrough which had been conceived in New Zealand.

We were the first to get it in Europe. It took months to commission and learn how to use it. The ROV men were getting impatient with the delays, but the Gibraltarians are much like the Spanish, nothing happens fast (unless $500mill treasure is at stake).

On 12th August 2007, a cargo vessel New Flame carrying scrap metal collided with a tanker Torm Gertrud after leaving Gibraltar. She sank bow down, stern up, just off Europa point, two miles from us. We were badly oiled and had a claim. The Spanish were involved in the cleanup and monitoring of oil pollution, and amongst others, they sent the Don Inda, the flagship vessel of the Salvamento Maritimo to the area.

On 5th September 2007, a two hundred ton fishing boat, the Nuevo Pepita Aurora, capsized in the straits of Gibraltar near Barbate in foul weather, after fishing off the coast of Morocco. As a patrol boat was towing them to sheltered waters, in order to dive under and perhaps rescue more crew, unfortunately the swell and the position of the towing line caused the vessel to right itself, and she promptly sank in one hundred and forty five metres with two poor fishermen trapped inside. Eight fishermen were rescued from the sixteen crew; only five bodies were eventually recovered.

My friend Julio, a boss in the port of Algeciras, called me to ask a very big favour. The media surrounding the tragedy were clamouring for the vessel to be recovered. A Spanish ROV company on-board the Don Inda had located the wreck, but lost their robot on the second dive. The Navy had also failed with their machine, only just recovering it damaged. The currents were savage where it had sunk. They needed an ROV and a crew who knew what they were doing, on-board ASAP.

I called the owners in China where they had an office, hiring ROV pilots to the government oil projects. We had one of their guys staying on-board arranging the servicing of the equipment we still had in storage. Within twenty four hours, I negotiated a contract and had the equipment loaded onto the Don Inda, awaiting the arrival of the two pilots.

I supervised the welding of components to the deck and the electrical supply. Their young lad Craig had only just joined as an apprentice, and was useless. The ship set sail. We would be transferred by fast boat, when everyone was ready.

Craig's brother Gary arrived along with a guy called Simon, both were experienced pilots; they would need to be. Julio insisted I went on-board as I spoke enough Spanish to get by. He spoke good

English and trusted me. I had to be Director of ROV, the Spanish like titles like that.

Within forty eight hours of the call, money was transferred to a bank in Belize via a bank in Northern Cyprus from the Salvamento Maritimo in Madrid. I was too busy to be suspicious of the instructions I was getting from the principals of the company, Jim and Lloyd, who themselves were offshore, on a job in Papa New Guinea.

The terms of the contact were ruthless. I was embarrassed to present them, but they were accepted, and we were on-board, ready to play for the media who were filming from helicopters, such was the public pressure. Even though we weren't ready to go, they insisted we dip the robot in the drink to appease the public.

A successful operation would put us in a great light with the authorities and would surely help our cause. Failure was not an option, we had to show them. The company who lost their equipment were still on-board, at our disposal. In reality they really wanted us to recover their robot, but there was also another reason.

After a survey of the wreck, I proposed a line be passed through the rudder post. The Director of Salvage on-board took nearly three days and advice from the ship builders to confirm what I said was correct. It was frustrating, anybody who knows boats should have known the answer – the rudder post is hugely strong!

The currents were so bad the robot only had a one hour window on the turn of the tide, meaning two short dives per day, much to the annoyance of the Spanish. The wreck had nets and lines flying about in the currents, endangering the umbilical cable. We wouldn't be rushed into losing the machine. We had a huge new salvage ship and crew doing anything we wanted. It was great!

I expressed concern a number of times about the rigging of pennants for the lifting cables on deck, and after they insisted it was safe, I made them move some conduit blocking a door, to allow our pilots to exit the control container on the other side to the cable rig.

After a week, the fishing boat was finally connected. I jumped ship by fast boat. Nicola's mum was getting married to her bloke Steve in the UK, and we just made it with hours to spare. I left the

ROV crew to decommission the equipment after the boat had been lifted and taken to port.

When the massive winches began to lift the fishing boat, a pennant to guide the cable parted, just as I'd predicted. The poor deckhand in the way of the cable was catapulted into the sea. If the positional thrusters had been going the other way, he'd have been liquidised. He was airlifted ashore, where surgeons fought to save his legs.

The next day, it was rigged as per my drawing before. The lift was successful. Amazingly, she was not brought to port but dropped again in thirty metres, where Guardia Civil Divers could conduct a search and recover two more bodies. I couldn't understand the mentality of this action, but it had nothing to do with us, our job was done.

I was due 20% of the contract plus wages for Nicola and me. The final bill was about £40k.

We stayed in the UK three days, during which time I got the distinct impression something was wrong. The ROV crew were in Gib. They were keen to get possession of the company car Jim had provided for me. He'd brought the new sonar gear down from Scotland in it before going to China. It was at Malaga airport seventy miles away. Surely they could hire a car for the few days they were in Gibraltar while waiting for flights. In any case, I had the keys with me.

I then got a farcical e-mail from Jim telling me they'd had enough of us and were sending their equipment back to Scotland. Their pilots paid Manoli his end to get the ROV and gear on a truck and sent it back to the UK, without paying the storage bill. We jumped on a plane, arriving to find they'd gone.

Simon phoned to tell me Jim and Lloyd had no intentions of honouring their deal with me, wages, commission or otherwise. The reason the money had gone to Belize via Cyprus was so it couldn't be traced. This system had been set up so their ex-wives would not be able to know their true earnings.

A shell company had been used for the contract, making it impossible to sue. The two of them, Jim and Lloyd, were quite proud of themselves with their little scam until they finally got ashore and realised, not only that I still had the car, but that Craig had failed to carry out specific instructions to move the sonar equipment from Rich Harvest to the container with the ROV spares and controls (in case it was needed by the Don Inda).

Of course the Don Inda had a far superior sonar system, so our jointly purchased gear wasn't needed. Suspicious, I refused to facilitate the moving, citing not enough time. Poor Jim and Lloyd had the jam taken right out of their donuts. They'd intended to screw us over completely, including our half of the equipment, which they thought was on route to Scotland when they dropped the bombshell.

Unfortunately for them, the plan backfired. Instead of £8k commission and wages they owed us, we ended up with all the new sonar equipment and Jim's car, which was nice! I also got the brownie points in the port, but the Spanish press gave the credit to the Spanish firm whose machine had been lost and recovered by us for free. Cheeky bastards said we'd "assisted"! There was no mention of the near fatal accident either.

CHAPTER THIRTY EIGHT

THE FINAL BLOW

I had a hearing to go to in May 2008 at Leeds where I would be applying for further disclosures relating to the forthcoming hearing. I left Nicola in Spain on-board to meet a potential buyer for the Mussasette, the classic motor sailor we'd salvaged and won, who was on route from the UK.

After dragging myself and bags through two airports, I went to Leeds centre for the hearing and just afterwards, had a big fat joint, went to lean against a bus stop and fell over. I really should have gone to the hospital but had a return flight to catch. I went to Doncaster airport but was refused boarding because my passport photo had been damaged when the car was 'broken into' near Malaga. Of course they wanted me to have a new type passport with the new data chip. I tried everything, but they wouldn't let me fly. It was the best thing they ever did for me.

It would take days to get a new passport, so I went to the hospital to get x-rayed. The pain in my back and right leg was excruciating. The doctor at A&E was absolutely horrified; he couldn't understand how I was walking, never mind carrying bags through two airports. My right hip joint was absolutely non-existent. I was walking on two broken sticks. His words I will never forget, "That's the worst hip I've ever seen."

Words couldn't express my joy, and it showed. The doctor couldn't understand why I was so happy until I told him. I'd been misdiagnosed with spinal damage, and expected to be in a wheelchair sometime soon. I'd been dragging my right leg about like a ten bob prosthetic in agony for years.

At first, I didn't care about the useless specialist and consultant who'd told me to keep moving on it. I was only looking at a new hip joint, after all that. I shook his hand, nicked the negatives, hobbled outside and telephoned Nicola, with the most fantastic news to date.

She couldn't believe it, and nor could I, the situation with the dirty bastards hiding behind the Queen's name paled into insignificance with the very dream of a solution to the suffering I'd endured for years. I don't know how she put up with me. I needed a Viagra to shag, a tablet to sleep, anti-inflammatory drugs, along with copious amounts of cannabis and alcohol to function, and still, I was a pain in the arse.

The following day, I was at my doctors, boy oh boy, was I mad! Luckily, a new doctor saw me. He winced, watching me walk. When I explained, he was horrified, especially when I asked him to check my records, showing how long I'd been complaining about it. The wheels were in motion in no time. He promised me, he'd sort it.

I applied for a new fast track passport. Of course, I still had my old one and other proof of ID, but yeah, you guessed it, I got passed about from pillar to post for almost a week before collecting it from Durham office. Clearly, they thought I was some sort of super villain. The place went deadly quiet when I gave my name. The lass behind the glass couldn't look me in the eye. I flew back to Nic and our boat, a much, much happier man than I'd been for a long time.

The next hearing back at Crown Court was scheduled for 21st July 2008, four years after the fact. I had no representation whatsoever. Trevor had reported the solicitors for fraud. He'd given them a cheque with a condition attached. They'd ignored the condition and cashed it anyway. I'd refused point blank, knowing just what they'd do.

I was furious; they'd played to the Customs tune for a nice payday in High Court. Despite Judge Taylor's insistence that the law was so complex only a barrister could present it, I was refused legal aid again. However, I was confident I'd plugged any weak points and applied for disclosure of some documents which would give us a boost. Phil Junior travelled from Tenerife to be a witness.

From the very start, it was all uphill with the judge. He was impatient, and often interrupted when Customs were struggling to answer, sticking up for them like an ignorant mother of a clearly horrible child. It was pathetic! We even got to see our stock outside on a truck. A blind man in a snowstorm could have seen it was all badly water damaged, and completely unsalable. He denied there was anything wrong with it.

Documents were held back, despite protests. I even recorded their barrister refusing me access to documents, then telling the judge he hadn't. The commander of the Valiant could not even explain his own abbreviations in the ship's log, which I say was re-written by someone else to counter my allegations. They completely denied coming anywhere near Little Flea and guess what? They stated no cameras were active. One wonders why, considering the high profile job they were on. This footage was priceless to their campaign. We've all seen such videos on TV; it was preposterous, but not even questioned by the judge

When I attempted to assert the regulations I was relying on, concerning UNCLOS (United Nations Convention on the law of the sea), which had been ratified (accepted into law) by the UK some time before, both the Judge and the barrister, along with his legal team from HMRC amazingly pretended they didn't know they had. Pathetic, of course they did!

As I'd obtained my copy of the regulations from a document printed before ratification, I simply checked and confirmed it had been done, but I couldn't produce the 'ratified' document. These regulations had been discussed at previous hearings without objection. Some very significant points were rejected, instead of the Judge giving us time to have it confirmed. I knew then that we weren't going to get a fair crack of the whip.

While I appreciate the transcripts of the hearings and the resulting judgements at the end of this are not so exciting to read. There's clear evidence that it all depends on which judge you get. Compare the favourable judgement we received from Judge Fox, who even praised Trevor and me for our honesty and integrity, to that of Judge Willkie, who basically concluded we were all devious liars.

The transcripts will show I did a fantastic job against a clearly biased Judge, and a bunch of lying cheating bastards who couldn't lie straight in bed! I tortured them in my opinion. Everyone in that court knew who was telling the truth, and who wasn't. Judge Fox should really have been the Judge for that hearing for a number of reasons.

He already had knowledge of the case, and with the guidance from the appeal court's judgement, he was far better placed to understand the complexities, and more importantly, he had already heard the case argued by a qualified QC on my behalf. As I was now unrepresented, justice would only be served properly if he heard it for the second time. But no, Willkie was drafted in for a purpose, no ifs or buts about it.

When I entered the court to hear the judgement handed down, the Customs team, who had been called in earlier, looked really devastated. I thought we'd won, and rightly so. When the Judge finished, and it was plainly obvious we'd lost, the Customs team still looked devastated. Their QC Puzey looked like a bull dog licking piss off a thistle.

I could only deduce the Judge had blasted them for really losing the case so convincingly, thereby making him appear even more unjust by finding against us. Highly significant to this point is the fact HMRC didn't even attempt to ask the Judge to award costs against us. Clearly they'd already been told beforehand. That's why they had faces like smacked arses, they'd only be getting wages.

The press behaved very oddly at this final hearing, especially when the judgement was handed down. Whereas before the court was filled with media representatives, and cameras waiting outside, this time was the opposite. There'd been many heated, even explosive allegations and exchanges, but none were reported.

The one reporter present whom I talked to from the local paper seemed very embarrassed, and totally avoided talking about anything other than the result. Most significantly, he made no notes of my statement. Nothing was mentioned in the press about perjury, sabotage, deception, or even attempted murder. We wonder if a gagging order was in force. We will never know!

In plain English, it was established that our activity in the North Sea was perfectly legal. However, Judge Wilkie concluded that Customs had the right to control my stock when the vessel entered port, even if seeking shelter from a storm. They could unload it into the pouring rain to devalue it, then hold it to ransom for outrageous transport and storage charges.

Trevor had complied with their requests to the letter; his half of the stock was disposed of without paperwork or proper notice within a couple of months. He asserts his solicitor was told to deal with it, but didn't. We never found out where it went. We know HMRC investigated their own operatives regarding cigarettes supplied to criminals at that time, but the door to the truth was slammed in our faces, again and again. It was only reported when the story broke on radio, then nothing was heard.

I did put in a letter of appeal and the transcripts were shown to various legal experts, who quite simply, were shocked and appalled! But I was advised to drop it and get on with my life. If I couldn't get legal aid so far, I had no chance of getting it in the future. The legal system put in place by the government would protect the government and its revenue.

As the case would also affect European revenues, it was considered futile to continue.

It'd taken four years of torture to get this far. My hip joint was replaced. I no longer had pain in my back or my leg. I was fit as a fiddle! What a joy!

Did we want to continue being abused wherever we went, without the support of the press or the public, or did we want to make a few quid with what we'd found at the bottom of the sea?

After considering, I had a new lease on life after the operation, and I'd found the perfect woman, who'd follow me to the end of the earth. We decided we needed a break from the stress of it all.

I'd made my point; they won't forget me in a hurry! And if I get any more shit, I'll be making complaints of perjury, attempted murder and sabotage! All transcripts are included for those with a legal mind. Readers in the legal profession will be astounded!

For the record, our operation offshore was legal, but a customer would get hassle if they were stopped coming ashore. At the time, the regulations in force didn't cover a person who had simply travelled to international waters to buy fags.

As you've read, we'd agreed a deal, where a symbolic seizure would be made, enabling us to have the law tested in court. Customs unloaded Trevor's goods by arrangement (again into the pouring rain), as the first part of the deal, and then changed their minds, refusing to honour their word.

Clearly, they were scared to have the law tested. This speaks volumes! I wouldn't recommend this operation to anyone. I certainly believe the powers in charge of any country that relies on such revenue, would go to any lengths to stop it happening.

I truly believe the HMCC Valiant was trying to run us down that day, and also we'd been lucky to survive the sabotage, and attempts to set us up.

From leaving the marina in Sotogrande in April 2006, our vessel Rich Harvest did not enter any port or marina until November 2010. We lived on her all that time, at sea or anchor, such was our fear of abuse!

The anti-mosquito towel project was destroyed by Customs interference.

We've been slandered, and vilified as drug smugglers through malicious and false intelligence, circulated by HMRC.

For the record, I don't blame any agency officer personally for acting on false and malicious intelligence; I've put up with it since the seventies when I made an enemy of a corrupt policeman who assaulted me with others in the police station, and got a good hiding, and broken arm in the process. I was exonerated, but he rose high up the ranks, before finally being exposed. He pulled strings throughout his police career to target me and anyone else who wouldn't do his dodgy bidding. I was horrendously bullied by my older brother as a child, and I've been fighting back ever since.

Another positive side to this saga was, because we endured years of constant high surveillance, that all of the agencies had to accept that I was not, or would not, break the law. I think we reached an agreement! To let sleeping dogs lie. I could live a normal life, well normal for me.

My advice? Don't do it! I had no idea I would piss them off so much. They have the power to mess you up, wherever you are, whatever you do. Play the game and pay your taxes. You need awfully deep pockets to take on the Crown, and the risks are very high, whether you're right or wrong.

CHAPTER THIRTY NINE

FROM THE WACCY BACCY BOAT TO CBD OIL AND CHANGING LIVES

After this, we stayed around Gibraltar, but to get a port operator's license to recover the chains and cables we'd found during our sonar surveys, we had to take on some Gibraltar nationals into a newly formed company Offshore Solutions Ltd Gibraltar. I had to undergo every training course and pass exams to become a commercial Captain. I'd done it all before, years ago, so it wasn't hard. We worked hard to bring the tug Aquarius up to standard while we continued identifying targets to lift for almost two years. The potential for serious money was huge. Our Gib partners had their eye on all of it, and became very difficult to deal with. It became very acrimonious, especially when all the hard work was done, they joined forces with a larger salvage company, and wanted us out of the picture.

Eventually one of the Giblets (an ex-lawyer) walked into Companies House, forged my signature, and resigned me as MD and appointed himself. I had 100% proof of this, but the authorities would do absolutely nothing. Again, we had an example of how helpless you are in another jurisdiction against the locals. It soon became clear, whatever happened, we were getting screwed. On top of everything else, Nicola was expecting our first child. What a shock that was to us both.

We'd been in the water for years and badly needed a lift out. We towed Rich Harvest across the straits to a boat yard in Ceuta, left Aquarius waiting and sailed Rich Harvest to Marina Smir in Morocco thirty miles away. The yard in Ceuta contacted us to say the tug had been taken away by our partners' 'new crew'. Given Nicola's condition, we had no choice but to sell Rich Harvest and return to the UK. Trevor was, quite rightly, putting us under pressure to settle an outstanding balance, so we advertised her. Boris got wind and landed at Marina Smir with a group of businessmen who wanted such a vessel for a grant-funded movie in Canada. They paid a deposit which was to be used to put her back in tip top condition.

When all was about finished, they cocked on the deal saying that the grants had not materialised, but were quite happy to lose their £20k deposit. We re-advertised her and relaxed for a couple of weeks, until disaster struck. Nicola went into labour early, and we lost our baby Joseph RIP the next day. She was an international hockey player, never drank, never smoked, and was as fit as a butcher's dog. We even had our own private doctor, the wife of a good friend we made. Dealing with such a tragedy in another continent was an absolute nightmare that left us scarred, but it didn't destroy us. It was a month before we could repatriate him for the funeral, and a month after, we returned to Smir. I must say, the people there were very supportive.

It wasn't long before Nicola was pregnant again, so we made arrangements to return to the UK to be on the safe side, and leave Rich Harvest out of the water until a buyer could be found. We moved in to her parents house in Essex, I caught up with John Nelson who brought me up to speed on the auto diagnostic job, and I made a decent living fixing and dealing a few cars until our son Teddy was born, early again. We knew there was a one in ten chance this would happen, and it was all very scary. We were panicking, but the hospital delivery room didn't see the urgency to get him oxygen. Very soon he had bad acid reflux, the doctors had no clue, and so we researched the far end of a fart, until we discovered he was dairy and soya intolerant. Meanwhile we had to find another house. The lad was keeping everybody awake. On a trip up north I took them to see the pub I was born in. It was for sale or rent. We moved in five weeks later in 2012, but it was two years before Teddy was diagnosed with cerebral palsy, and then later epilepsy, with partial sight and digestive issues.

Before that terrible day, we'd found another buyer for the Rich Harvest, but he wanted to part-ex a French chateau. We were about to look at it when the first buyers came back saying the grants were forthcoming and they wanted her again. They had a fair bit of pull in the area, and when I refused, they said the vessel would be seized if they 'asked' the right people. The marina fees were over thirty thousand by then, and despite me asking Trevor for help, I never heard from him. I had little choice. They paid the marina bill by way of a deposit, but wanted the vessel clear of Morocco as she'd been there three years, and there was a tax problem. I organised a bunch of good lads, along with Nicola and Teddy for a sailing jolly, we parted with a slack handful of cash, dropped her back in the drink, and we sailed her to Spain.

We cleared out all of the stuff we'd acquired and sold it, from salvage airbags to spring loaded fishing hooks. We were three tons lighter, and had enough money to buy a smaller boat, a classic 1910 gaff cutter, and rent a house in Caleta, east of Malaga, where she was berthed. The firm buying Rich Harvest employed an engineer, and delivery skipper with catastrophic consequences. They failed to open the sea-cocks before starting machinery, and ruined the main engine, generator and hydraulics. Weeks turned to months and then a year later, after being lifted out again, they forged documents, and took her to Brazil.

After we had the devastating diagnosis for Teddy, I knew I needed a business which would leave both Teddy and Nicola comfortable. My retirement was over before it began. We got into a pharmaceutical merry-go-round, and spent all our time researching natural remedies and new treatments to get him off the horrendous class A drugs they prescribed, which destroyed his character, and dumbed him down. Our boy could recite his phonetic alphabet before he was three. We wanted him back.

And that's what set me on my new path in life.

Medicinal cannabis, especially oil, is having fantastic results with epilepsy, and despite opposition from Nicola, I could clearly see it was an option in the future. I set about cross-breeding plants in Spain, and after three years of buying, begging and even stealing genetics to work with, I have a strain so high in CBD and low in THC that we can make a CBD oil which is legal to sell in the UK. Our son Teddy, at nearly seven, is a photographic model for River Island, M&S, Very, and has been featured on children's TV a number of times, a far cry from where he was a couple of years before.

Nicola is now a convert; she even takes CBD oil herself. I'm obsessed with helping others with similar problems. All the oil I made before the final strain was perfected was given to people with cancer and other problems. The results are mind blowing. It's not a magic bullet, but it's a must along with other protocols, such as diet and supplements. The buzz we get from helping people is addictive, the job satisfaction through the roof. Our oils are making us famous, even where the big players have struggled to get results. We must be doing something right.

The Healing Cauldron Ltd is growing month by month, and we're getting better at it all the time. My son Phil Junior has stepped right up, and become quite an expert. We can't see a better way of making a reasonable income that comes with so much good Karma. However the battle to get cannabis oil to the people that need it, when they need it, consumes me.

I just know I'm going to have to be a pain in the arse again, sometime soon.